ANTHONY BOURDAIN's
HUNGRY GHOSTS ™

BERGER BOOKS

AN IMPRINT OF
DARK HORSE COMICS

Written by
Anthony Bourdain
& Joel Rose

Color *José Villarrubia*
Letters *Sal Cipriano*

KAIDAN

Alberto Ponticelli

THE STARVING SKELETON

Alberto Ponticelli

THE PIRATES

Vanesa Del Rey

SALTY HORSE

Leonardo Manco

KAIDAN

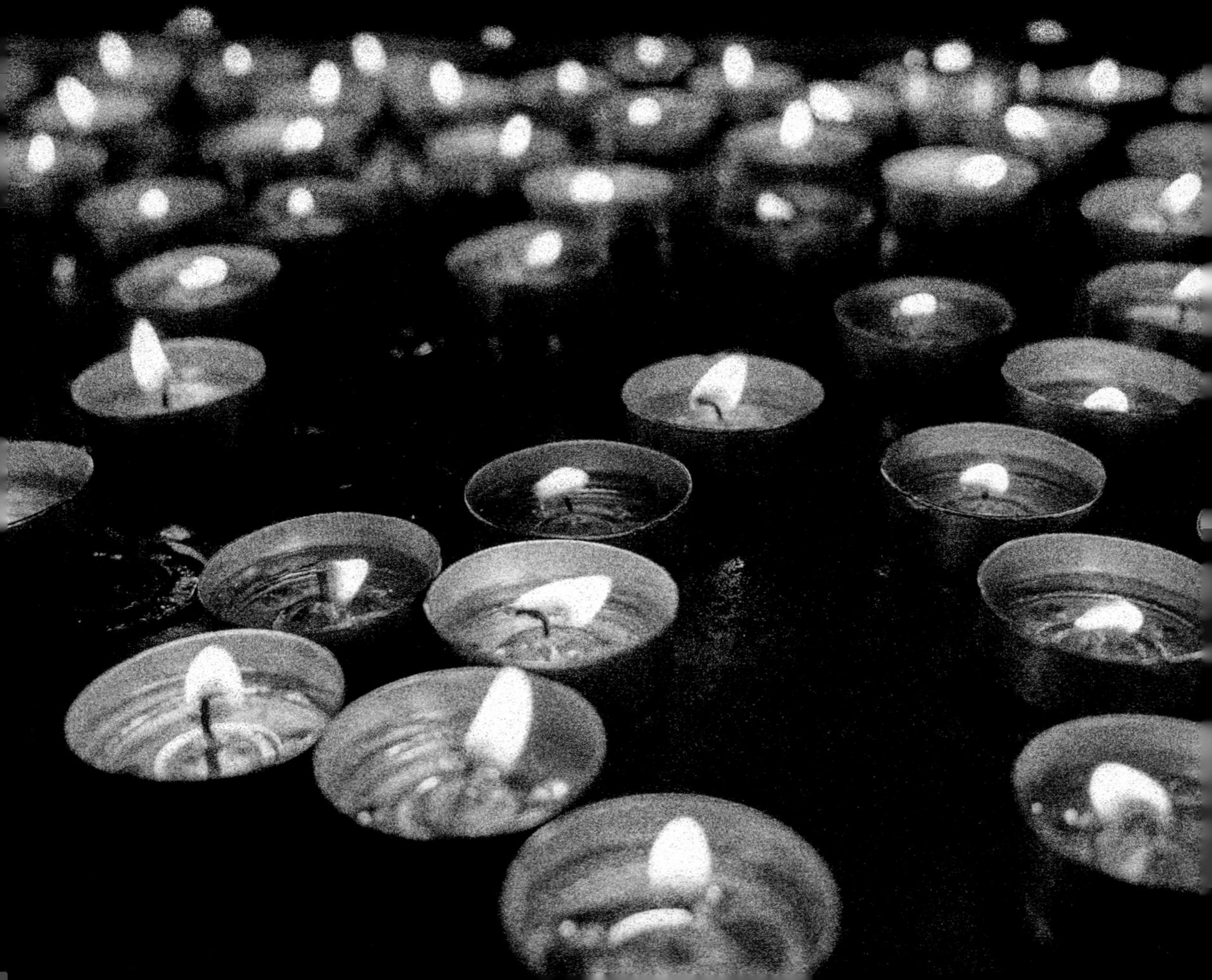

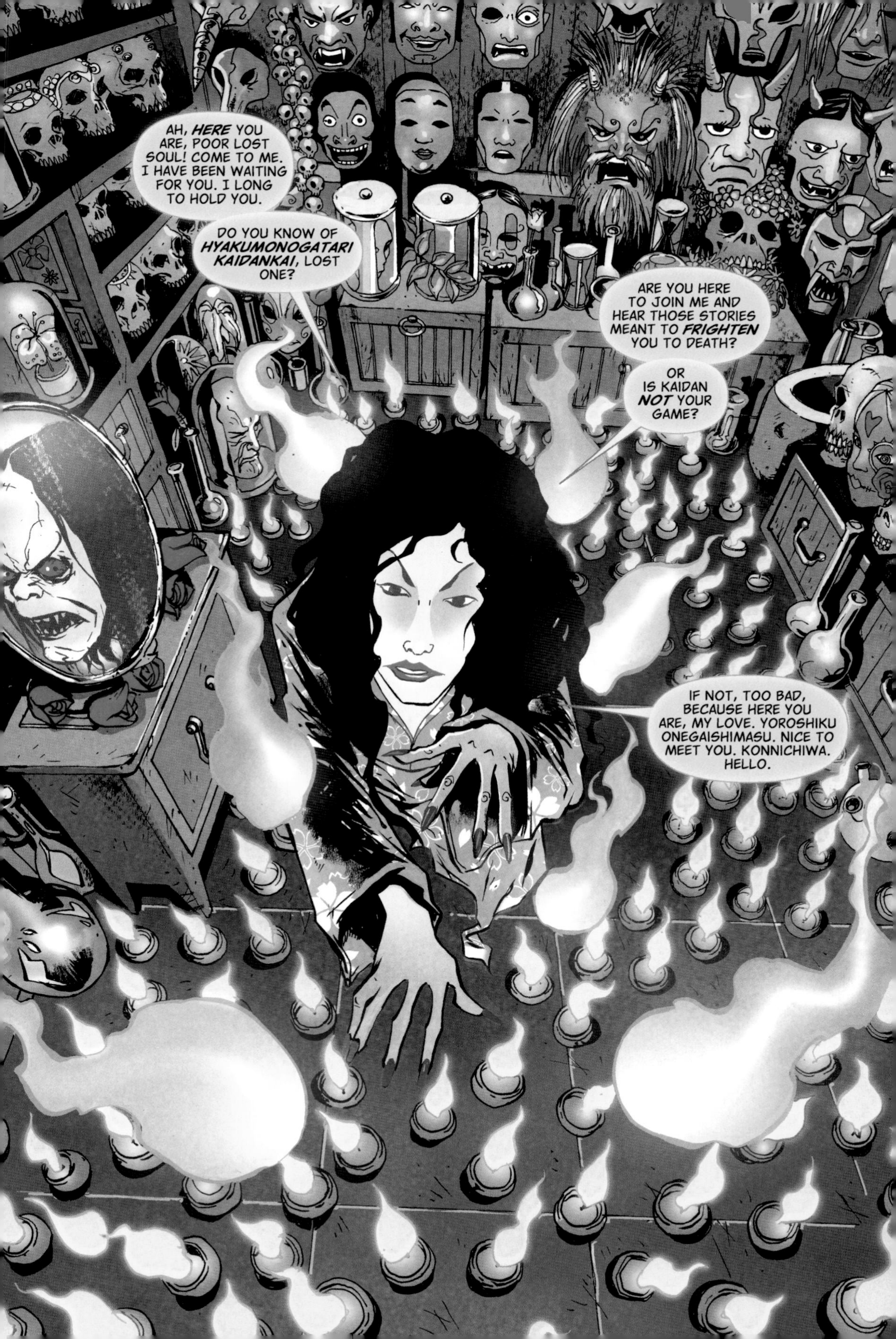
AH, **HERE** YOU ARE, POOR LOST SOUL! COME TO ME. I HAVE BEEN WAITING FOR YOU. I LONG TO HOLD YOU.
DO YOU KNOW OF **HYAKUMONOGATARI KAIDANKAI**, LOST ONE?
ARE YOU HERE TO JOIN ME AND HEAR THOSE STORIES MEANT TO **FRIGHTEN** YOU TO DEATH?
OR IS KAIDAN **NOT** YOUR GAME?
IF NOT, TOO BAD, BECAUSE HERE YOU ARE, MY LOVE. YOROSHIKU ONEGAISHIMASU. NICE TO MEET YOU. KONNICHIWA. HELLO.

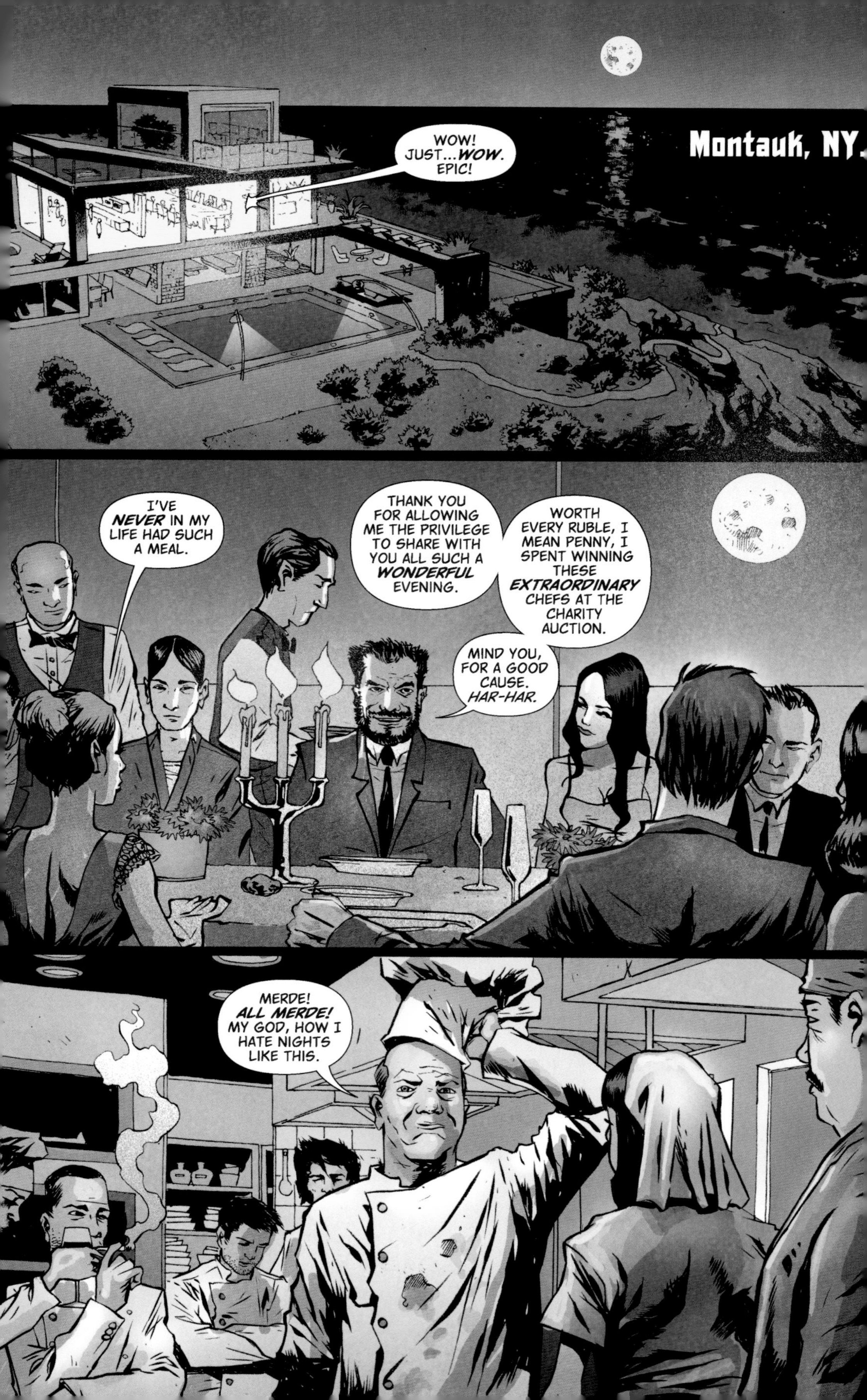
Montauk, NY.
WOW! JUST...WOW. EPIC!
I'VE NEVER IN MY LIFE HAD SUCH A MEAL.
THANK YOU FOR ALLOWING ME THE PRIVILEGE TO SHARE WITH YOU ALL SUCH A WONDERFUL EVENING.
WORTH EVERY RUBLE, I MEAN PENNY, I SPENT WINNING THESE EXTRAORDINARY CHEFS AT THE CHARITY AUCTION.
MIND YOU, FOR A GOOD CAUSE. HAR-HAR.
MERDE! ALL MERDE! MY GOD, HOW I HATE NIGHTS LIKE THIS.

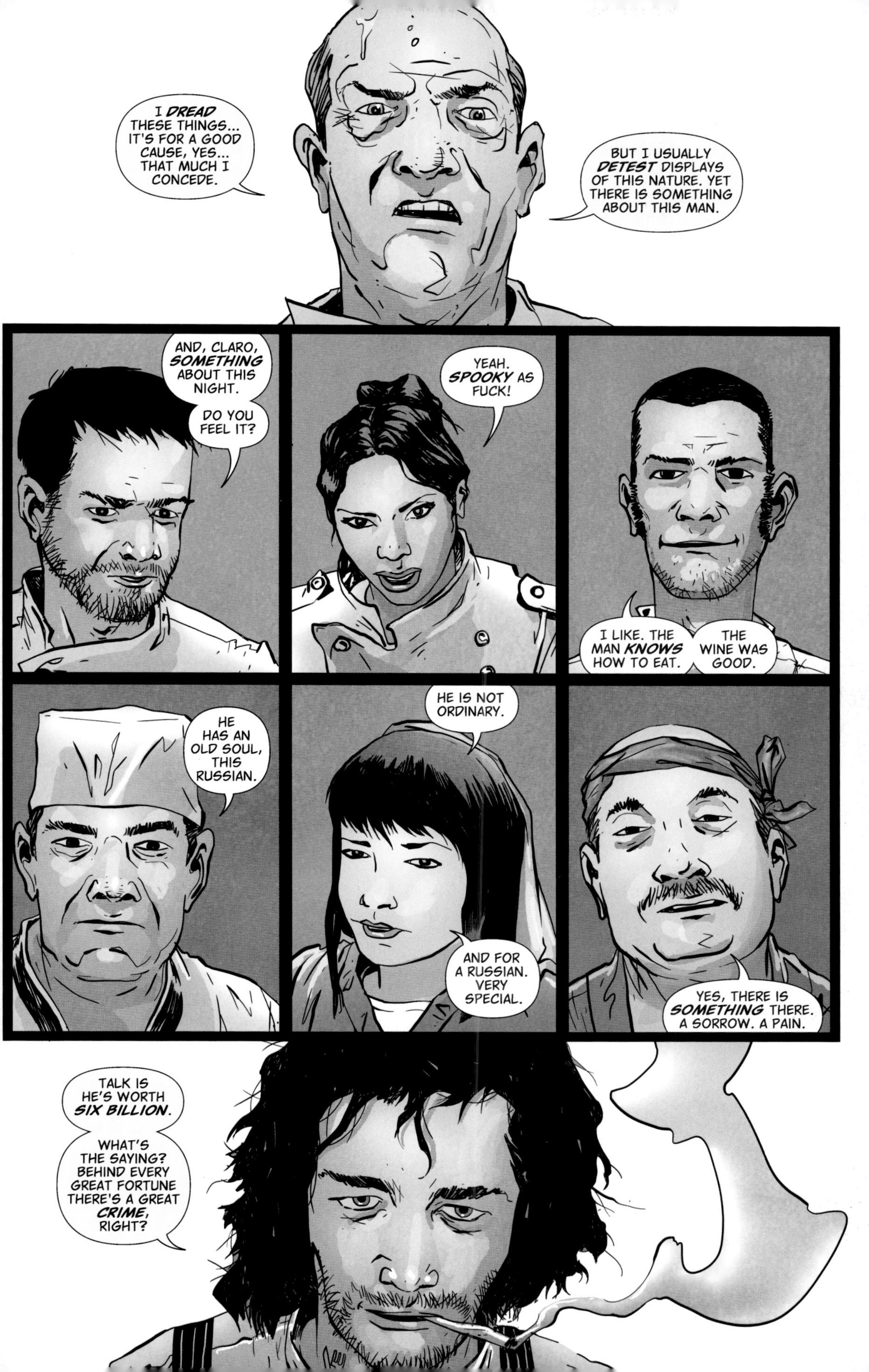
I DREAD THESE THINGS... IT'S FOR A GOOD CAUSE, YES... THAT MUCH I CONCEDE.
BUT I USUALLY DETEST DISPLAYS OF THIS NATURE. YET THERE IS SOMETHING ABOUT THIS MAN.
AND, CLARO, SOMETHING ABOUT THIS NIGHT.
DO YOU FEEL IT?
YEAH. SPOOKY AS FUCK!
I LIKE. THE MAN KNOWS HOW TO EAT.
THE WINE WAS GOOD.
HE HAS AN OLD SOUL, THIS RUSSIAN.
HE IS NOT ORDINARY.
AND FOR A RUSSIAN. VERY SPECIAL.
YES, THERE IS SOMETHING THERE. A SORROW. A PAIN.
TALK IS HE'S WORTH SIX BILLION.
WHAT'S THE SAYING? BEHIND EVERY GREAT FORTUNE THERE'S A GREAT CRIME, RIGHT?

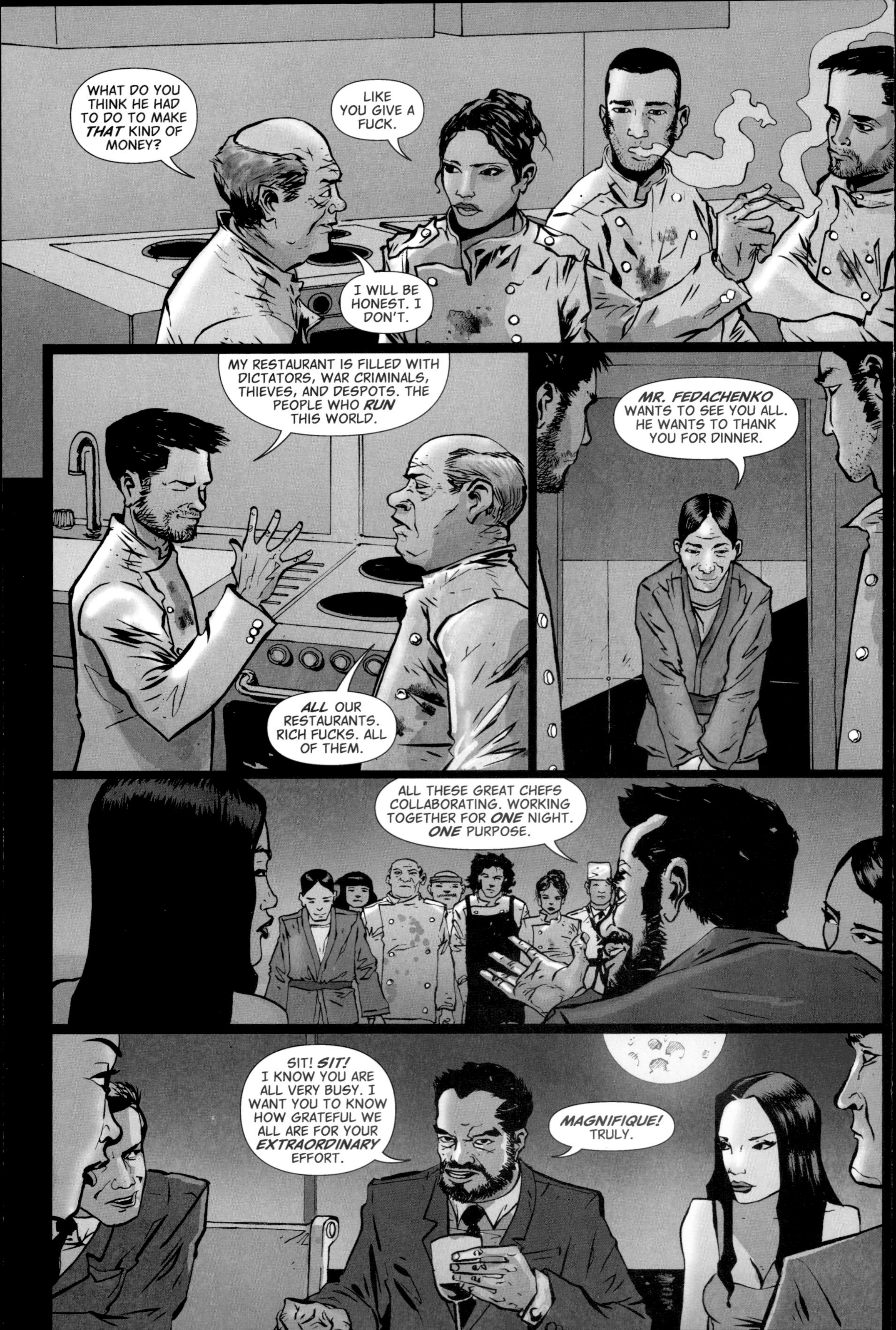
WHAT DO YOU THINK HE HAD TO DO TO MAKE THAT KIND OF MONEY?
LIKE YOU GIVE A FUCK.
I WILL BE HONEST. I DON'T.
MY RESTAURANT IS FILLED WITH DICTATORS, WAR CRIMINALS, THIEVES, AND DESPOTS. THE PEOPLE WHO RUN THIS WORLD.
ALL OUR RESTAURANTS. RICH FUCKS. ALL OF THEM.
MR. FEDACHENKO WANTS TO SEE YOU ALL. HE WANTS TO THANK YOU FOR DINNER.
ALL THESE GREAT CHEFS COLLABORATING. WORKING TOGETHER FOR ONE NIGHT. ONE PURPOSE.
SIT! SIT! I KNOW YOU ARE ALL VERY BUSY. I WANT YOU TO KNOW HOW GRATEFUL WE ALL ARE FOR YOUR EXTRAORDINARY EFFORT.
MAGNIFIQUE! TRULY.

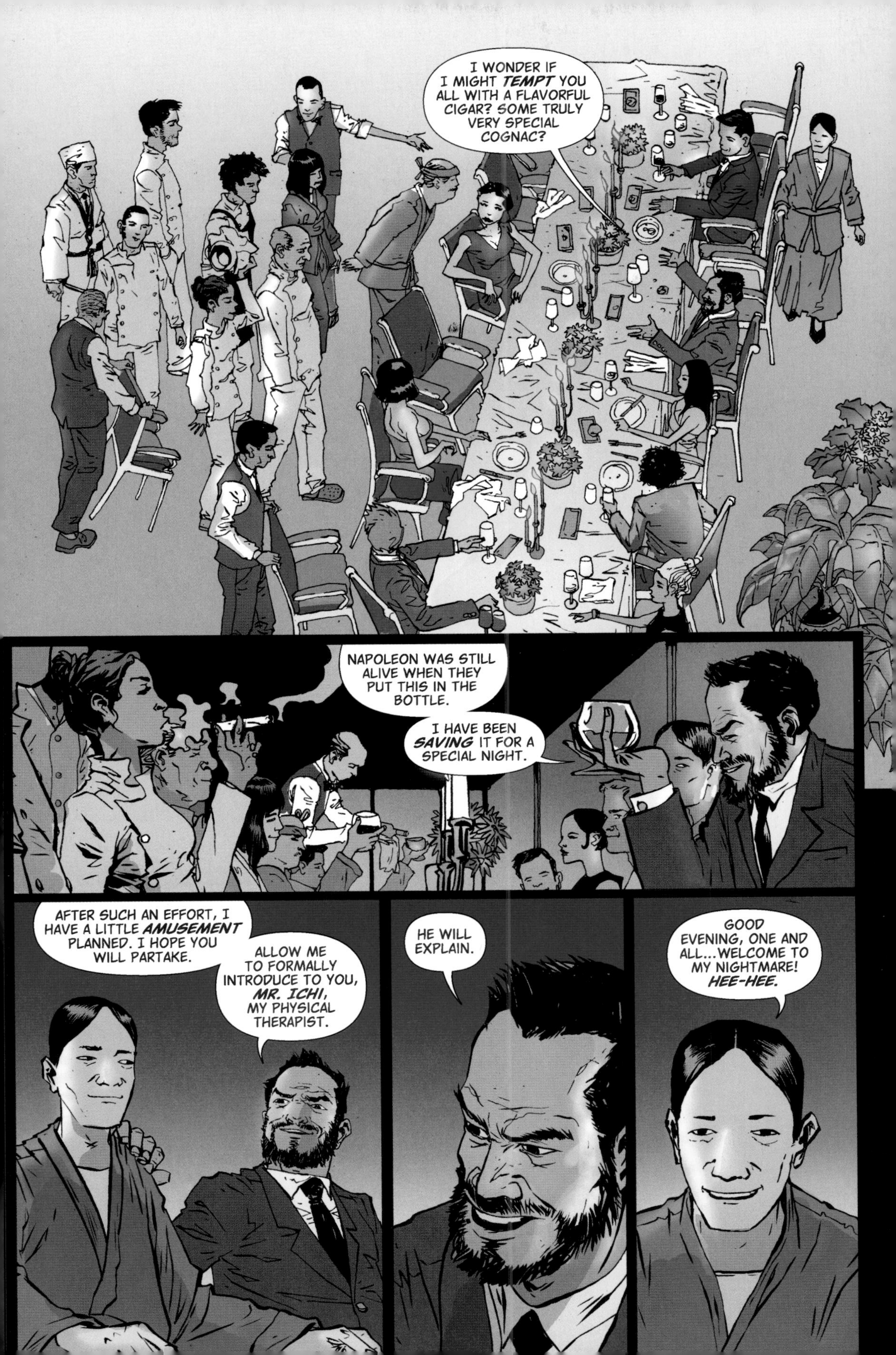
I WONDER IF I MIGHT TEMPT YOU ALL WITH A FLAVORFUL CIGAR? SOME TRULY VERY SPECIAL COGNAC?
NAPOLEON WAS STILL ALIVE WHEN THEY PUT THIS IN THE BOTTLE.
I HAVE BEEN SAVING IT FOR A SPECIAL NIGHT.
AFTER SUCH AN EFFORT, I HAVE A LITTLE AMUSEMENT PLANNED. I HOPE YOU WILL PARTAKE.
ALLOW ME TO FORMALLY INTRODUCE TO YOU, MR. ICHI, MY PHYSICAL THERAPIST.
HE WILL EXPLAIN.
GOOD EVENING, ONE AND ALL...WELCOME TO MY NIGHTMARE! HEE-HEE.

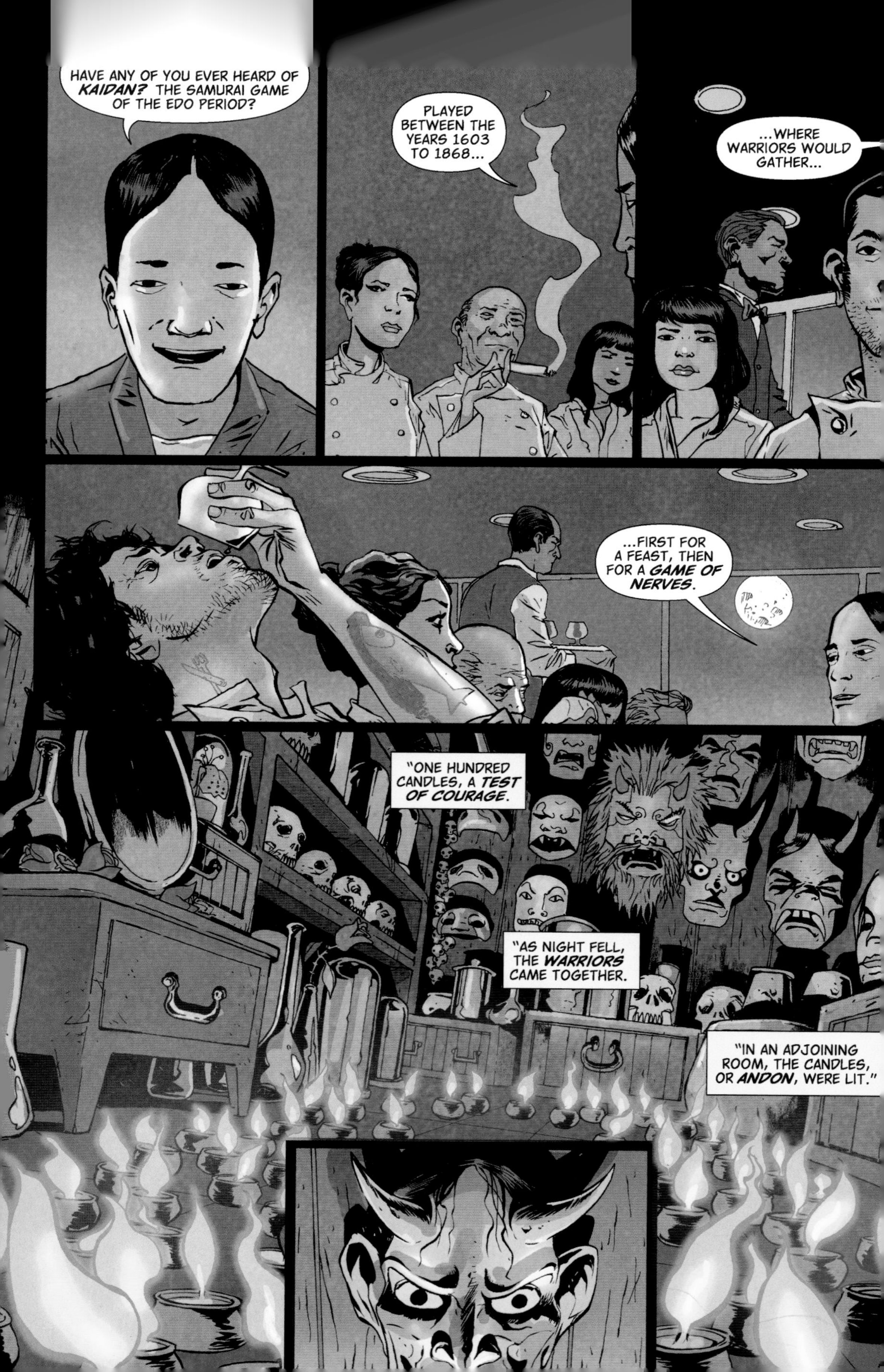

HAVE ANY OF YOU EVER HEARD OF *KAIDAN?* THE SAMURAI GAME OF THE EDO PERIOD?
PLAYED BETWEEN THE YEARS 1603 TO 1868...
...WHERE WARRIORS WOULD GATHER...
...FIRST FOR A FEAST, THEN FOR A *GAME OF NERVES*.
"ONE HUNDRED CANDLES, A *TEST OF COURAGE*.
"AS NIGHT FELL, THE *WARRIORS* CAME TOGETHER.
"IN AN ADJOINING ROOM, THE CANDLES, OR *ANDON*, WERE LIT."

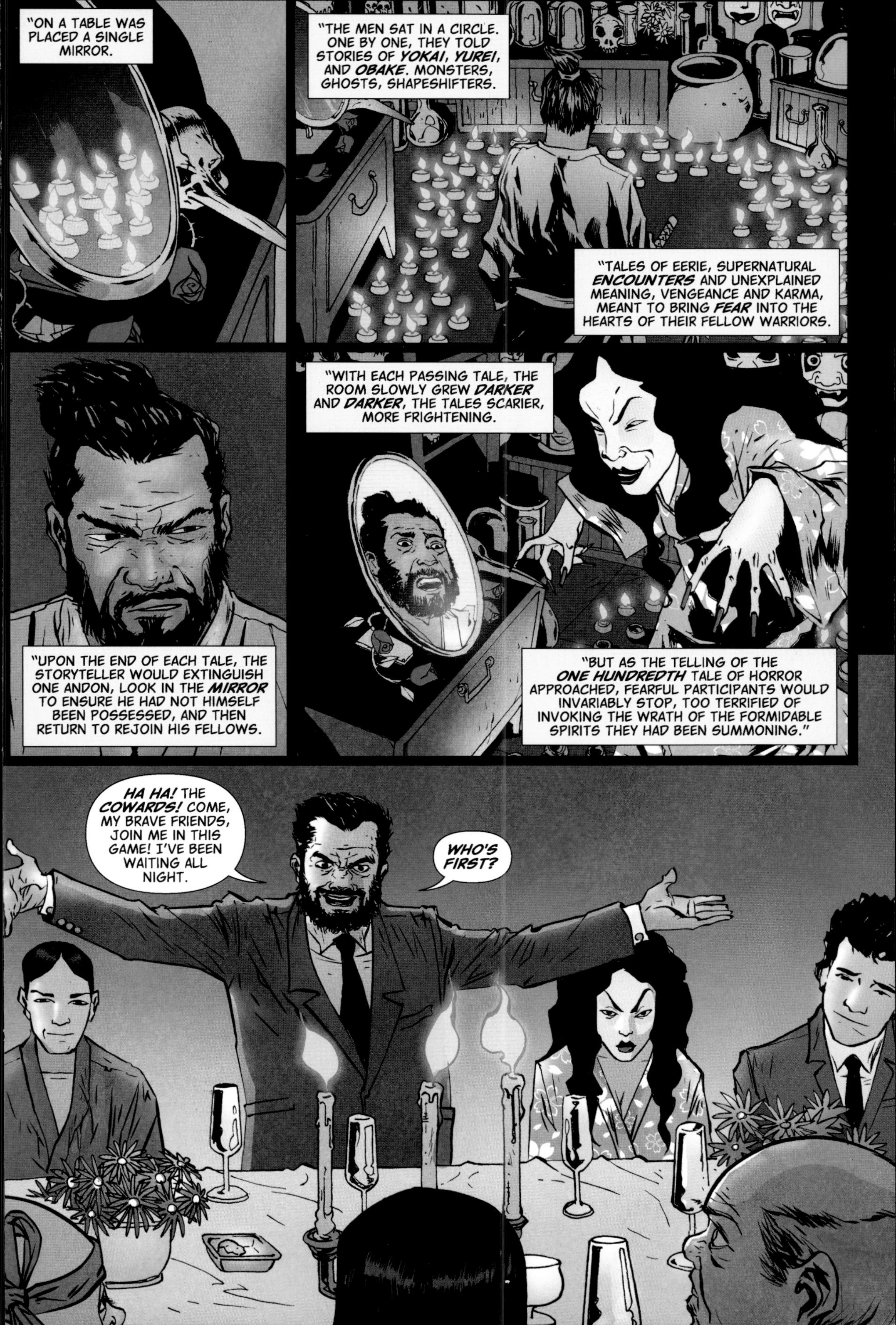
"ON A TABLE WAS PLACED A SINGLE MIRROR.
"THE MEN SAT IN A CIRCLE. ONE BY ONE, THEY TOLD STORIES OF YOKAI, YUREI, AND OBAKE. MONSTERS, GHOSTS, SHAPESHIFTERS.
"TALES OF EERIE, SUPERNATURAL ENCOUNTERS AND UNEXPLAINED MEANING, VENGEANCE AND KARMA, MEANT TO BRING FEAR INTO THE HEARTS OF THEIR FELLOW WARRIORS.
"UPON THE END OF EACH TALE, THE STORYTELLER WOULD EXTINGUISH ONE ANDON, LOOK IN THE MIRROR TO ENSURE HE HAD NOT HIMSELF BEEN POSSESSED, AND THEN RETURN TO REJOIN HIS FELLOWS.
"WITH EACH PASSING TALE, THE ROOM SLOWLY GREW DARKER AND DARKER, THE TALES SCARIER, MORE FRIGHTENING.
"BUT AS THE TELLING OF THE ONE HUNDREDTH TALE OF HORROR APPROACHED, FEARFUL PARTICIPANTS WOULD INVARIABLY STOP, TOO TERRIFIED OF INVOKING THE WRATH OF THE FORMIDABLE SPIRITS THEY HAD BEEN SUMMONING."
HA HA! THE COWARDS! COME, MY BRAVE FRIENDS, JOIN ME IN THIS GAME! I'VE BEEN WAITING ALL NIGHT.
WHO'S FIRST?

THE STARVING SKELETON

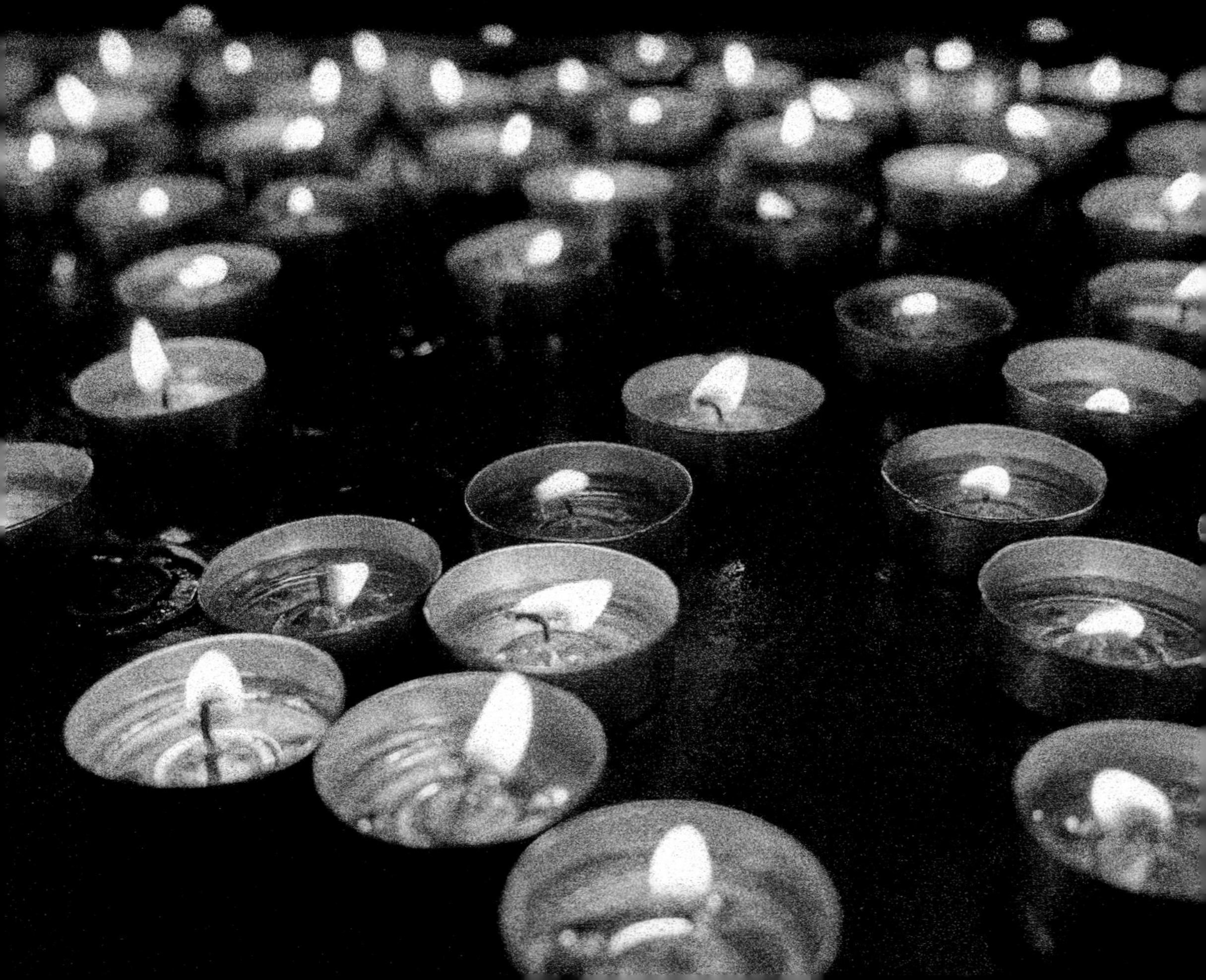

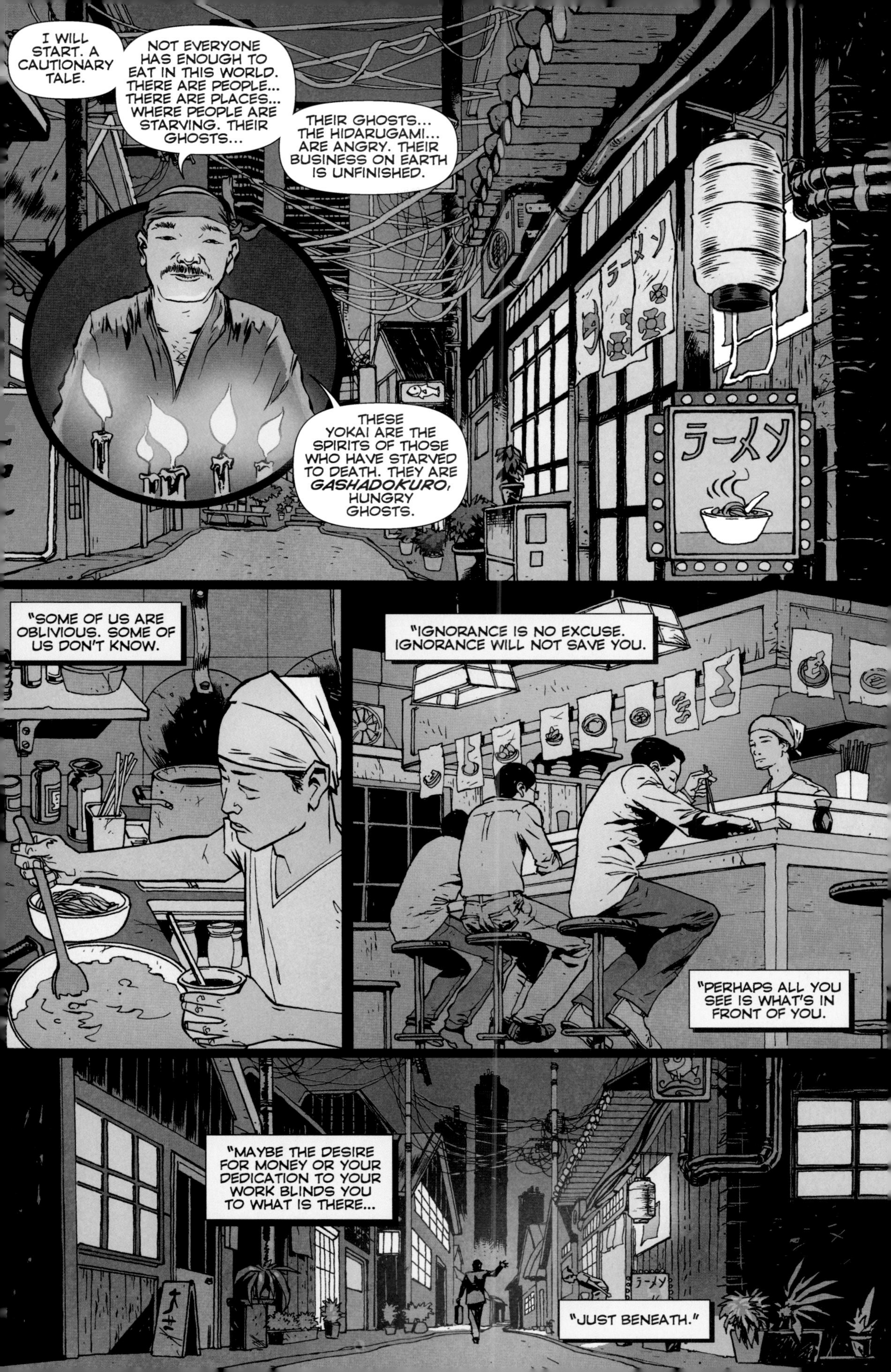
I WILL START. A CAUTIONARY TALE.
NOT EVERYONE HAS ENOUGH TO EAT IN THIS WORLD. THERE ARE PEOPLE... THERE ARE PLACES... WHERE PEOPLE ARE STARVING. THEIR GHOSTS...
THEIR GHOSTS... THE HIDARUGAMI... ARE ANGRY. THEIR BUSINESS ON EARTH IS UNFINISHED.
ラーメン
ラーメン
THESE YOKAI ARE THE SPIRITS OF THOSE WHO HAVE STARVED TO DEATH. THEY ARE *GASHADOKURO*, HUNGRY GHOSTS.
"SOME OF US ARE OBLIVIOUS. SOME OF US DON'T KNOW.
"IGNORANCE IS NO EXCUSE. IGNORANCE WILL NOT SAVE YOU.
"PERHAPS ALL YOU SEE IS WHAT'S IN FRONT OF YOU.
"MAYBE THE DESIRE FOR MONEY OR YOUR DEDICATION TO YOUR WORK BLINDS YOU TO WHAT IS THERE...
ラーメン
"JUST BENEATH."

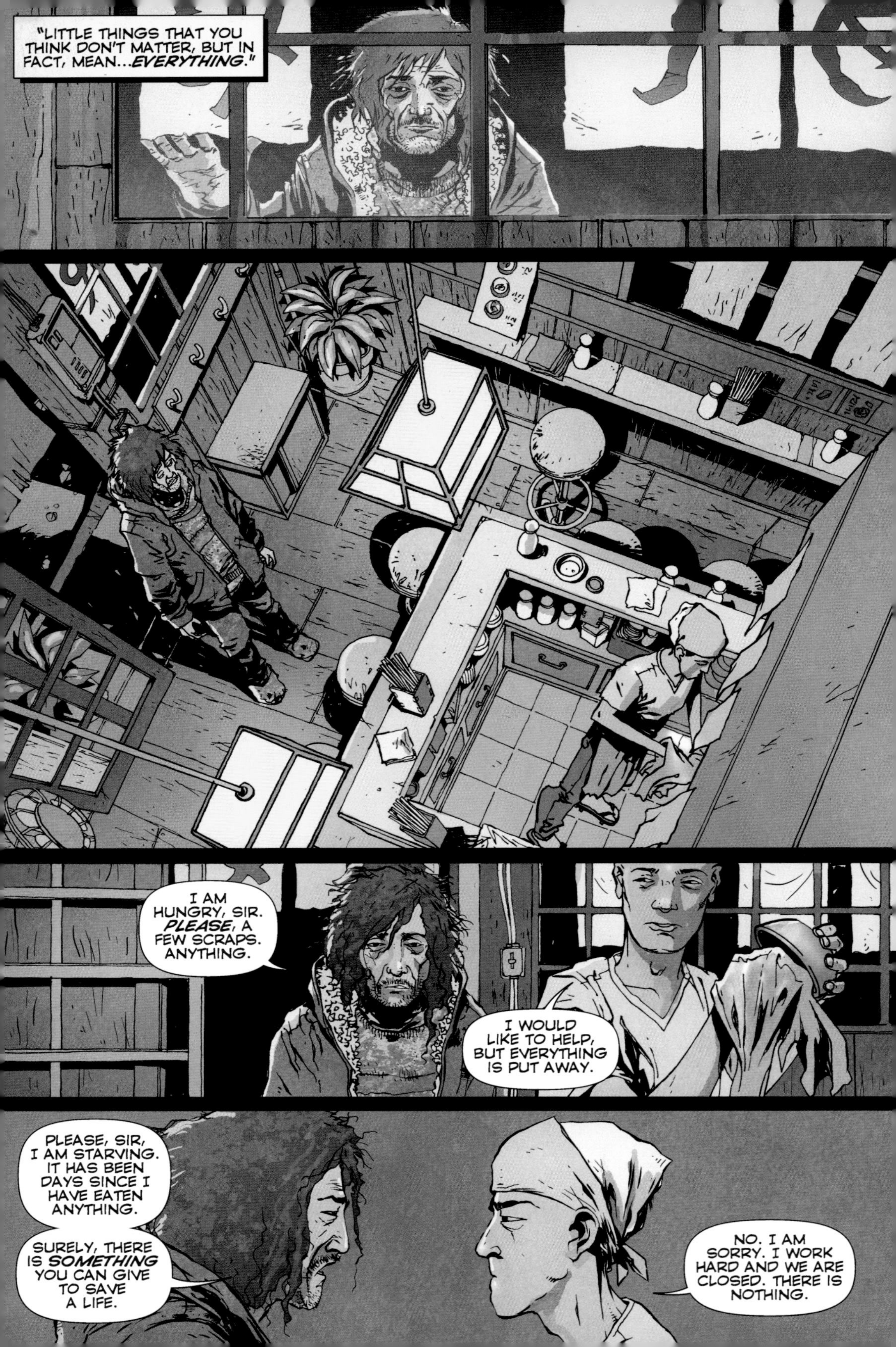
"LITTLE THINGS THAT YOU THINK DON'T MATTER, BUT IN FACT, MEAN...*EVERYTHING*."
I AM HUNGRY, SIR. *PLEASE*, A FEW SCRAPS. ANYTHING.
I WOULD LIKE TO HELP, BUT EVERYTHING IS PUT AWAY.
PLEASE, SIR, I AM STARVING. IT HAS BEEN DAYS SINCE I HAVE EATEN ANYTHING.
SURELY, THERE IS *SOMETHING* YOU CAN GIVE TO SAVE A LIFE.
NO. I AM SORRY. I WORK HARD AND WE ARE CLOSED. THERE IS NOTHING.

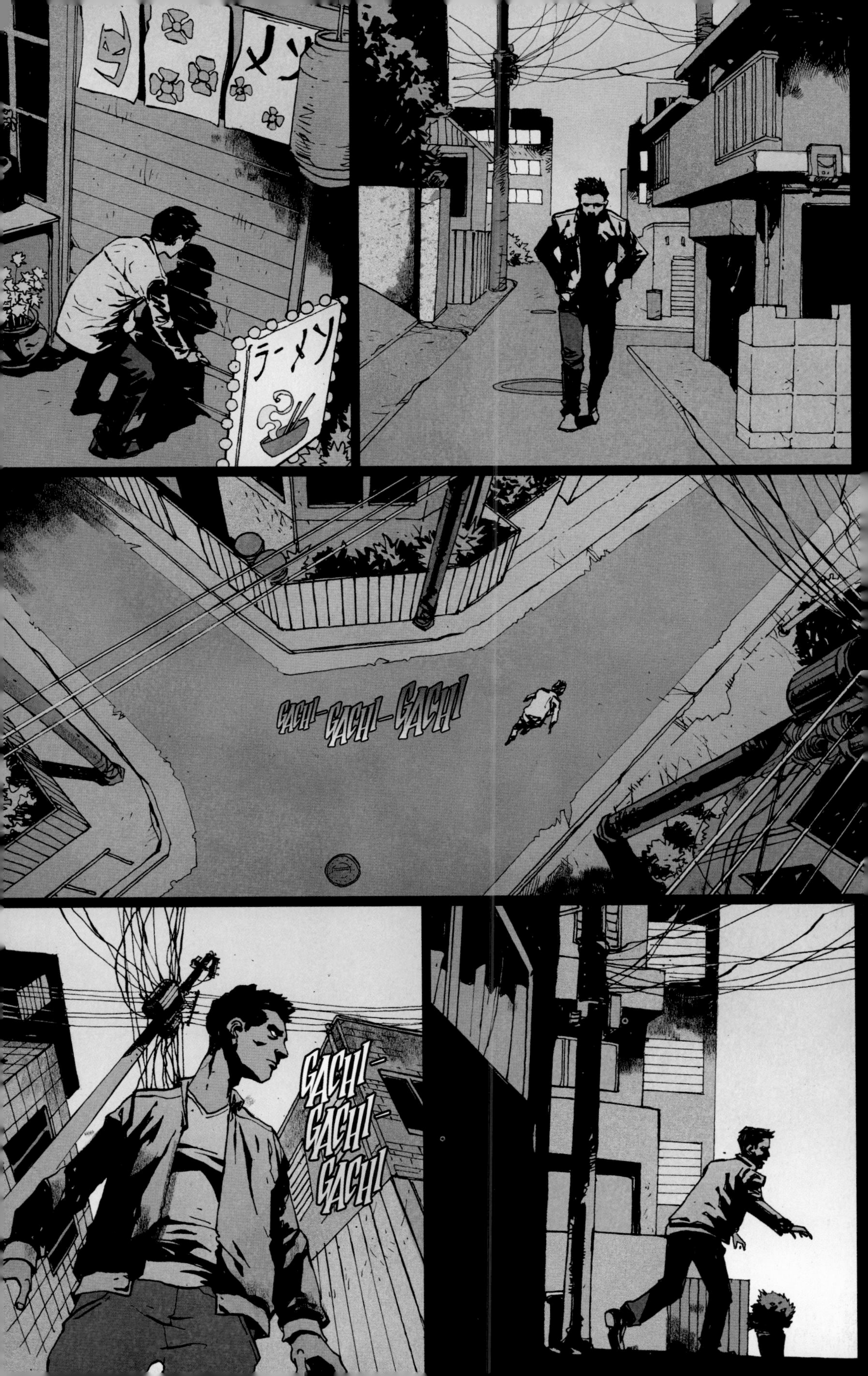
ラーメン
GACHI-GACHI-GACHI
GACHI-GACHI-GACHI

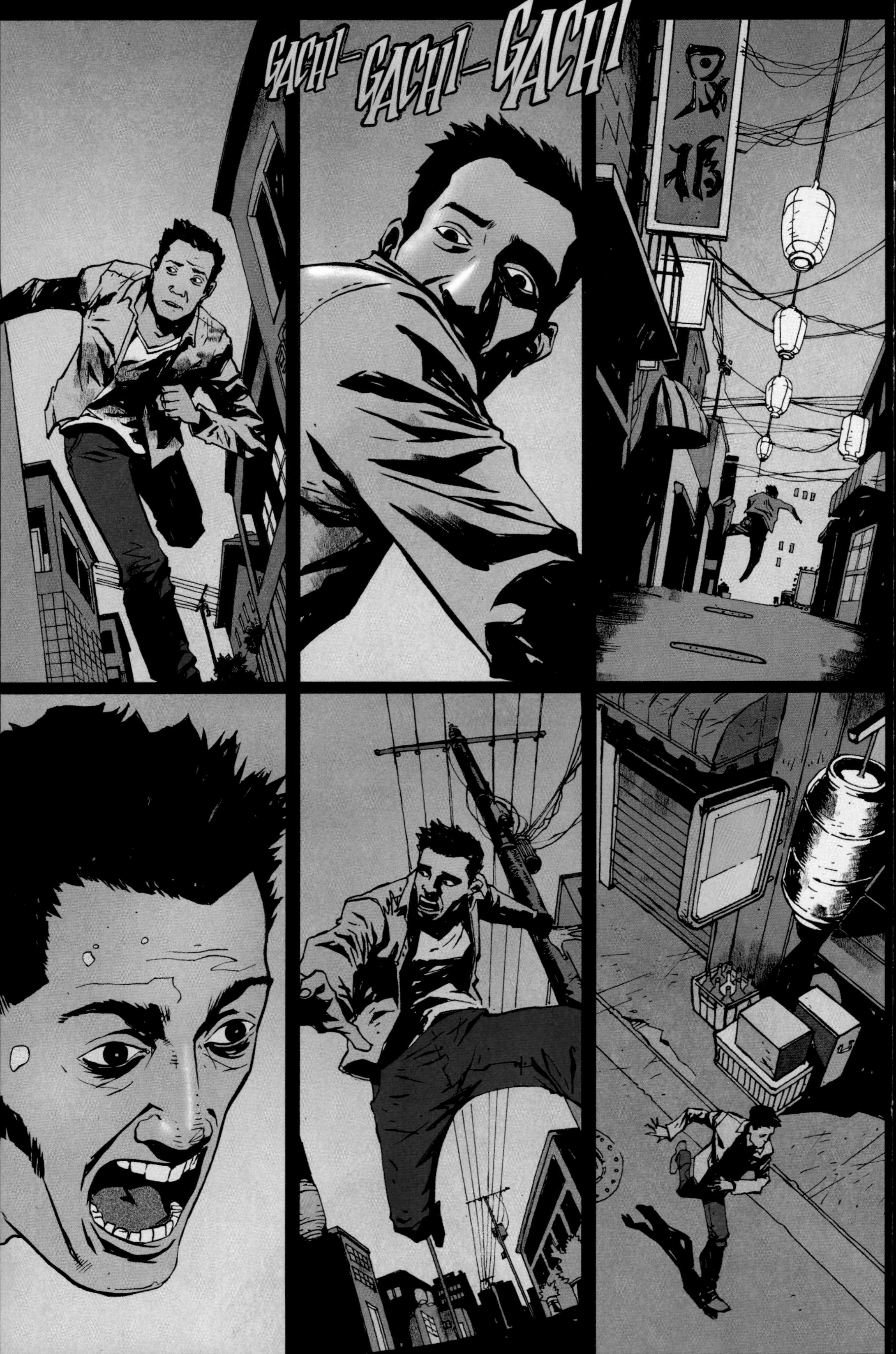
GACHI-GACHI-GACHI

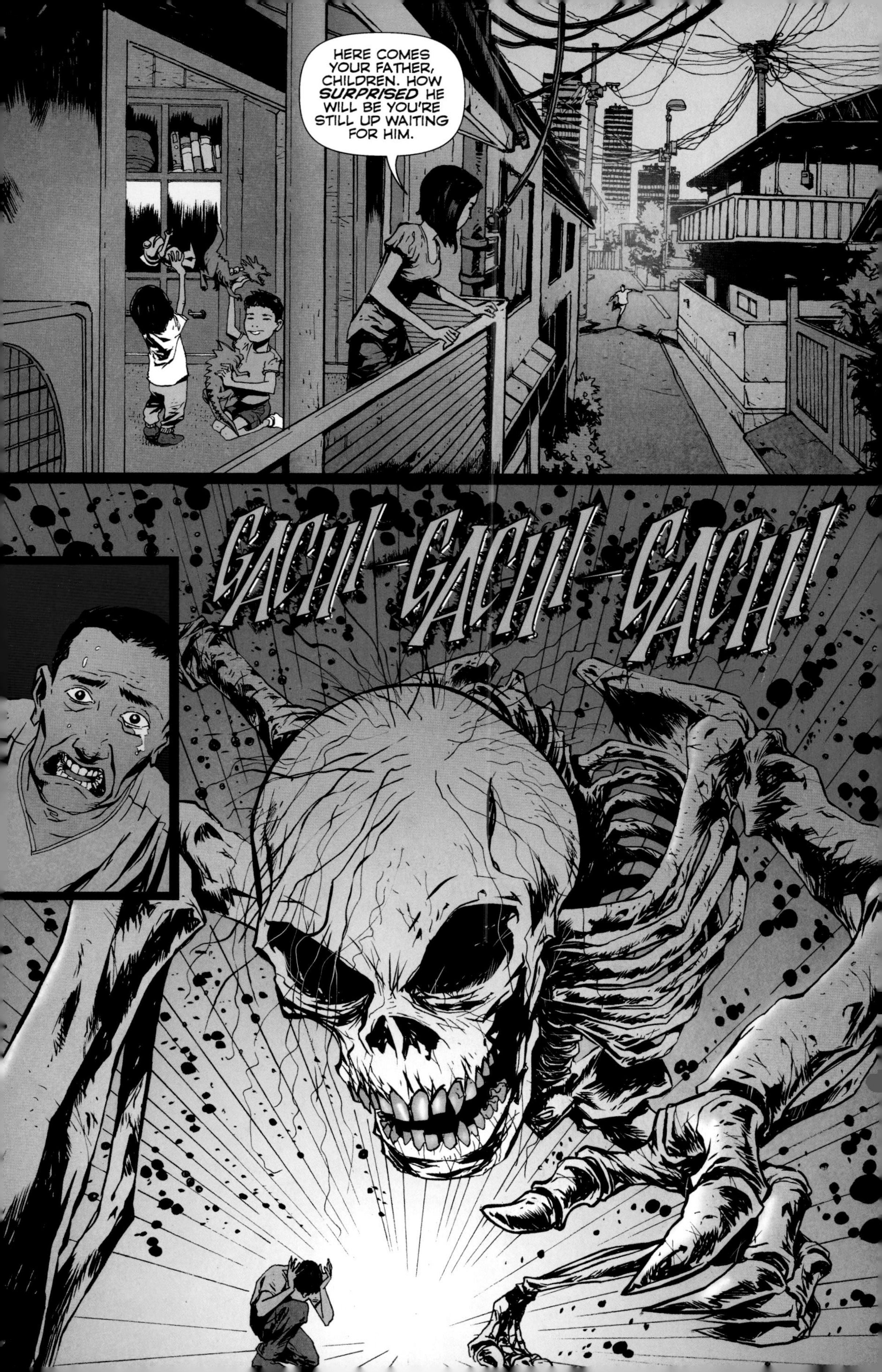
HERE COMES YOUR FATHER, CHILDREN. HOW SURPRISED HE WILL BE YOU'RE STILL UP WAITING FOR HIM.
GACHI-GACHI-GACHI

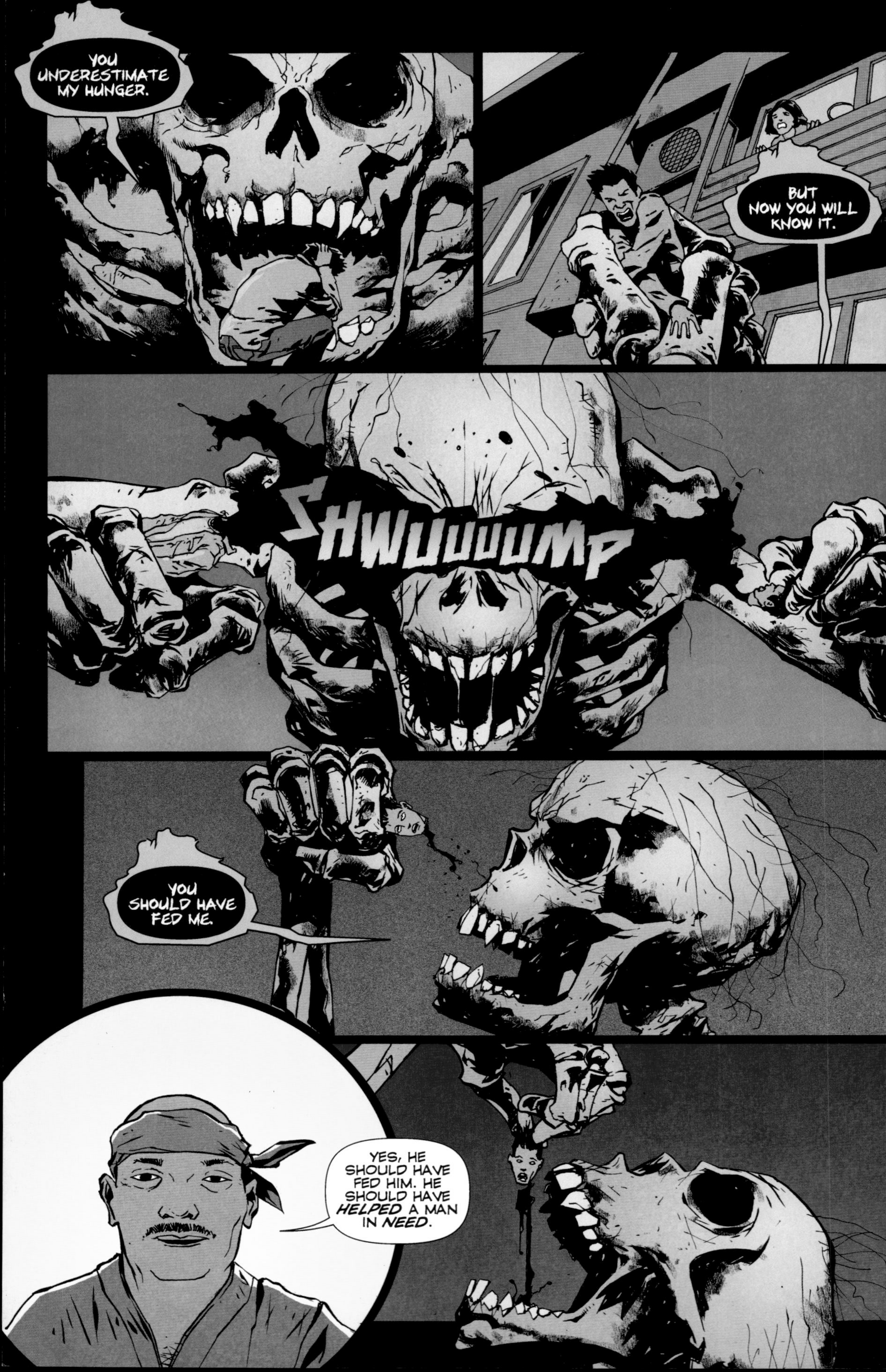
YOU UNDERESTIMATE MY HUNGER.
BUT NOW YOU WILL KNOW IT.
SHWUUUUMP
YOU SHOULD HAVE FED ME.
YES, HE SHOULD HAVE FED HIM. HE SHOULD HAVE *HELPED* A MAN IN *NEED*.

THE PIRATES

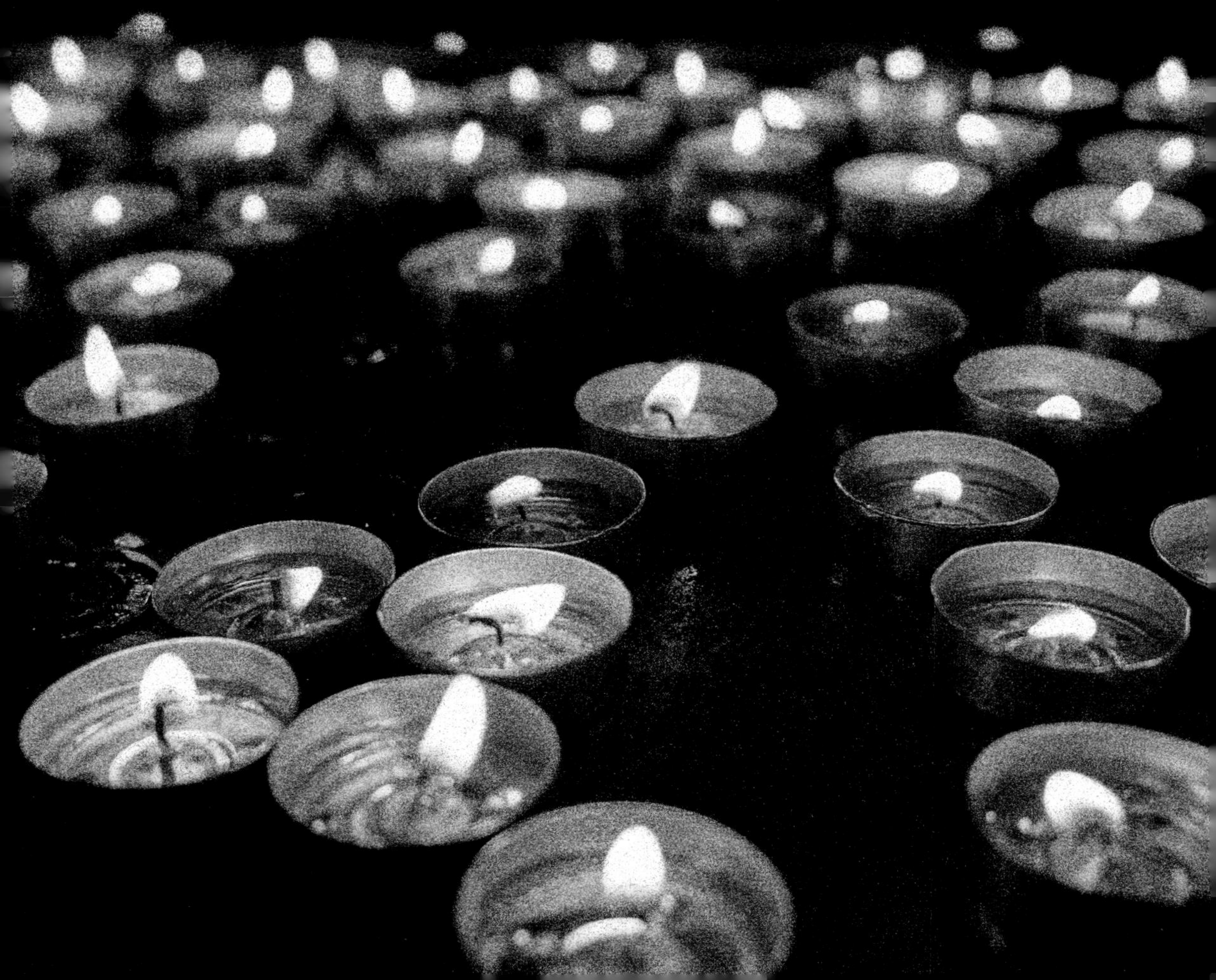

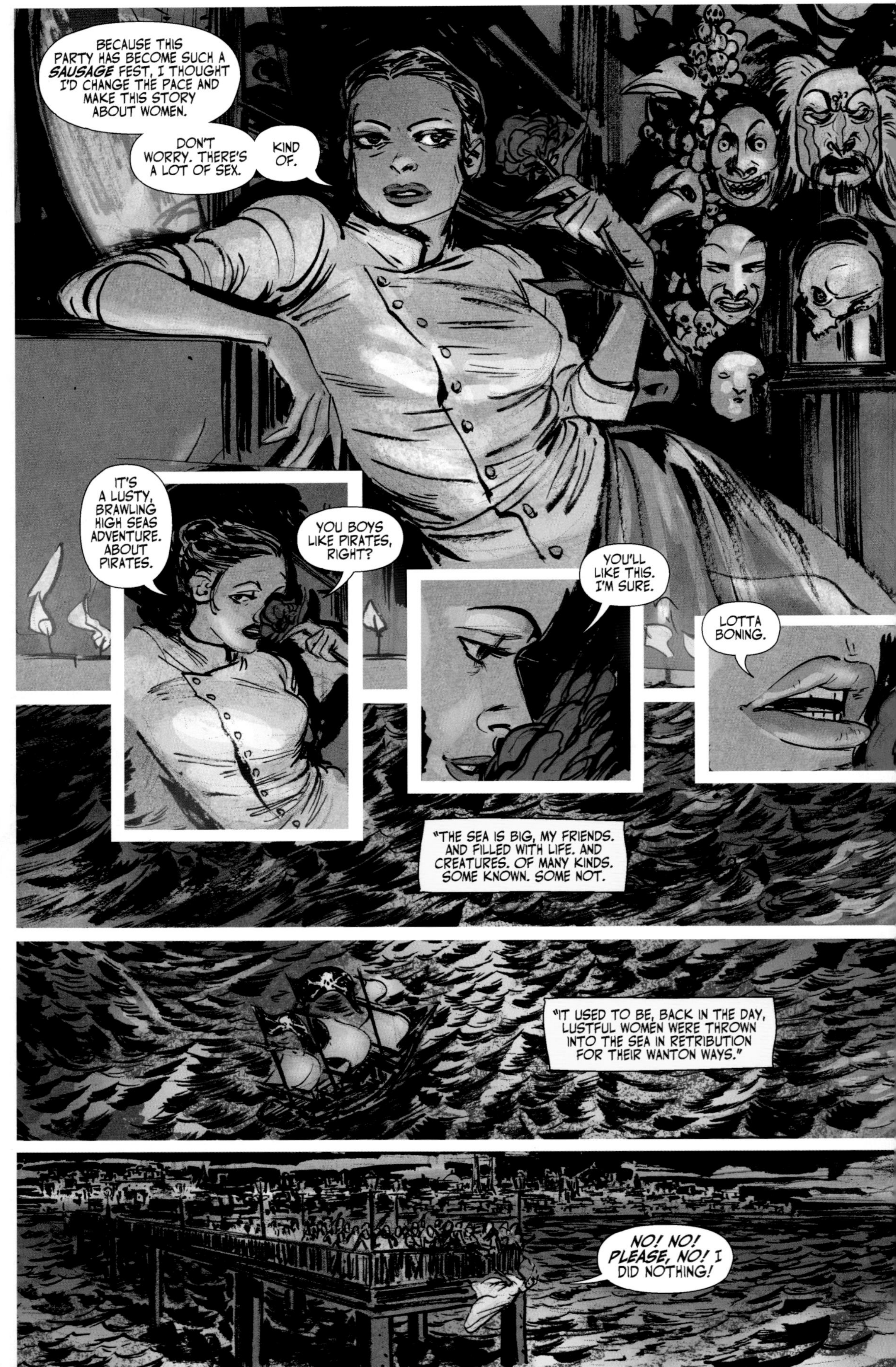
BECAUSE THIS PARTY HAS BECOME SUCH A SAUSAGE FEST, I THOUGHT I'D CHANGE THE PACE AND MAKE THIS STORY ABOUT WOMEN.
DON'T WORRY. THERE'S A LOT OF SEX.
KIND OF.
IT'S A LUSTY, BRAWLING HIGH SEAS ADVENTURE. ABOUT PIRATES.
YOU BOYS LIKE PIRATES, RIGHT?
YOU'LL LIKE THIS. I'M SURE.
LOTTA BONING.
"THE SEA IS BIG, MY FRIENDS. AND FILLED WITH LIFE. AND CREATURES. OF MANY KINDS. SOME KNOWN. SOME NOT.
"IT USED TO BE, BACK IN THE DAY, LUSTFUL WOMEN WERE THROWN INTO THE SEA IN RETRIBUTION FOR THEIR WANTON WAYS."
NO! NO! PLEASE, NO! I DID NOTHING!

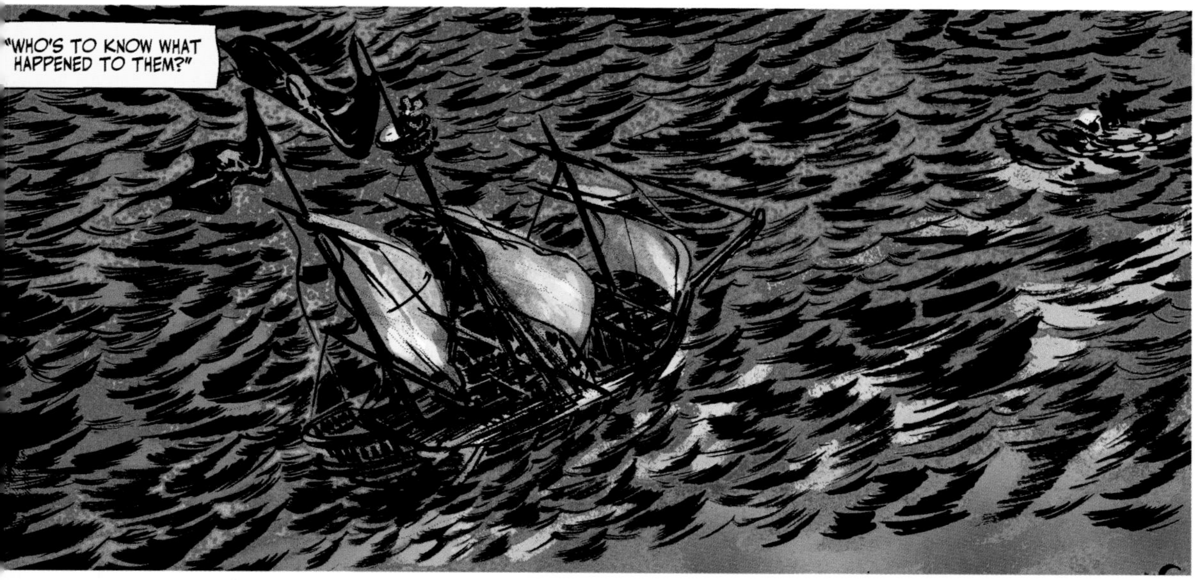
"WHO'S TO KNOW WHAT HAPPENED TO THEM?"

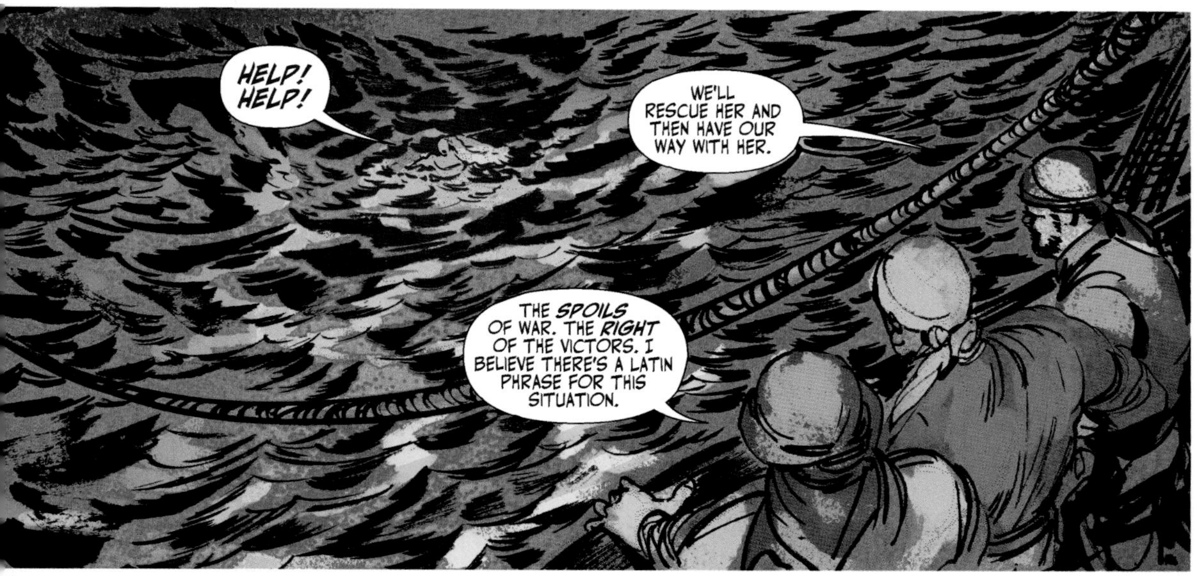
HELP! HELP!
WE'LL RESCUE HER AND THEN HAVE OUR WAY WITH HER.
THE SPOILS OF WAR. THE RIGHT OF THE VICTORS. I BELIEVE THERE'S A LATIN PHRASE FOR THIS SITUATION.

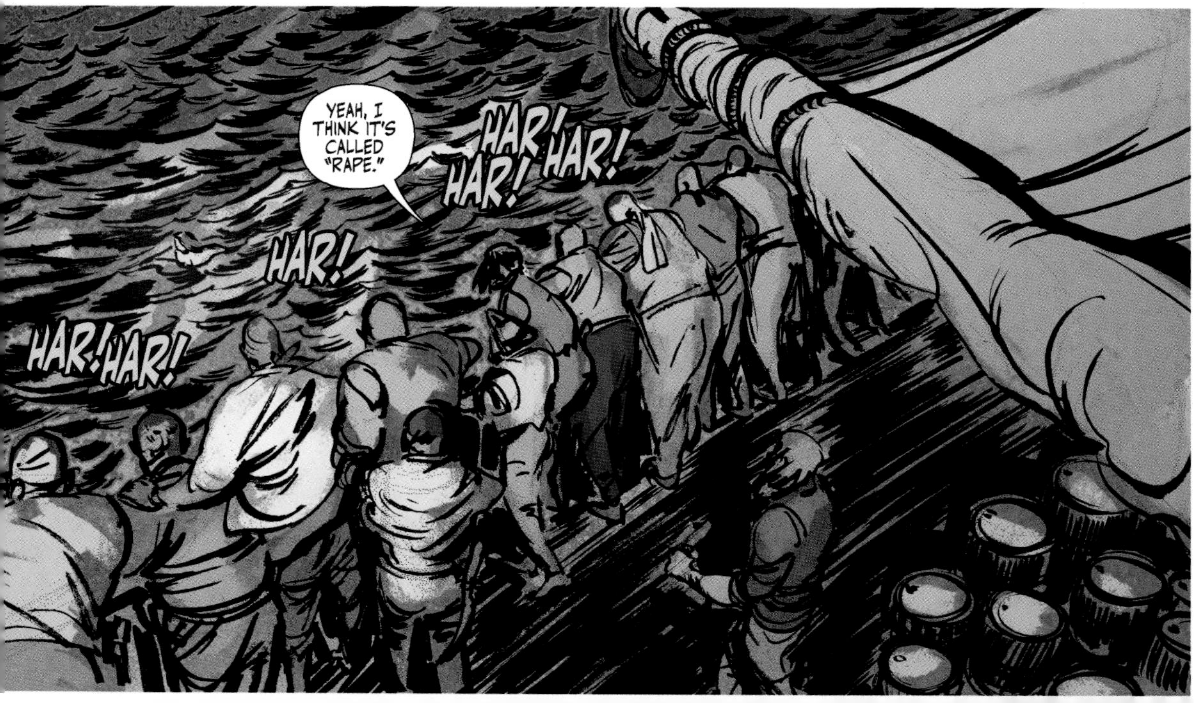
YEAH, I THINK IT'S CALLED "RAPE."
HAR! HAR!
HAR!
HAR!
HAR! HAR!

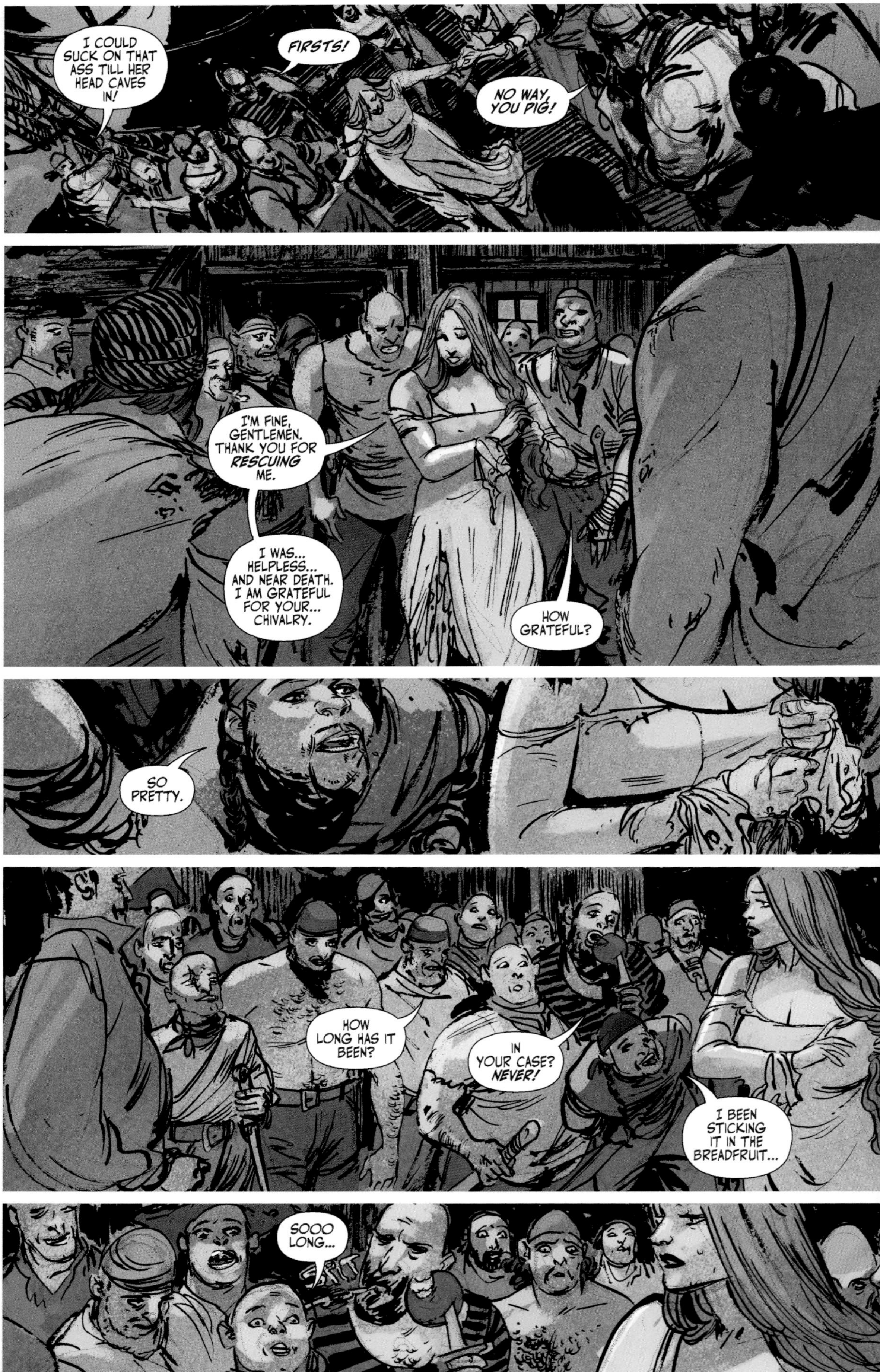
I COULD SUCK ON THAT ASS TILL HER HEAD CAVES IN!
FIRSTS!
NO WAY, YOU PIG!
I'M FINE, GENTLEMEN. THANK YOU FOR RESCUING ME.
I WAS... HELPLESS... AND NEAR DEATH. I AM GRATEFUL FOR YOUR... CHIVALRY.
HOW GRATEFUL?
SO PRETTY.
HOW LONG HAS IT BEEN?
IN YOUR CASE? NEVER!
I BEEN STICKING IT IN THE BREADFRUIT...
SOOO LONG...

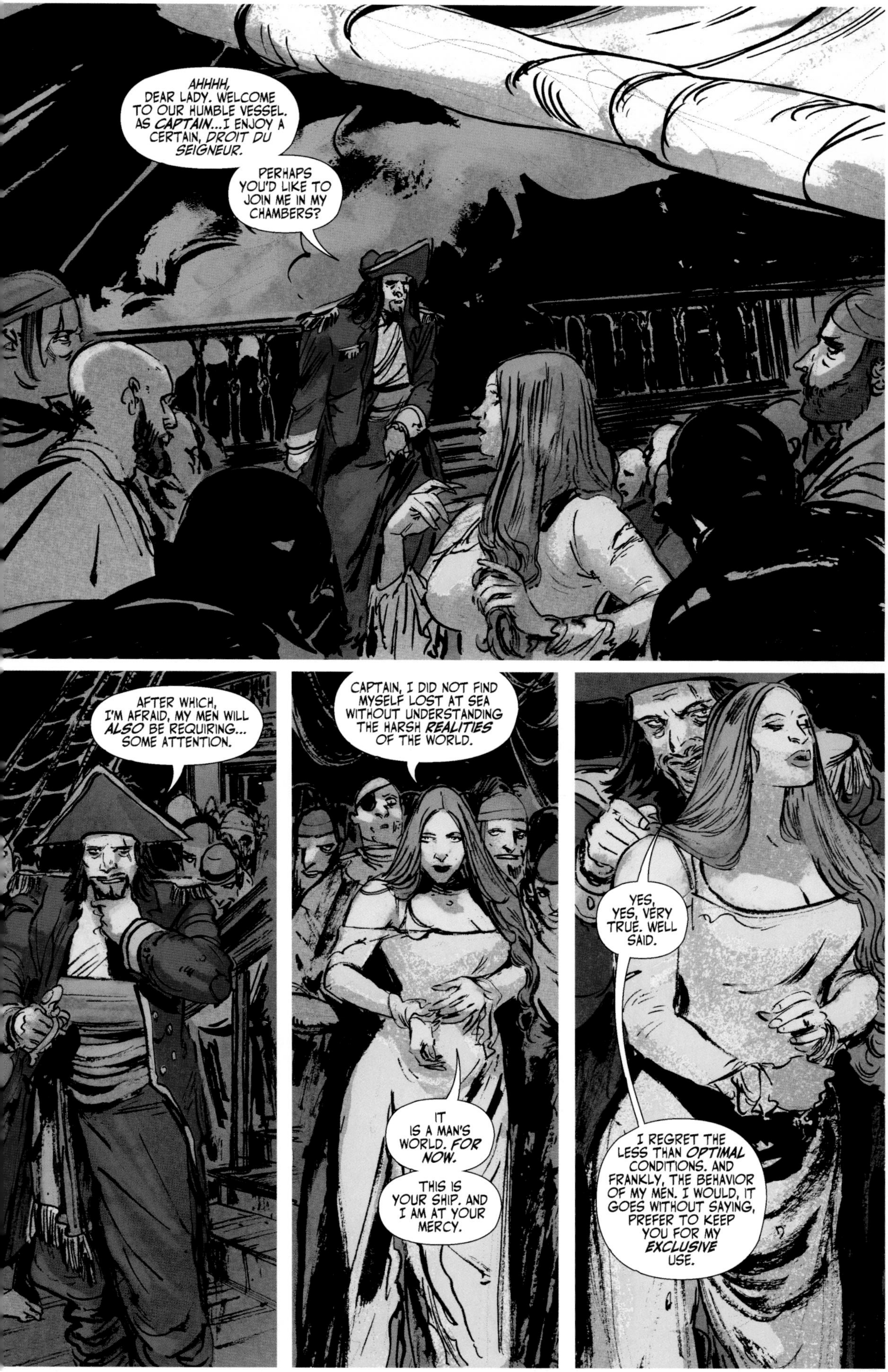
AHHHH, DEAR LADY. WELCOME TO OUR HUMBLE VESSEL. AS CAPTAIN...I ENJOY A CERTAIN, DROIT DU SEIGNEUR.
PERHAPS YOU'D LIKE TO JOIN ME IN MY CHAMBERS?
AFTER WHICH, I'M AFRAID, MY MEN WILL ALSO BE REQUIRING... SOME ATTENTION.
CAPTAIN, I DID NOT FIND MYSELF LOST AT SEA WITHOUT UNDERSTANDING THE HARSH REALITIES OF THE WORLD.
IT IS A MAN'S WORLD. FOR NOW.
THIS IS YOUR SHIP. AND I AM AT YOUR MERCY.
YES, YES, VERY TRUE. WELL SAID.
I REGRET THE LESS THAN OPTIMAL CONDITIONS. AND FRANKLY, THE BEHAVIOR OF MY MEN. I WOULD, IT GOES WITHOUT SAYING, PREFER TO KEEP YOU FOR MY EXCLUSIVE USE.

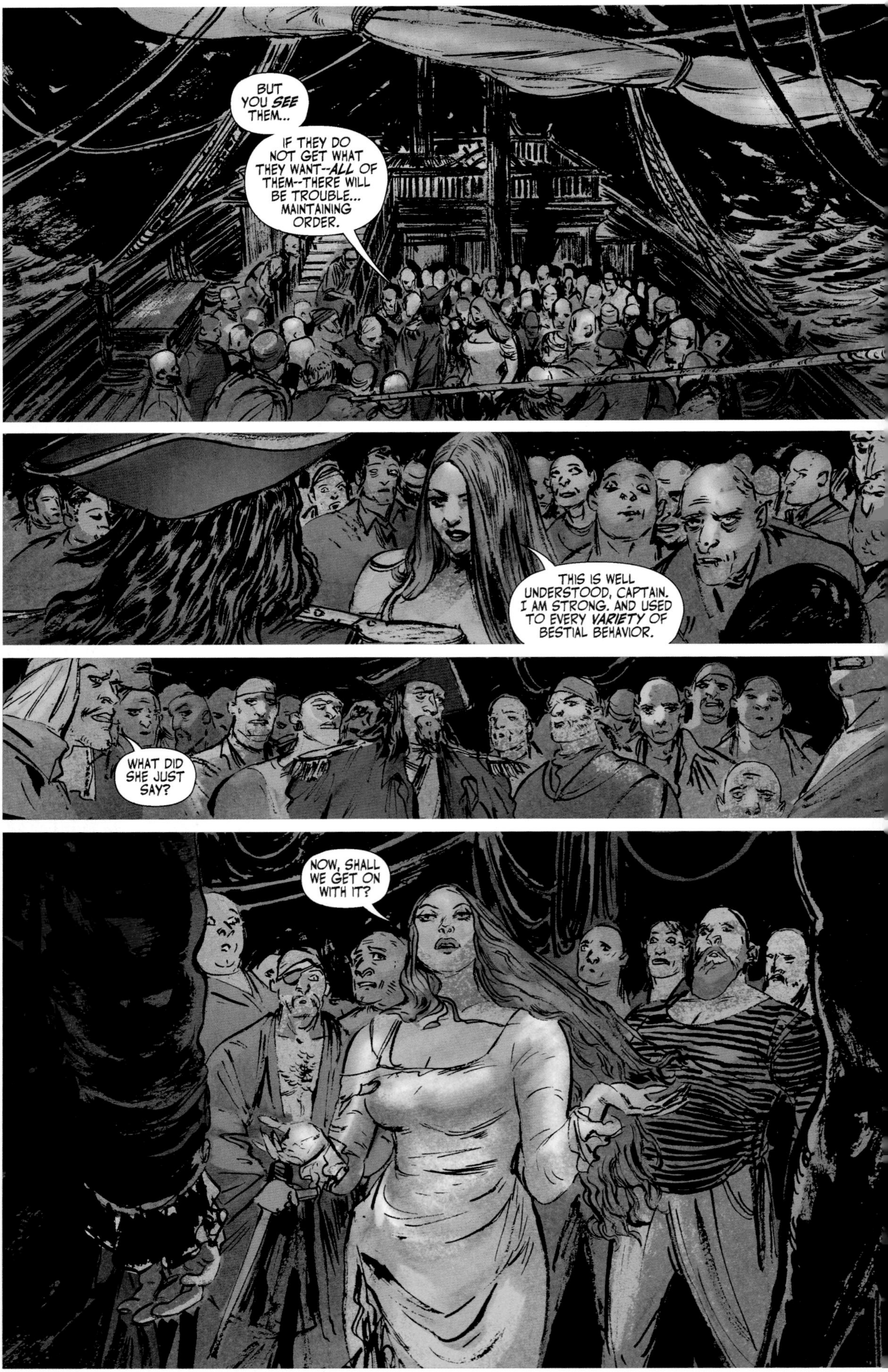
BUT YOU *SEE* THEM...
IF THEY DO NOT GET WHAT THEY WANT--*ALL* OF THEM--THERE WILL BE TROUBLE... MAINTAINING ORDER.
THIS IS WELL UNDERSTOOD, CAPTAIN. I AM STRONG. AND USED TO EVERY *VARIETY* OF BESTIAL BEHAVIOR.
WHAT DID SHE JUST SAY?
NOW, SHALL WE GET ON WITH IT?

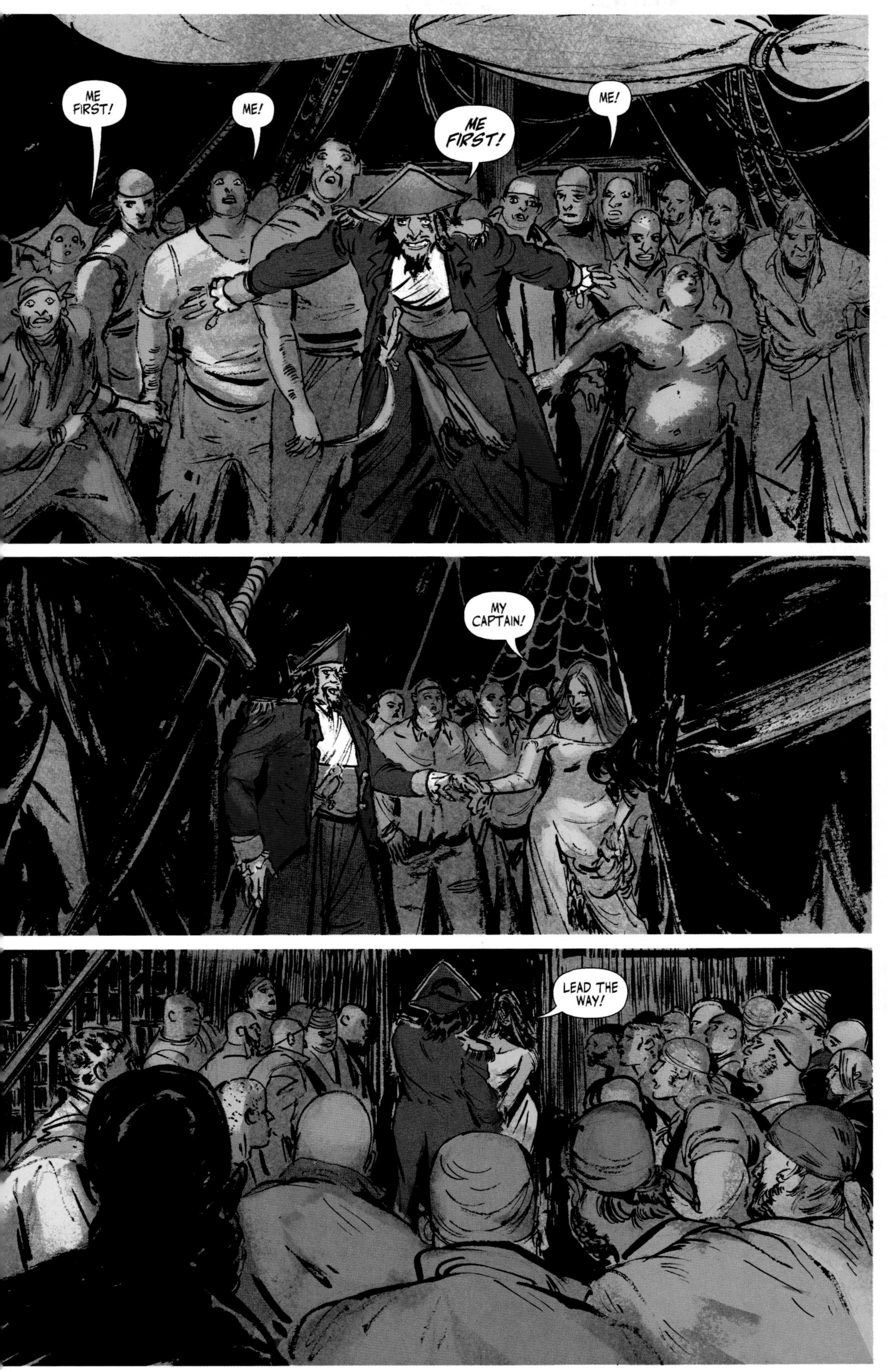
ME FIRST!
ME!
ME FIRST!
ME!
MY CAPTAIN!
LEAD THE WAY!

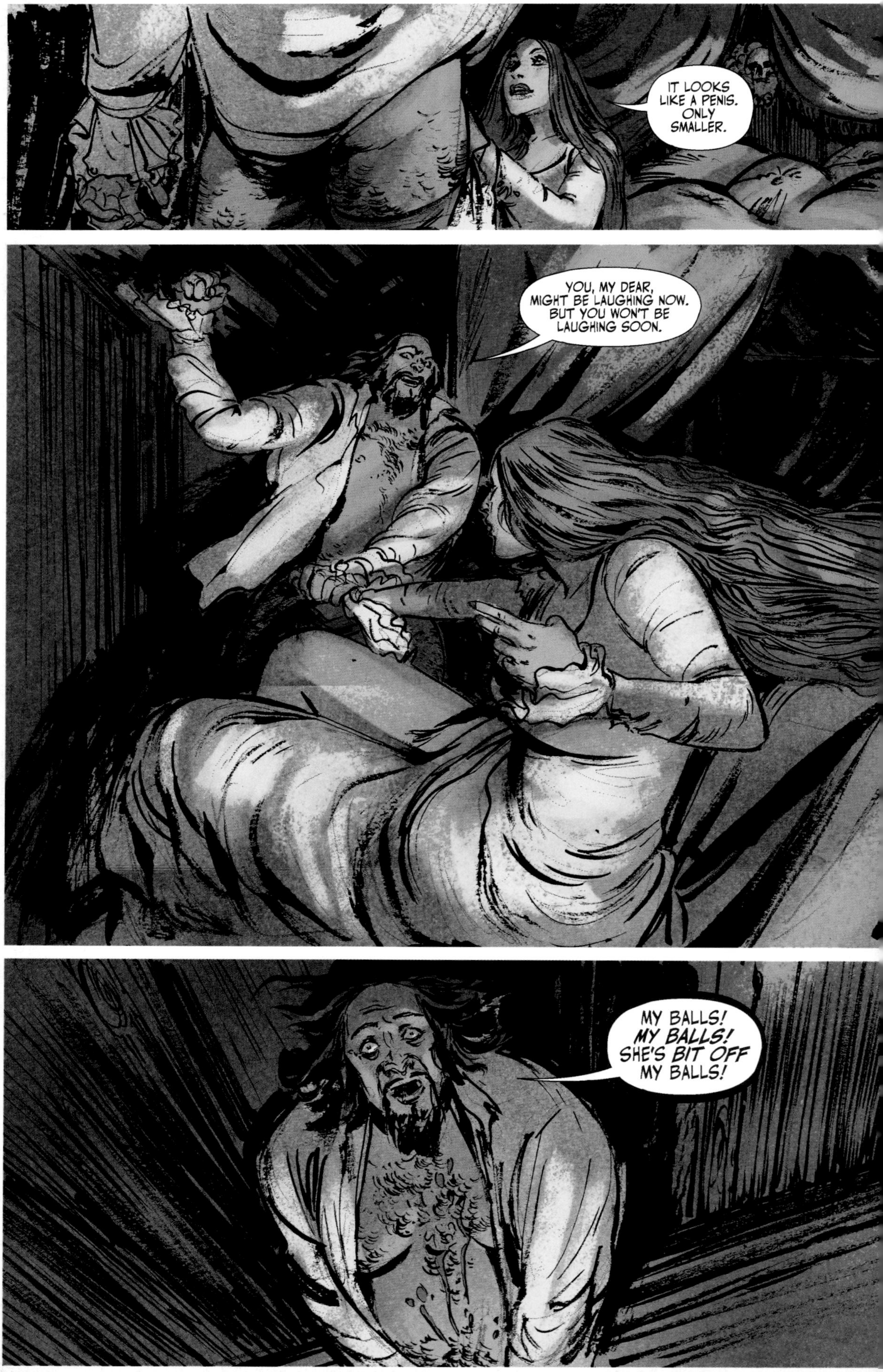
IT LOOKS LIKE A PENIS. ONLY SMALLER.
YOU, MY DEAR, MIGHT BE LAUGHING NOW. BUT YOU WON'T BE LAUGHING SOON.
MY BALLS! *MY BALLS!* SHE'S *BIT OFF* MY BALLS!

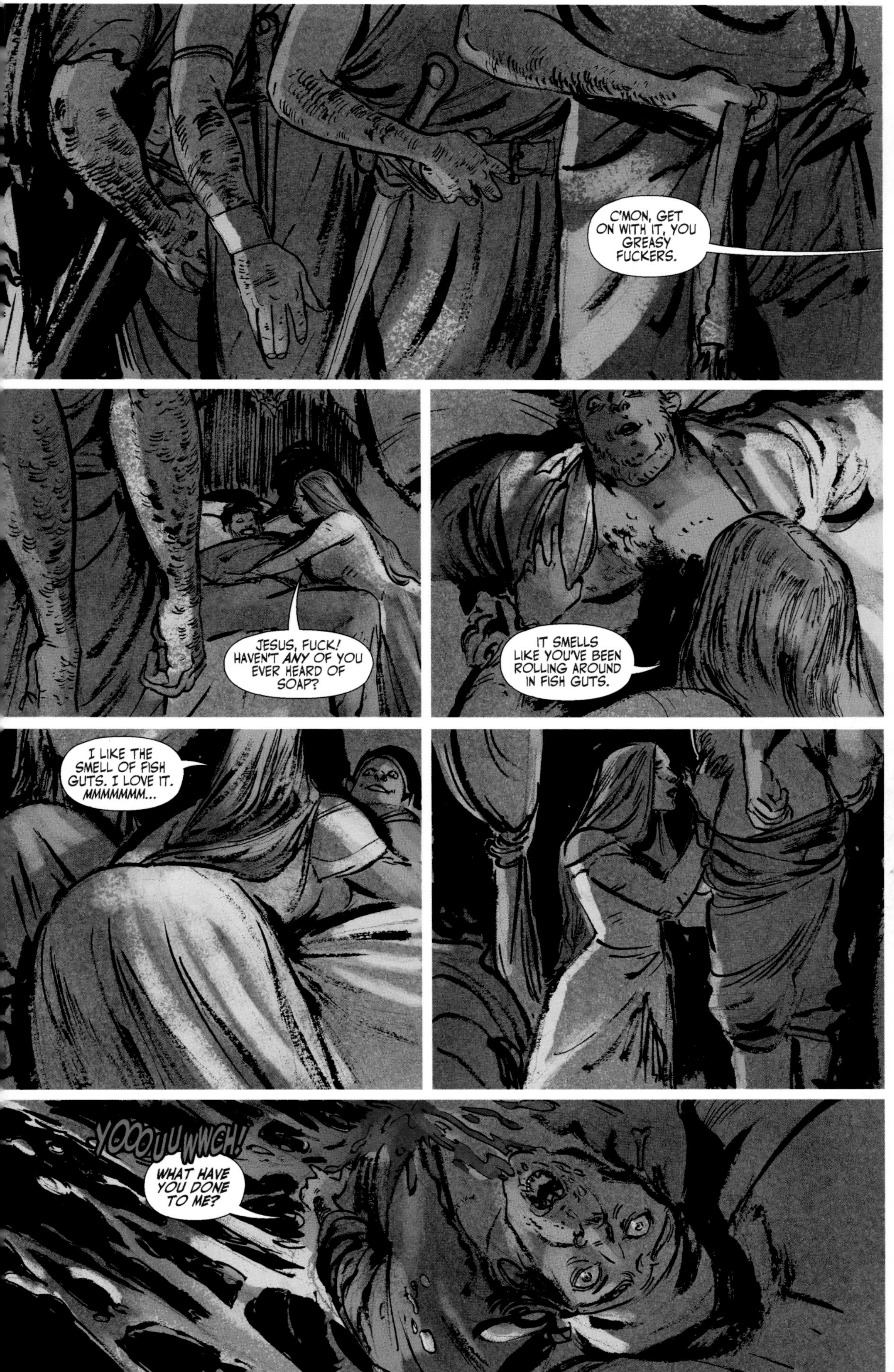
C'MON, GET ON WITH IT, YOU GREASY FUCKERS.
JESUS, FUCK! HAVEN'T ANY OF YOU EVER HEARD OF SOAP?
IT SMELLS LIKE YOU'VE BEEN ROLLING AROUND IN FISH GUTS.
I LIKE THE SMELL OF FISH GUTS. I LOVE IT. MMMMMMM...
YOOOUUWWCH!
WHAT HAVE YOU DONE TO ME?

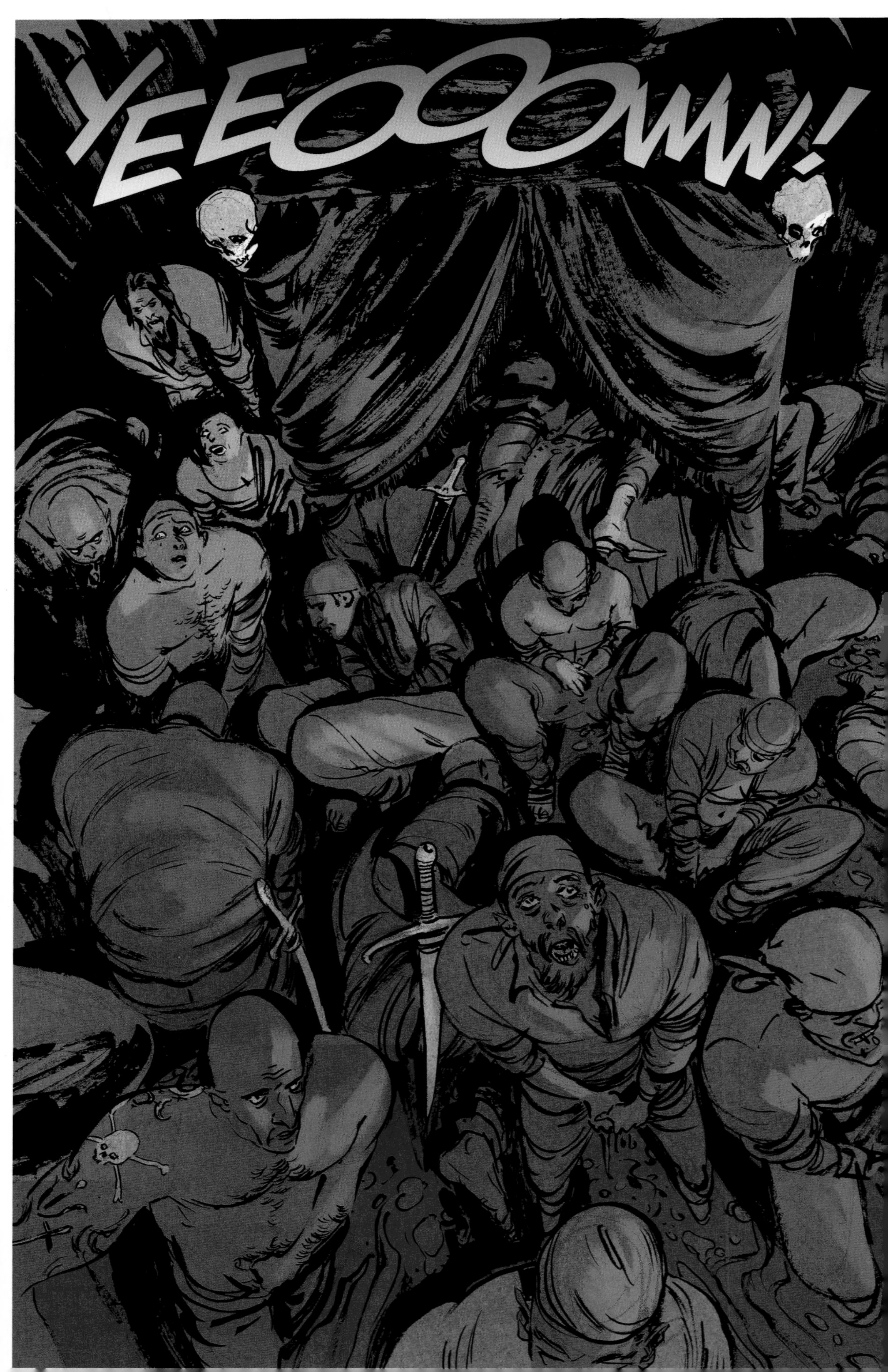
YEEOOOWW!

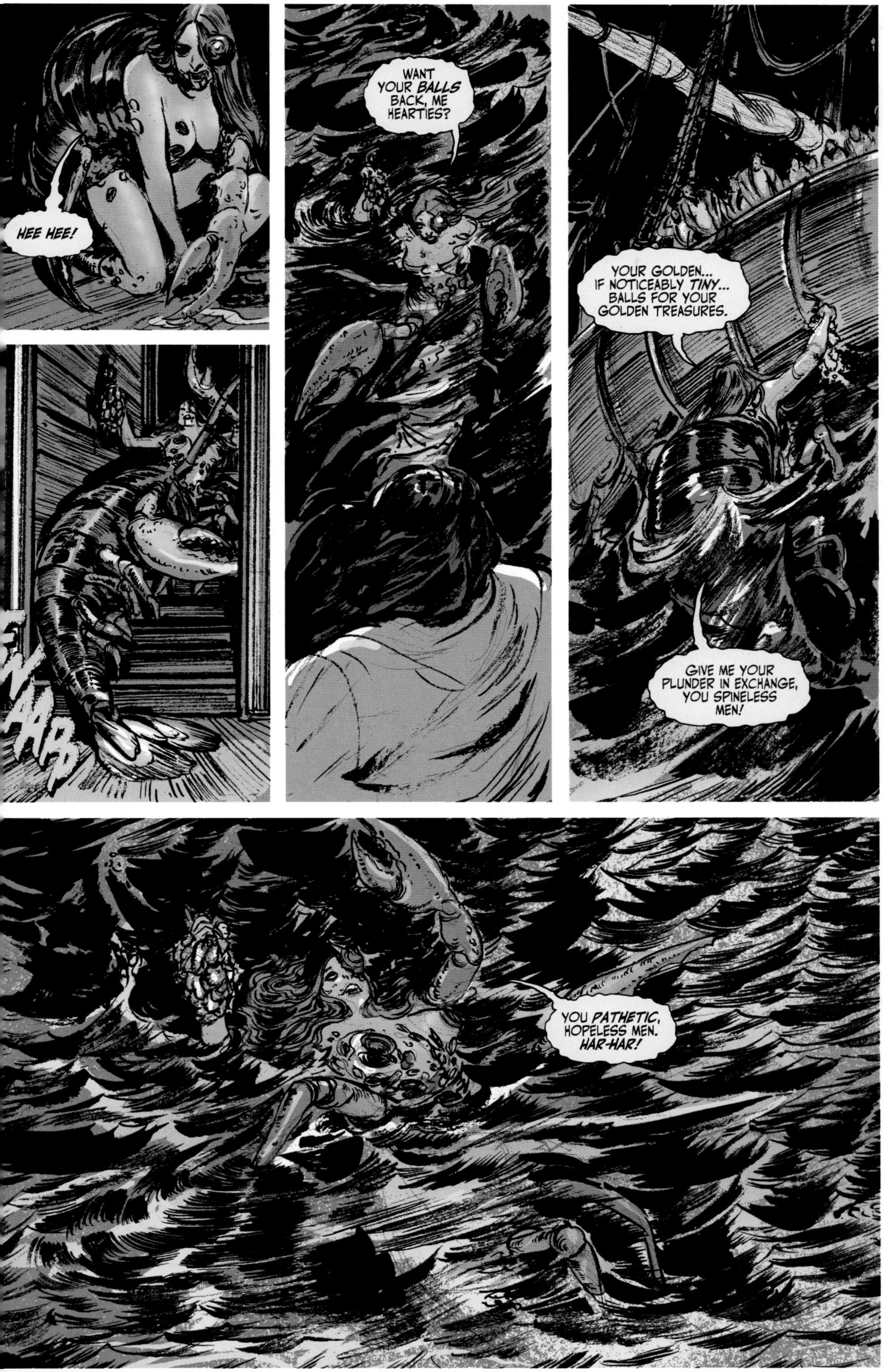
HEE HEE!
WANT YOUR BALLS BACK, ME HEARTIES?
YOUR GOLDEN... IF NOTICEABLY TINY... BALLS FOR YOUR GOLDEN TREASURES.
GIVE ME YOUR PLUNDER IN EXCHANGE, YOU SPINELESS MEN!
YOU PATHETIC, HOPELESS MEN. HAR-HAR!

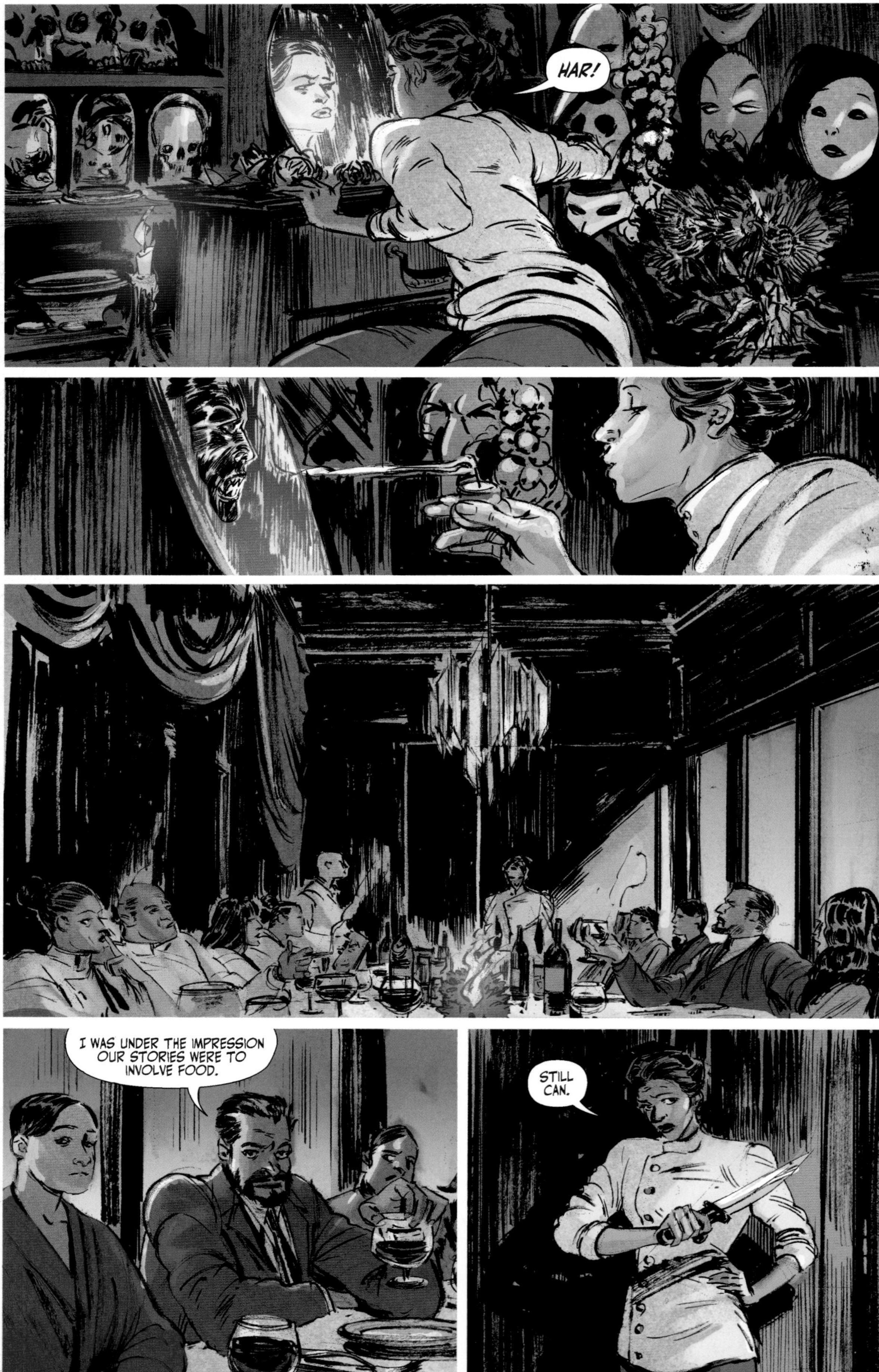
HAR!
I WAS UNDER THE IMPRESSION OUR STORIES WERE TO INVOLVE FOOD.
STILL CAN.

SALTY HORSE

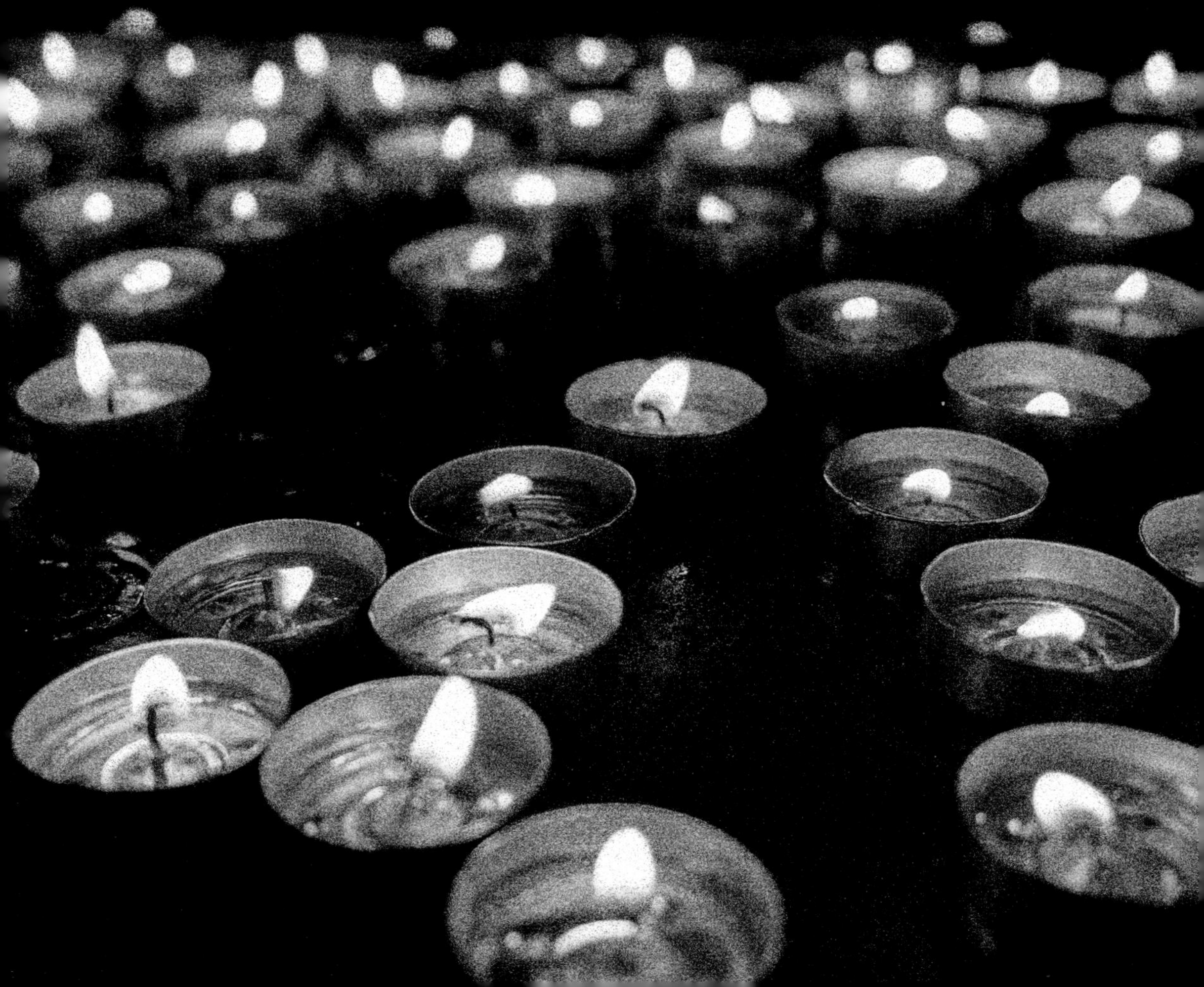

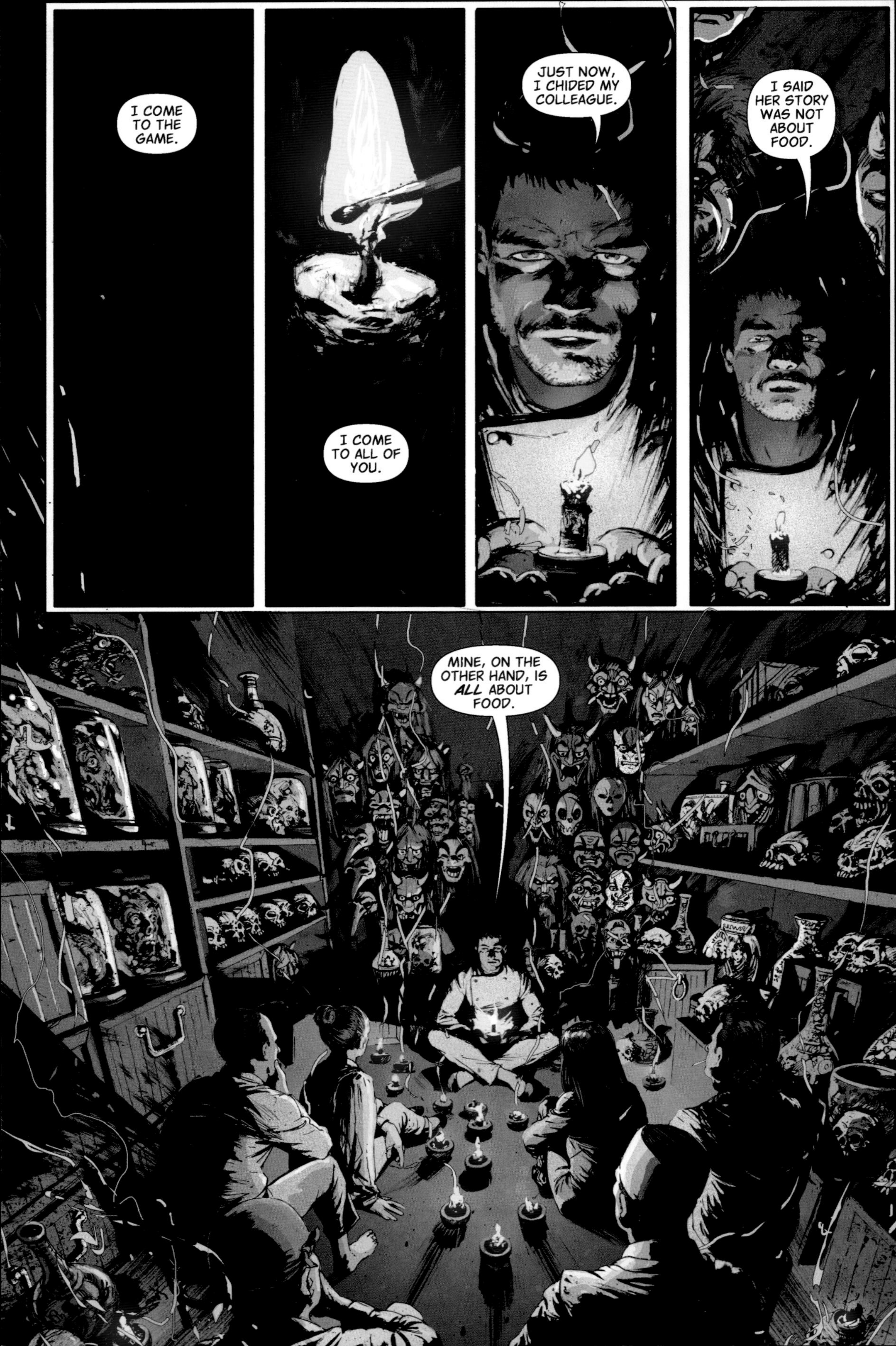
I COME TO THE GAME.
I COME TO ALL OF YOU.
JUST NOW, I CHIDED MY COLLEAGUE.
I SAID HER STORY WAS NOT ABOUT FOOD.
MINE, ON THE OTHER HAND, IS ***ALL*** ABOUT FOOD.

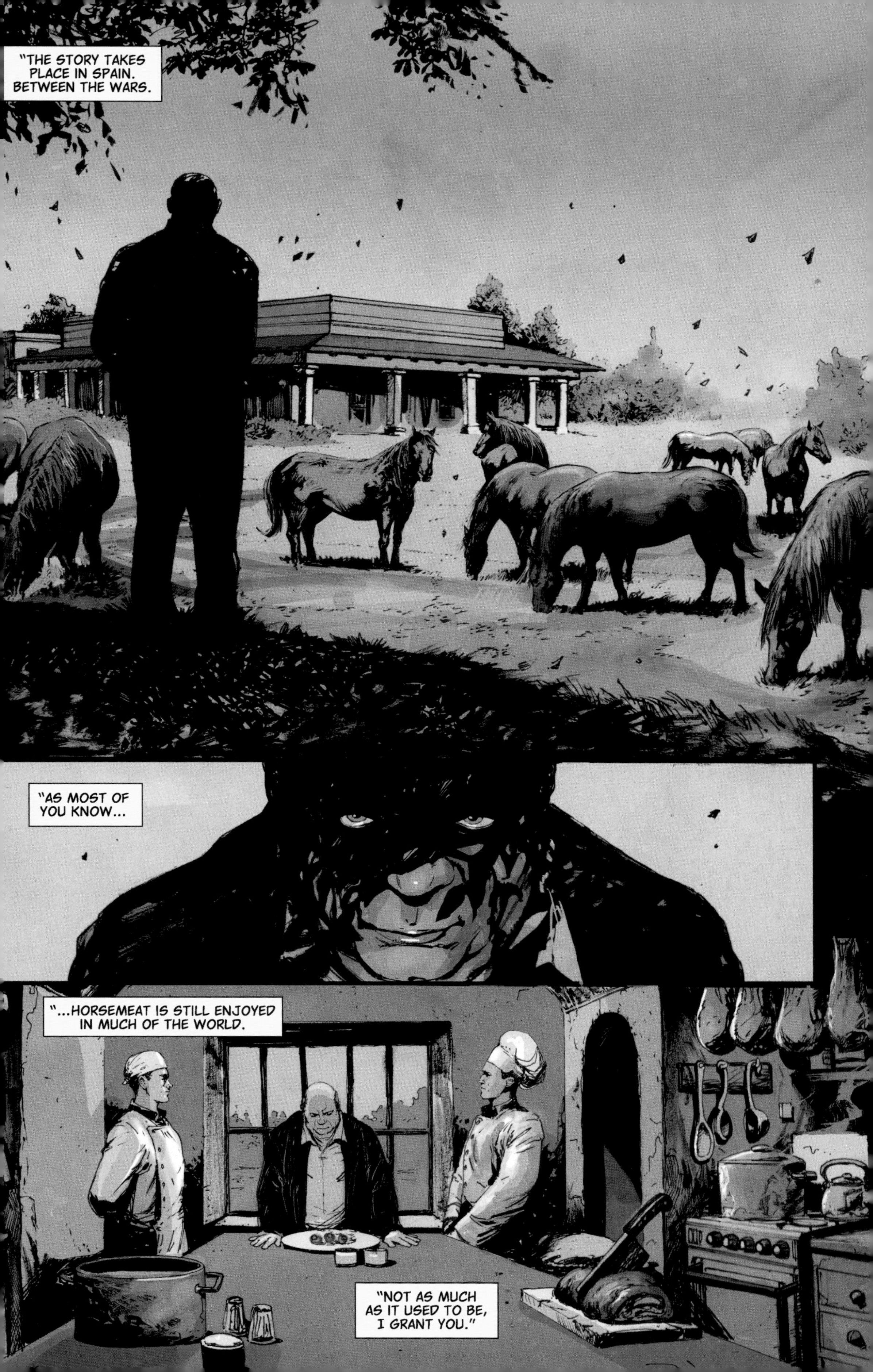
"THE STORY TAKES PLACE IN SPAIN. BETWEEN THE WARS.
"AS MOST OF YOU KNOW...
"...HORSEMEAT IS STILL ENJOYED IN MUCH OF THE WORLD.
"NOT AS MUCH AS IT USED TO BE, I GRANT YOU."

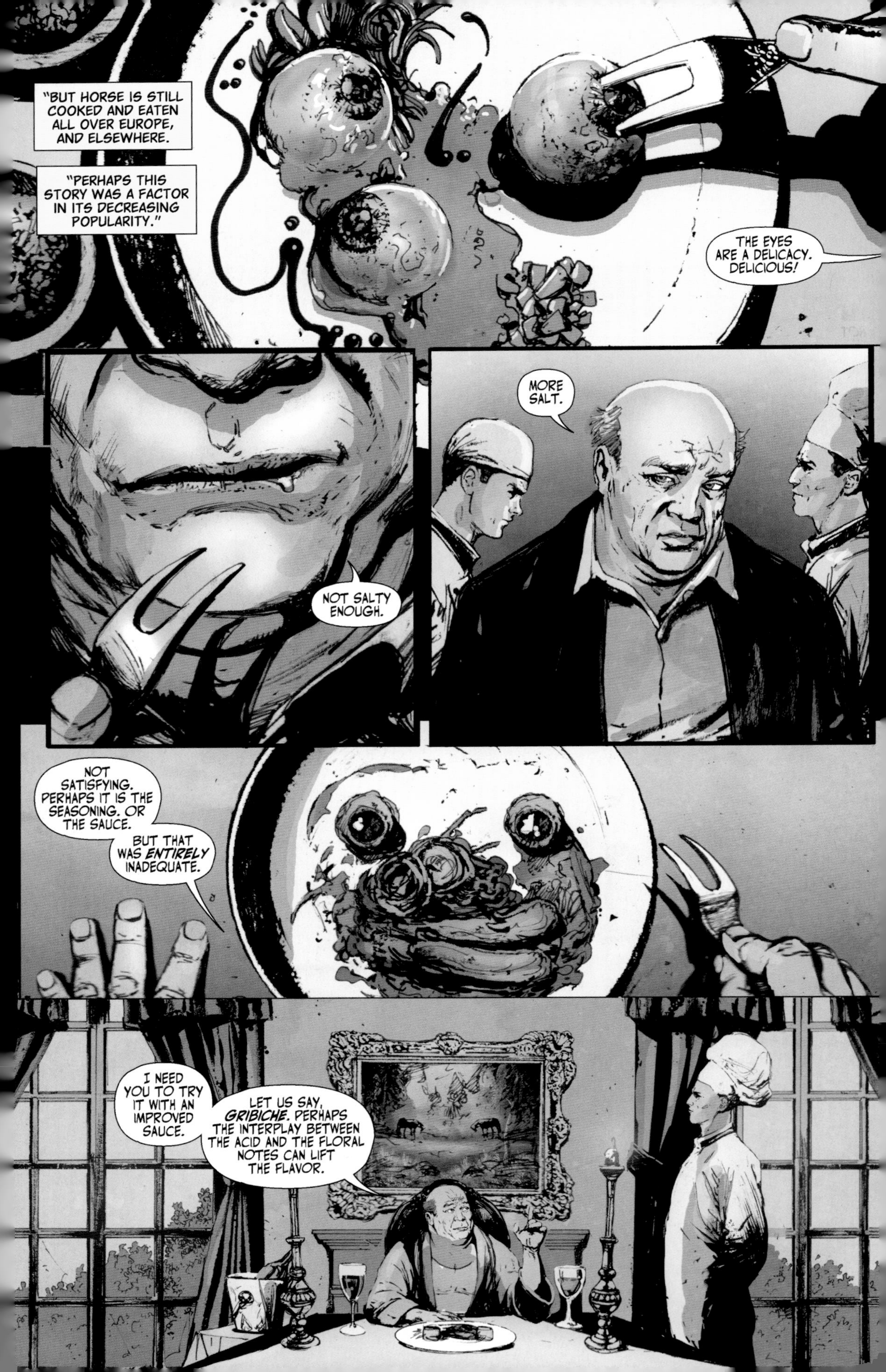
"BUT HORSE IS STILL COOKED AND EATEN ALL OVER EUROPE, AND ELSEWHERE.
"PERHAPS THIS STORY WAS A FACTOR IN ITS DECREASING POPULARITY."
THE EYES ARE A DELICACY. DELICIOUS!
NOT SALTY ENOUGH.
MORE SALT.
NOT SATISFYING. PERHAPS IT IS THE SEASONING. OR THE SAUCE.
BUT THAT WAS *ENTIRELY* INADEQUATE.
I NEED YOU TO TRY IT WITH AN IMPROVED SAUCE.
LET US SAY, ***GRIBICHE***. PERHAPS THE INTERPLAY BETWEEN THE ACID AND THE FLORAL NOTES CAN LIFT THE FLAVOR.

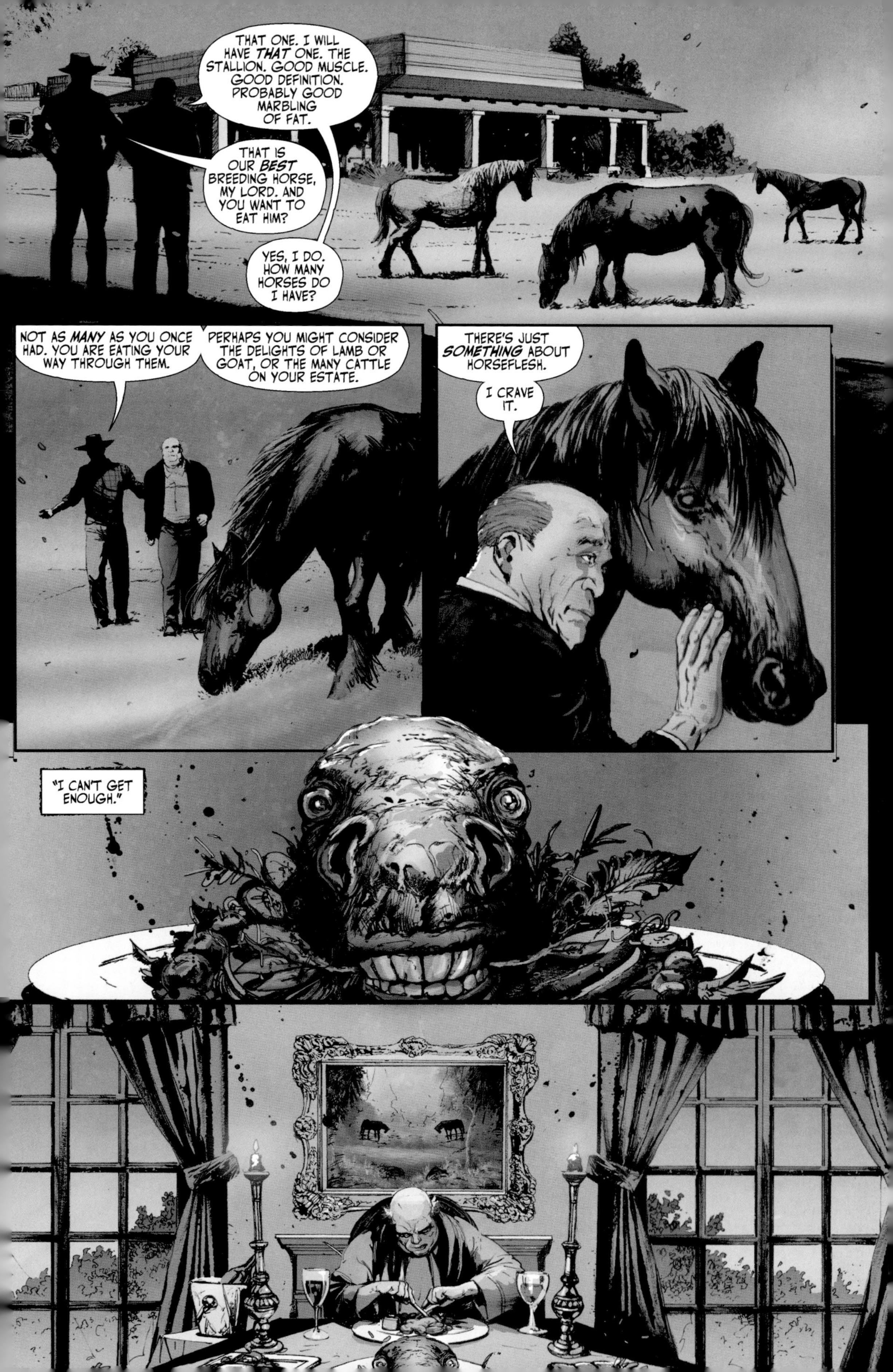
THAT ONE. I WILL HAVE THAT ONE. THE STALLION. GOOD MUSCLE. GOOD DEFINITION. PROBABLY GOOD MARBLING OF FAT.
THAT IS OUR BEST BREEDING HORSE, MY LORD. AND YOU WANT TO EAT HIM?
YES, I DO. HOW MANY HORSES DO I HAVE?
NOT AS MANY AS YOU ONCE HAD. YOU ARE EATING YOUR WAY THROUGH THEM.
PERHAPS YOU MIGHT CONSIDER THE DELIGHTS OF LAMB OR GOAT, OR THE MANY CATTLE ON YOUR ESTATE.
THERE'S JUST SOMETHING ABOUT HORSEFLESH.
I CRAVE IT.
"I CAN'T GET ENOUGH."

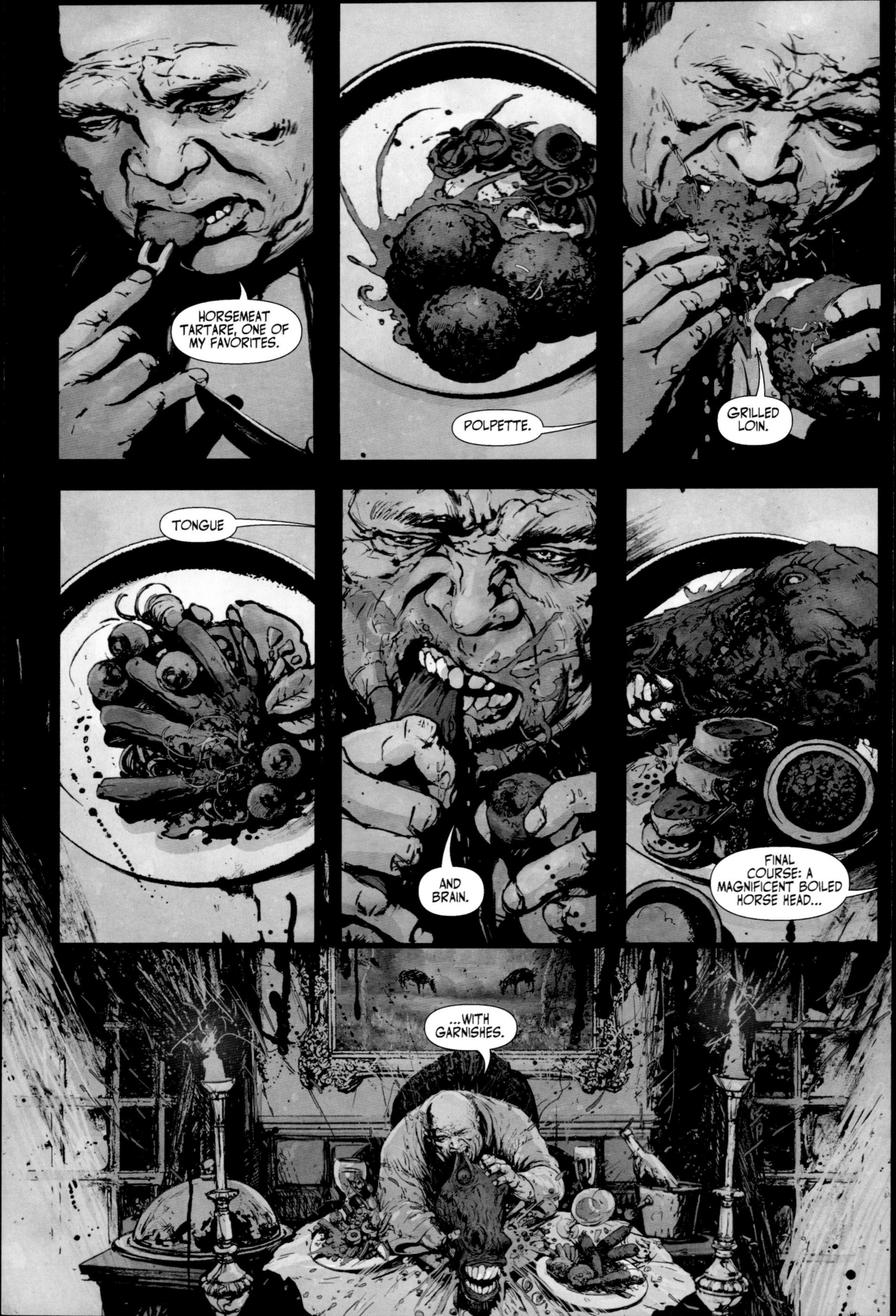
HORSEMEAT TARTARE, ONE OF MY FAVORITES.
POLPETTE.
GRILLED LOIN.
TONGUE
AND BRAIN.
FINAL COURSE: A MAGNIFICENT BOILED HORSE HEAD...
...WITH GARNISHES.

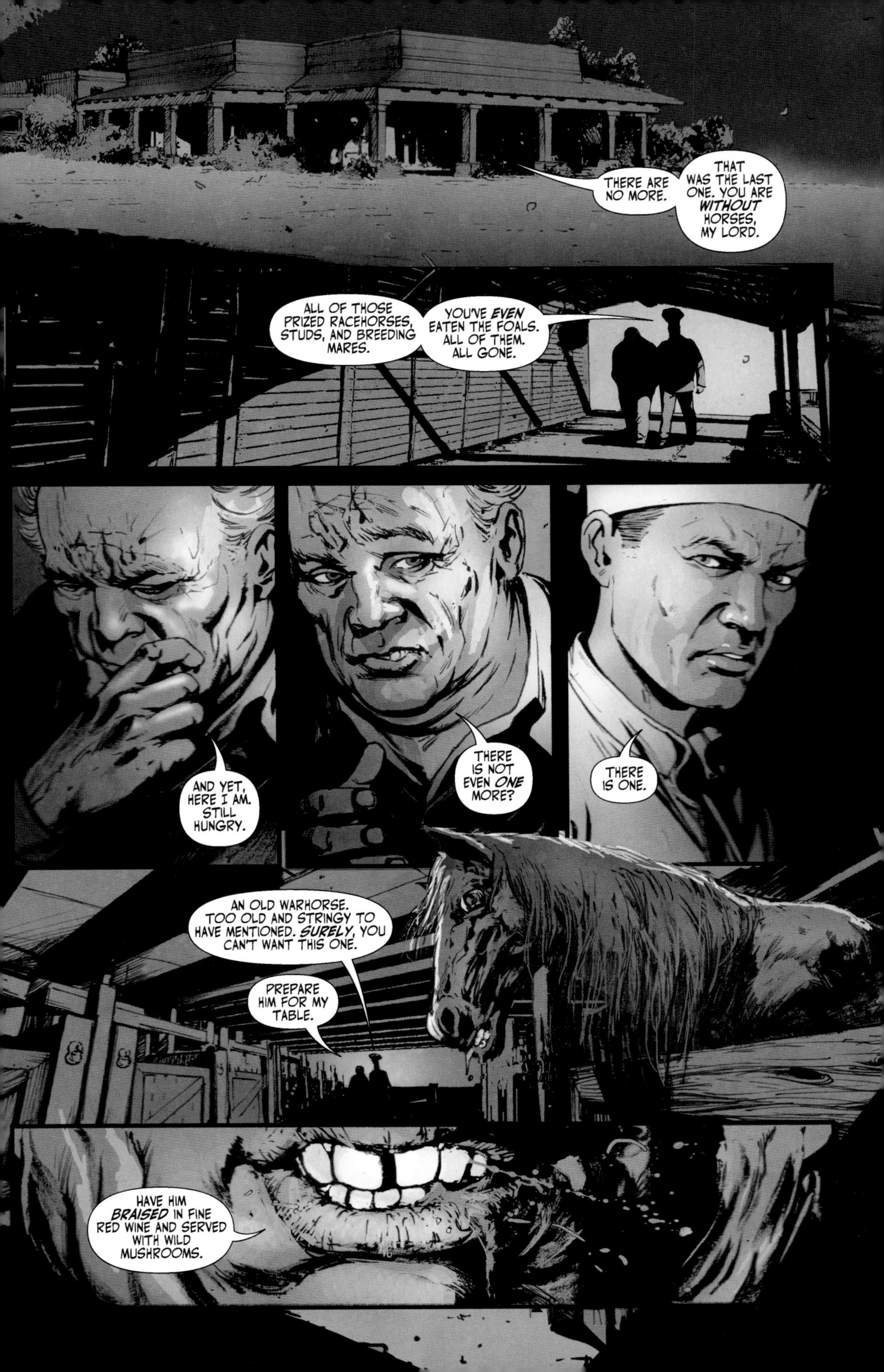
THERE ARE NO MORE.
THAT WAS THE LAST ONE. YOU ARE *WITHOUT* HORSES, MY LORD.
ALL OF THOSE PRIZED RACEHORSES, STUDS, AND BREEDING MARES.
YOU'VE *EVEN* EATEN THE FOALS. ALL OF THEM. ALL GONE.
AND YET, HERE I AM. STILL HUNGRY.
THERE IS NOT EVEN *ONE* MORE?
THERE IS ONE.
AN OLD WARHORSE. TOO OLD AND STRINGY TO HAVE MENTIONED. *SURELY*, YOU CAN'T WANT THIS ONE.
PREPARE HIM FOR MY TABLE.
HAVE HIM *BRAISED* IN FINE RED WINE AND SERVED WITH WILD MUSHROOMS.

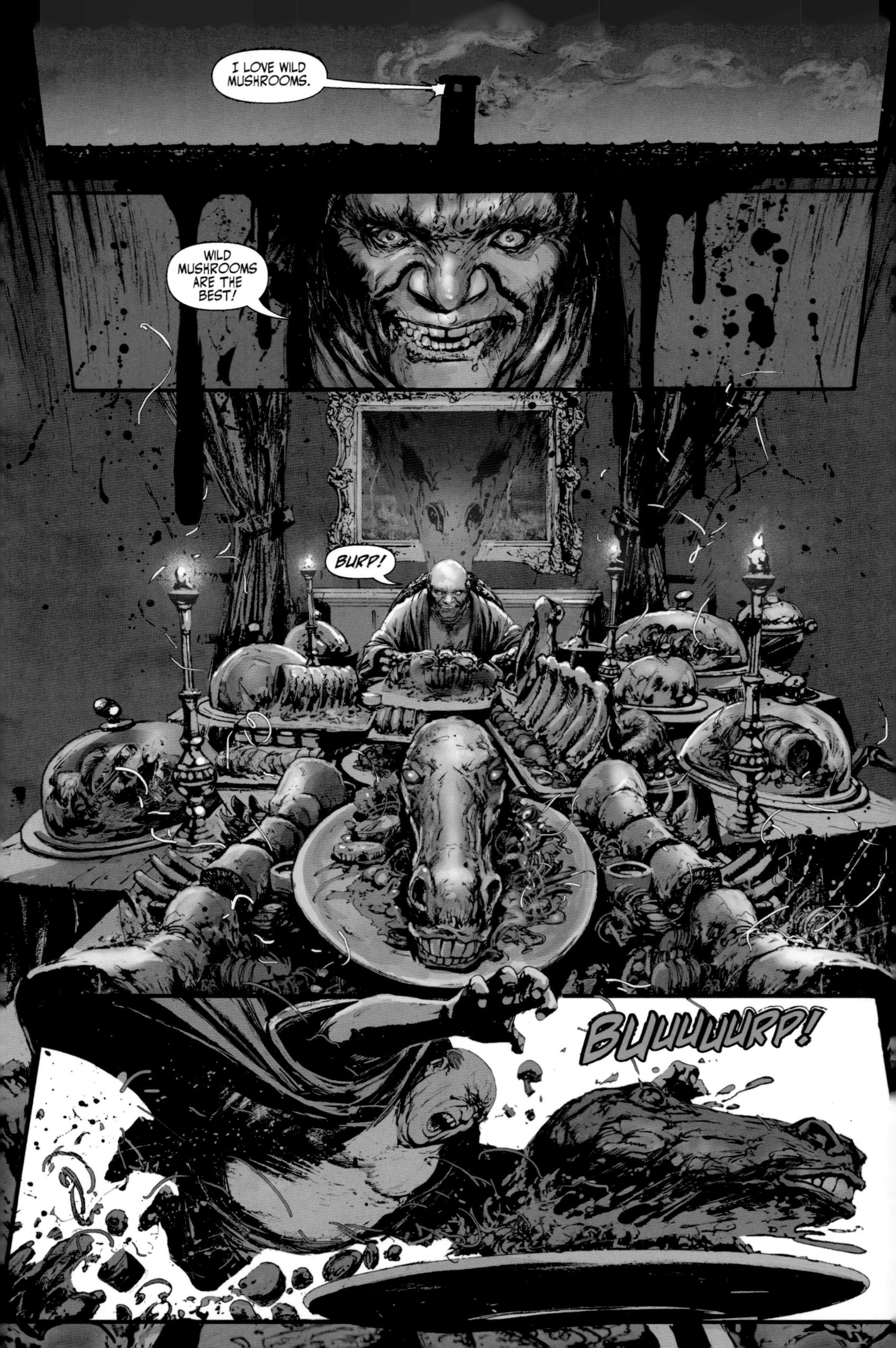
I LOVE WILD MUSHROOMS.
WILD MUSHROOMS ARE THE BEST!
BURP!
BUUUURP!

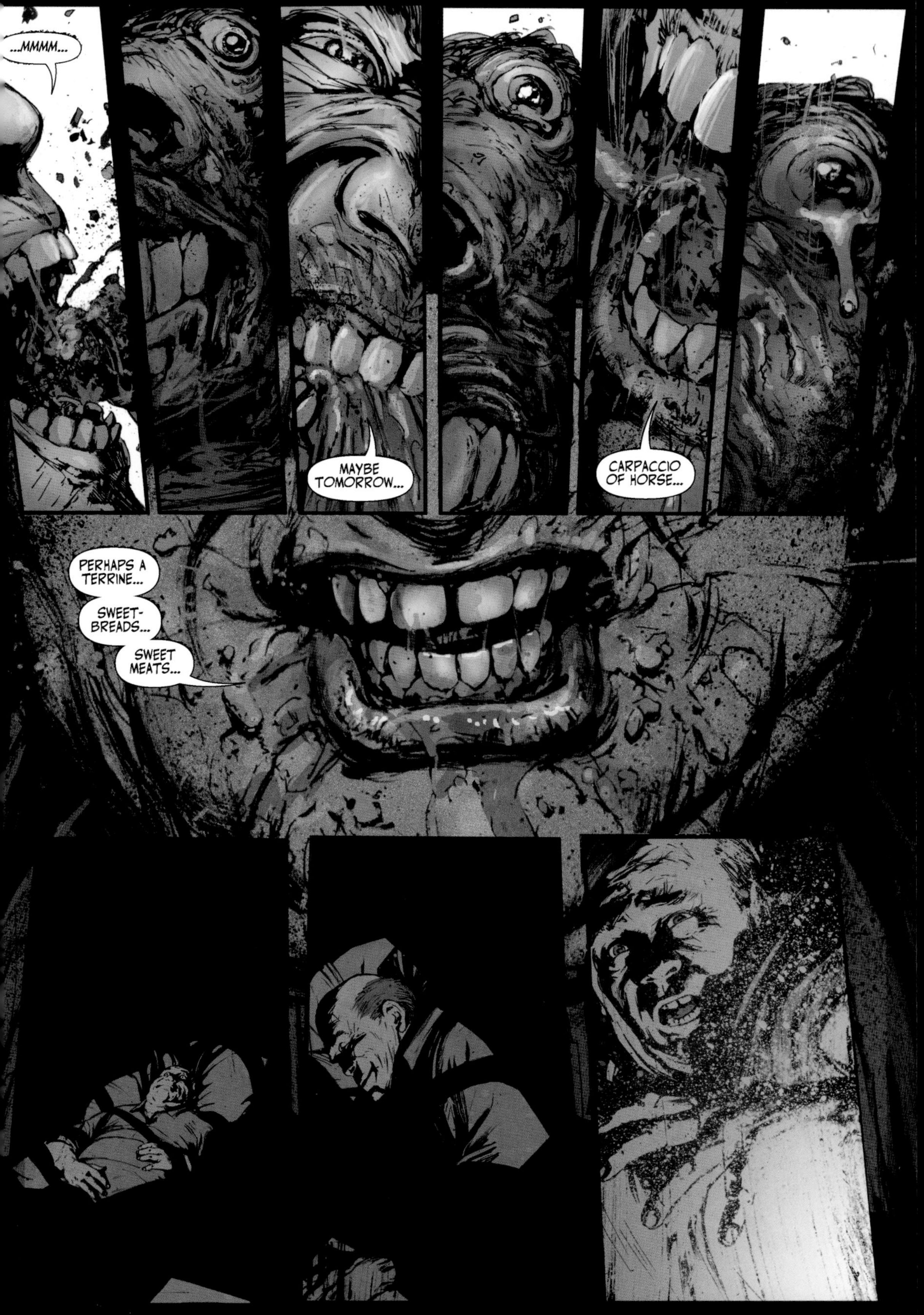
...MMMM...
MAYBE TOMORROW...
CARPACCIO OF HORSE...
PERHAPS A TERRINE...
SWEET-BREADS...
SWEET MEATS...

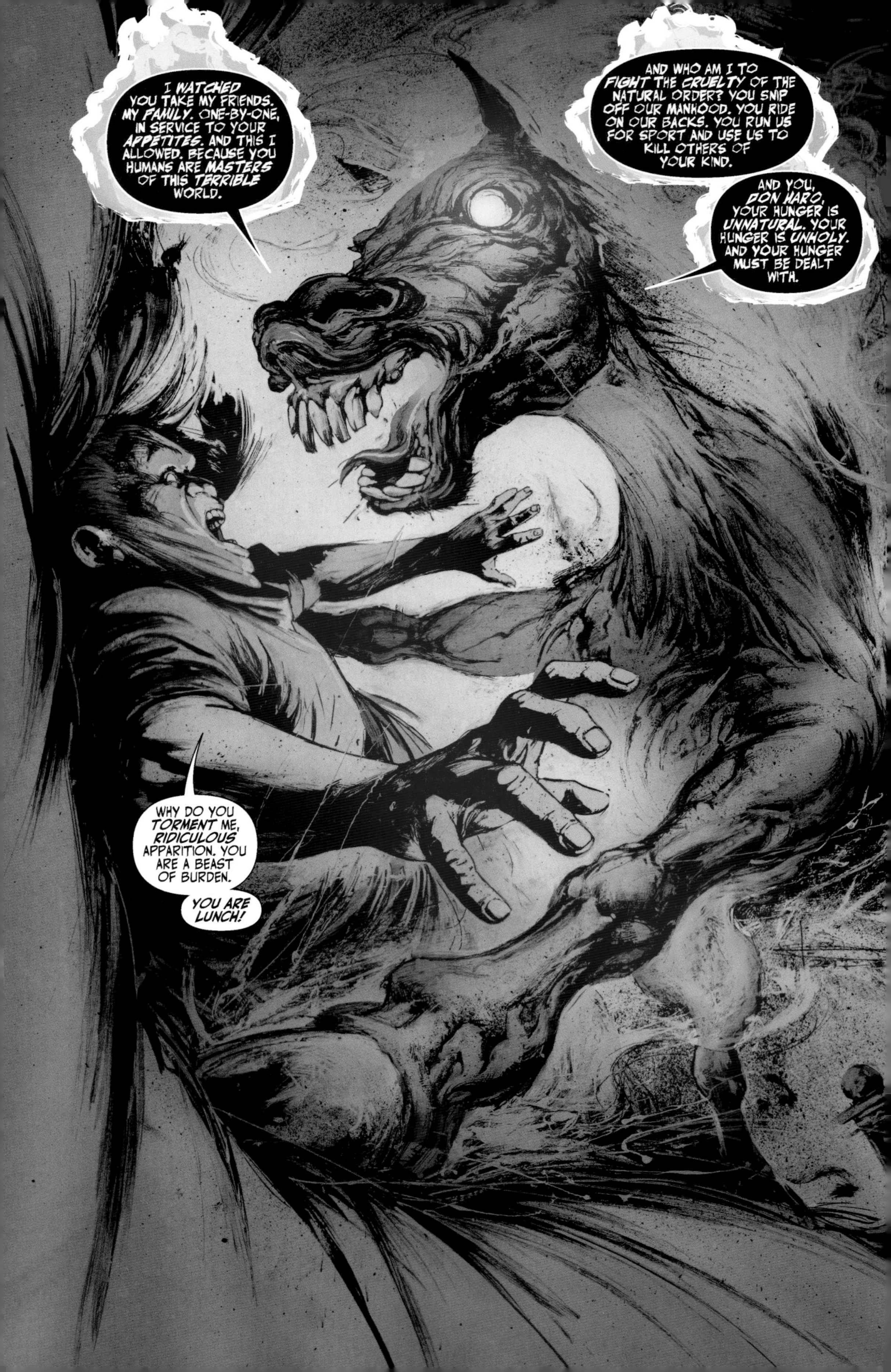
I WATCHED YOU TAKE MY FRIENDS. MY FAMILY. ONE-BY-ONE, IN SERVICE TO YOUR APPETITES. AND THIS I ALLOWED. BECAUSE YOU HUMANS ARE MASTERS OF THIS TERRIBLE WORLD.
AND WHO AM I TO FIGHT THE CRUELTY OF THE NATURAL ORDER? YOU SNIP OFF OUR MANHOOD. YOU RIDE ON OUR BACKS. YOU RUN US FOR SPORT AND USE US TO KILL OTHERS OF YOUR KIND.
AND YOU, DON HARO, YOUR HUNGER IS UNNATURAL. YOUR HUNGER IS UNHOLY. AND YOUR HUNGER MUST BE DEALT WITH.
WHY DO YOU TORMENT ME, RIDICULOUS APPARITION. YOU ARE A BEAST OF BURDEN.
YOU ARE LUNCH!

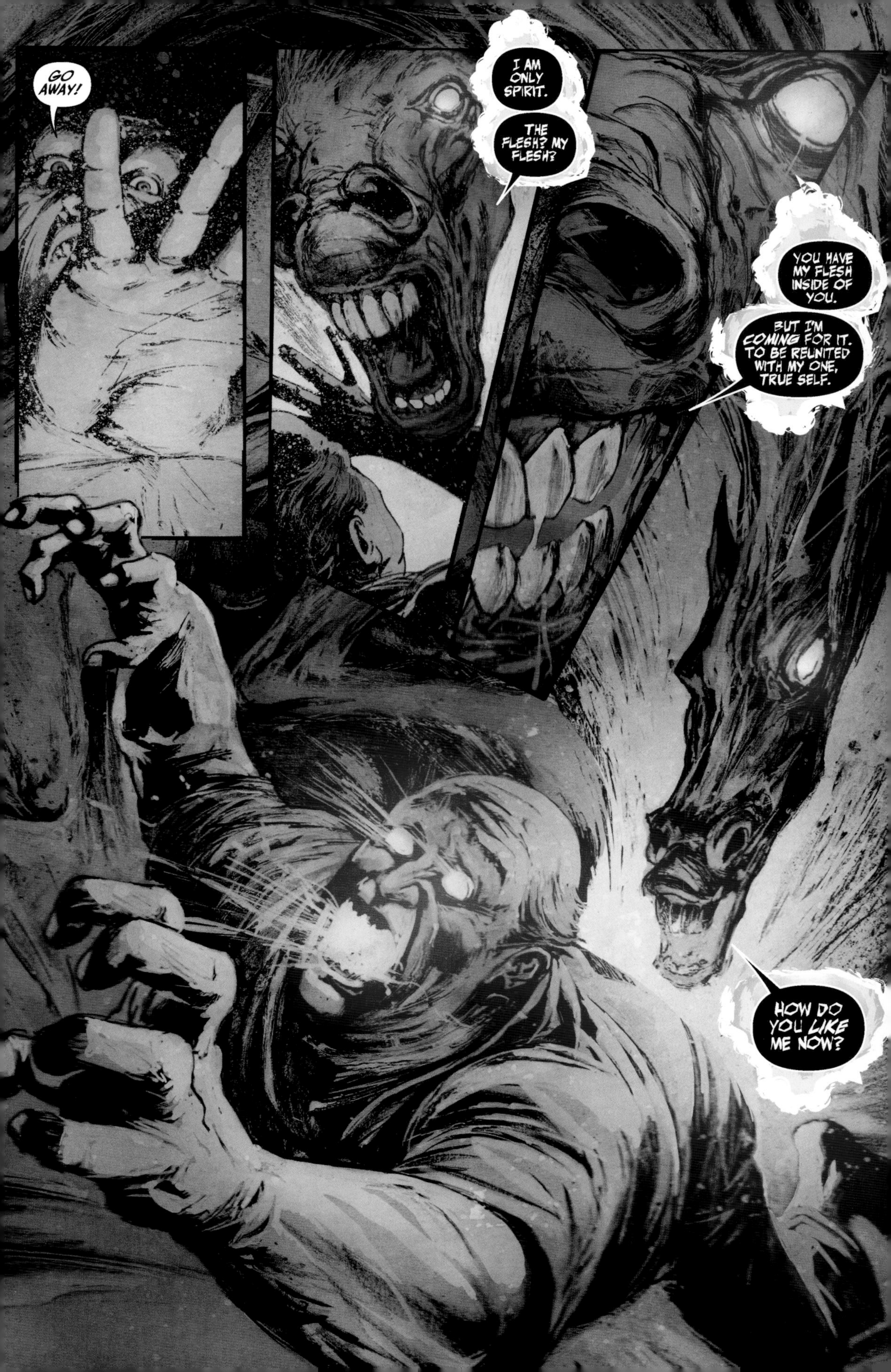
GO AWAY!
I AM ONLY SPIRIT.
THE FLESH? MY FLESH?
YOU HAVE MY FLESH INSIDE OF YOU.
BUT I'M COMING FOR IT. TO BE REUNITED WITH MY ONE, TRUE SELF.
HOW DO YOU LIKE ME NOW?

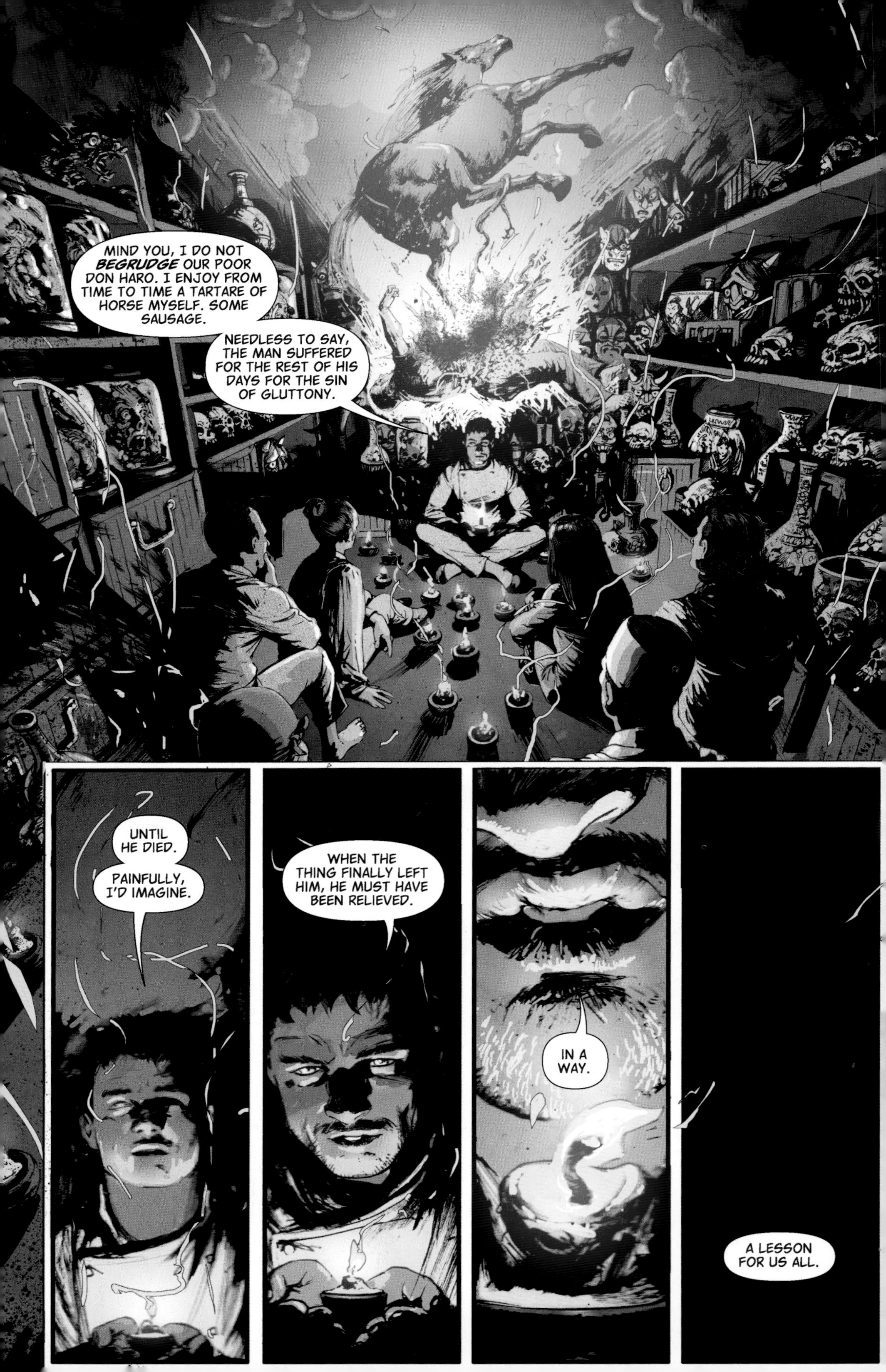
MIND YOU, I DO NOT BEGRUDGE OUR POOR DON HARO. I ENJOY FROM TIME TO TIME A TARTARE OF HORSE MYSELF. SOME SAUSAGE.
NEEDLESS TO SAY, THE MAN SUFFERED FOR THE REST OF HIS DAYS FOR THE SIN OF GLUTTONY.
UNTIL HE DIED.
PAINFULLY, I'D IMAGINE.
WHEN THE THING FINALLY LEFT HIM, HE MUST HAVE BEEN RELIEVED.
IN A WAY.
A LESSON FOR US ALL.

THE HEADS

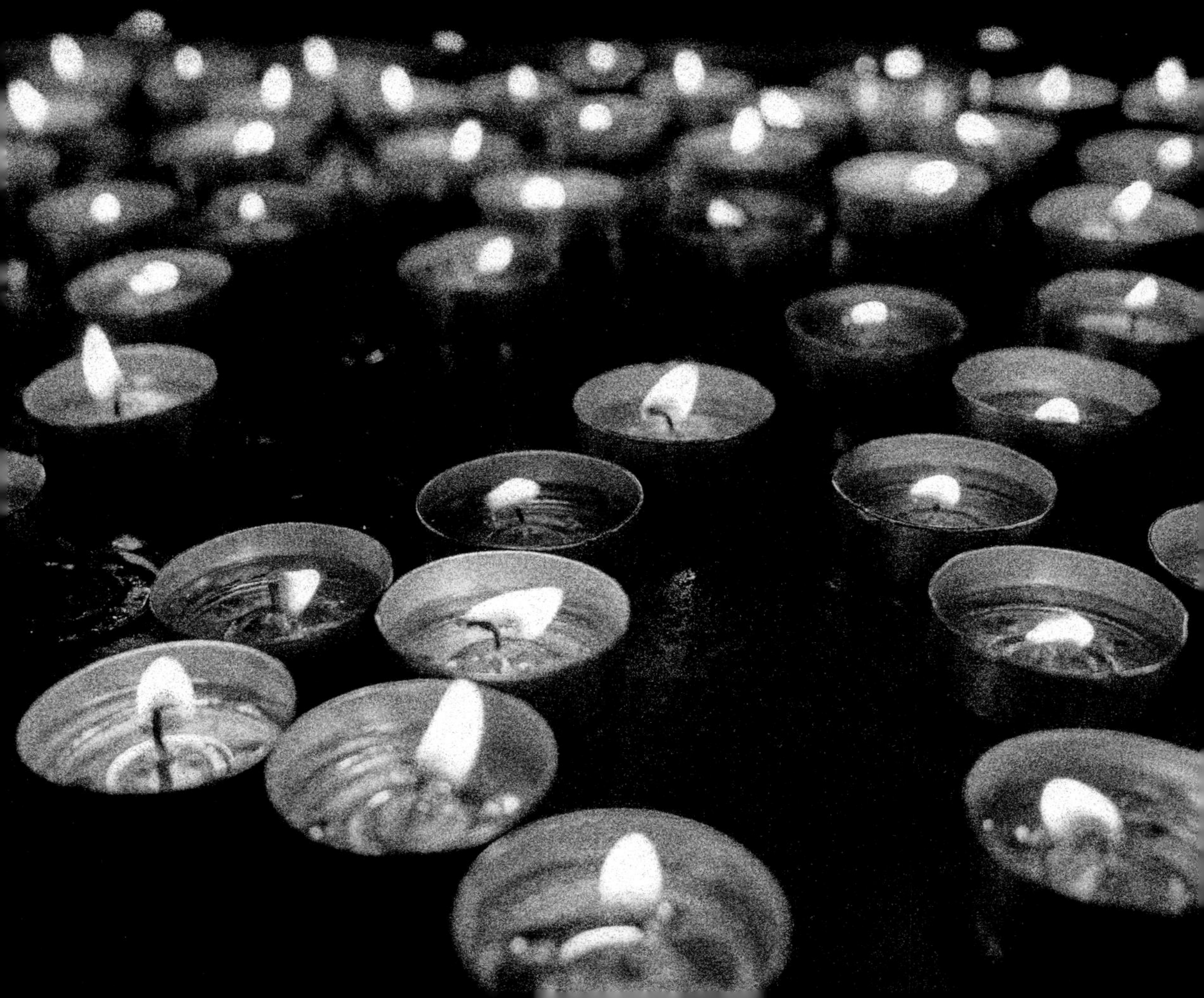

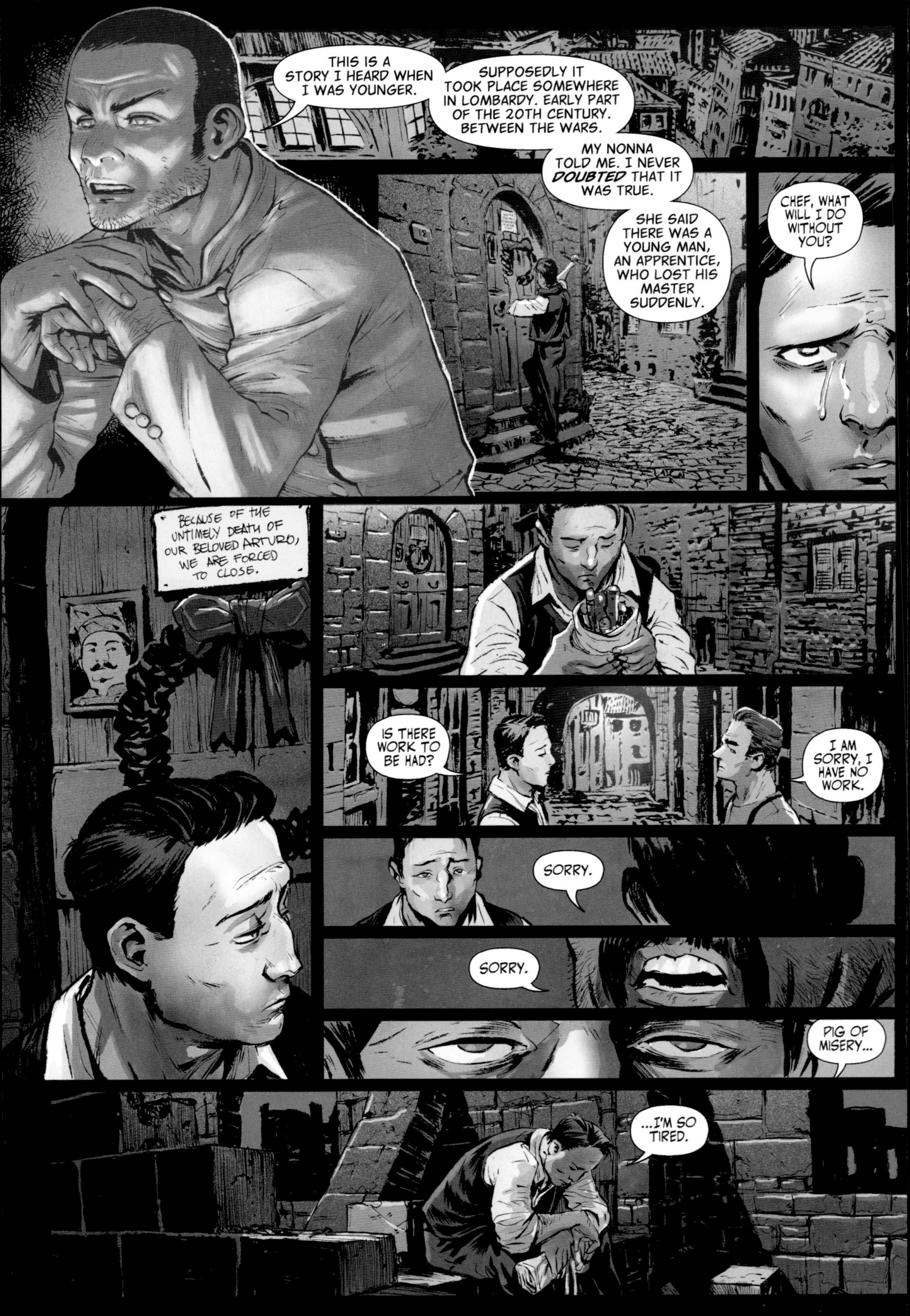
THIS IS A STORY I HEARD WHEN I WAS YOUNGER.
SUPPOSEDLY IT TOOK PLACE SOMEWHERE IN LOMBARDY. EARLY PART OF THE 20TH CENTURY. BETWEEN THE WARS.
MY NONNA TOLD ME. I NEVER DOUBTED THAT IT WAS TRUE.
SHE SAID THERE WAS A YOUNG MAN, AN APPRENTICE, WHO LOST HIS MASTER SUDDENLY.
CHEF, WHAT WILL I DO WITHOUT YOU?
BECAUSE OF THE UNTIMELY DEATH OF OUR BELOVED ARTURO, WE ARE FORCED TO CLOSE.
IS THERE WORK TO BE HAD?
I AM SORRY, I HAVE NO WORK.
SORRY.
SORRY.
PIG OF MISERY...
...I'M SO TIRED.

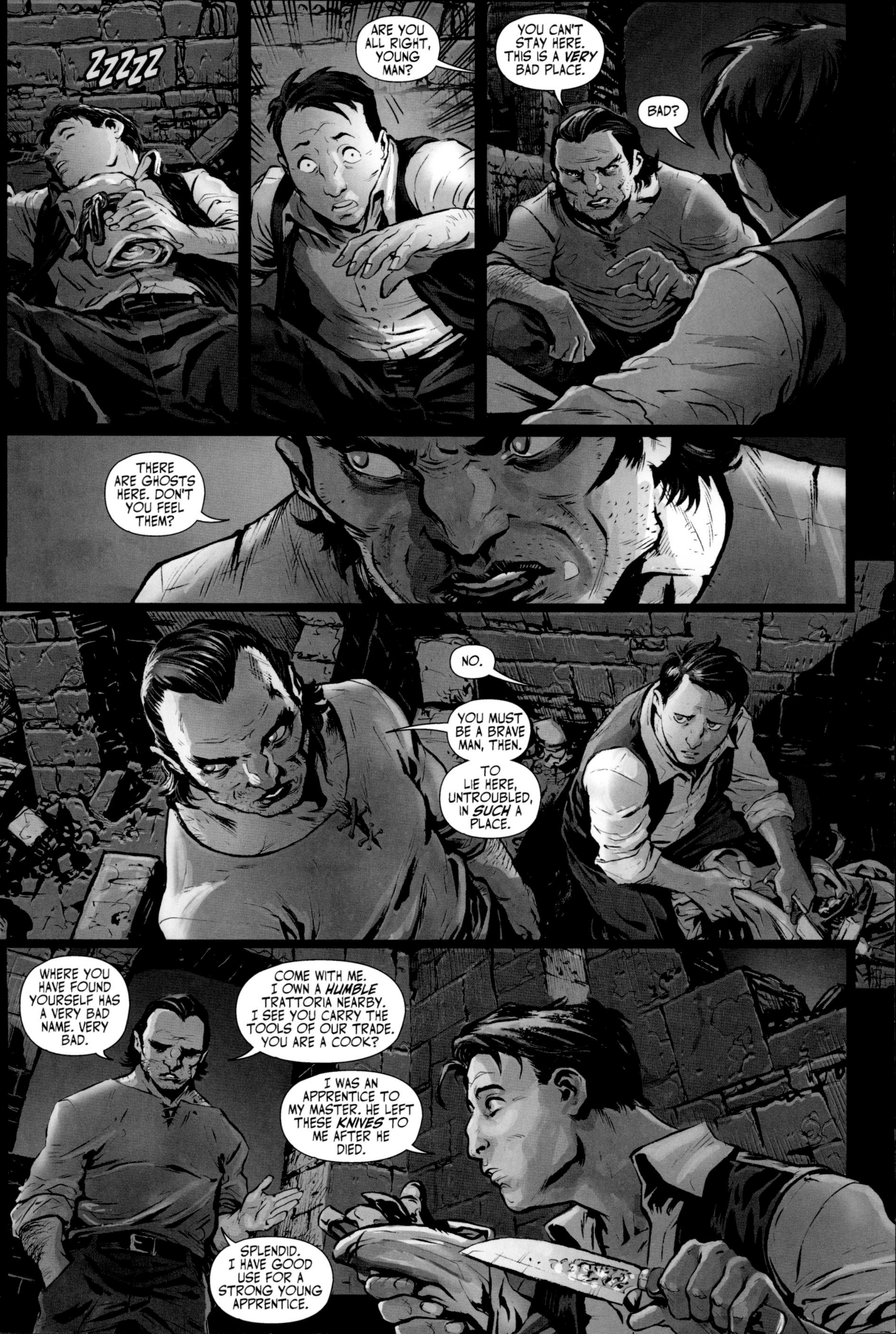
ZZZZZ
ARE YOU ALL RIGHT, YOUNG MAN?
YOU CAN'T STAY HERE. THIS IS A *VERY* BAD PLACE.
BAD?
THERE ARE GHOSTS HERE. DON'T YOU FEEL THEM?
NO.
YOU MUST BE A BRAVE MAN, THEN.
TO LIE HERE, UNTROUBLED, IN *SUCH* A PLACE.
WHERE YOU HAVE FOUND YOURSELF HAS A VERY BAD NAME. VERY BAD.
COME WITH ME. I OWN A *HUMBLE* TRATTORIA NEARBY. I SEE YOU CARRY THE TOOLS OF OUR TRADE. YOU ARE A COOK?
I WAS AN APPRENTICE TO MY MASTER. HE LEFT THESE *KNIVES* TO ME AFTER HE DIED.
SPLENDID. I HAVE GOOD USE FOR A STRONG YOUNG APPRENTICE.

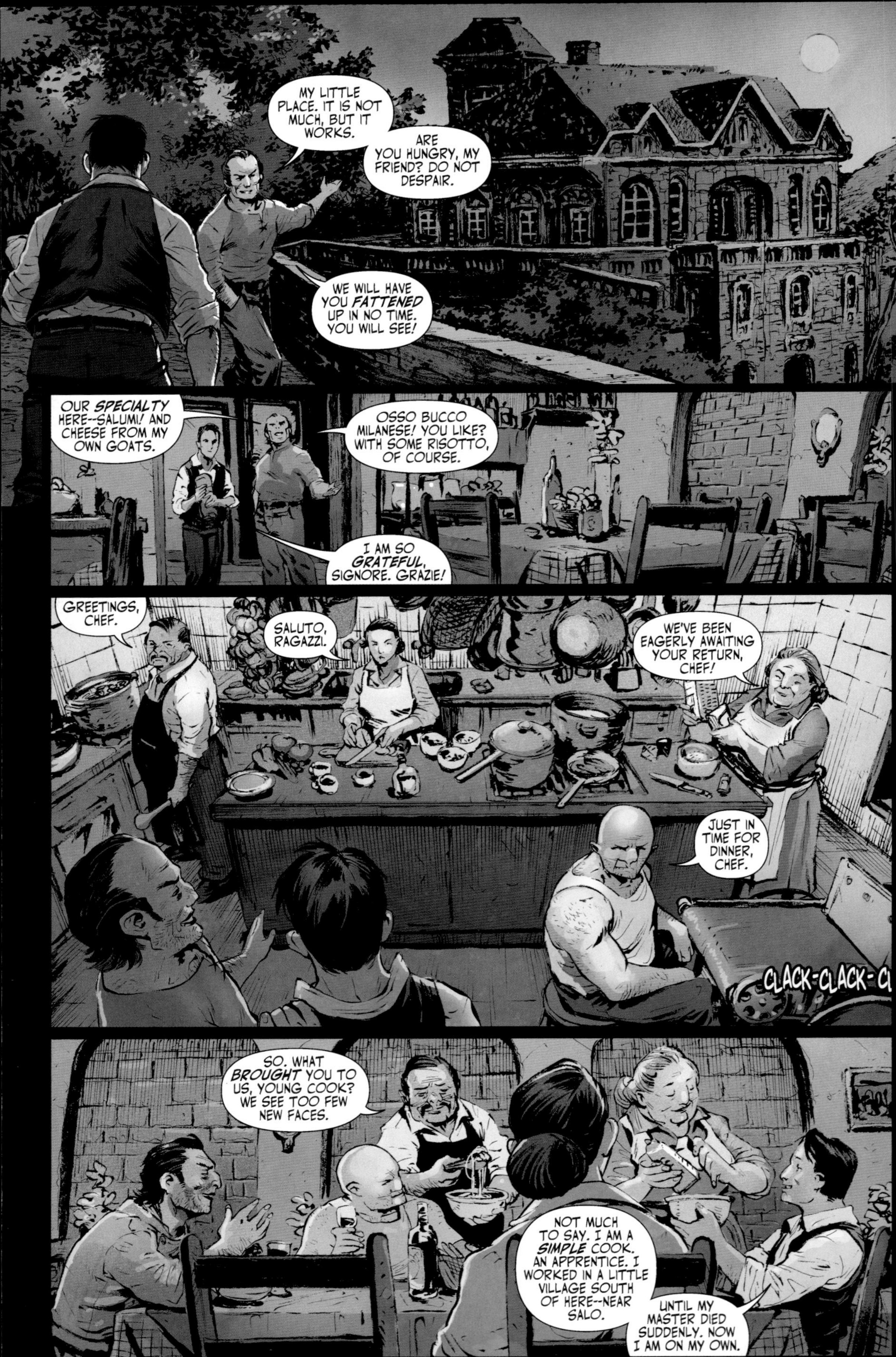
MY LITTLE PLACE. IT IS NOT MUCH, BUT IT WORKS.
ARE YOU HUNGRY, MY FRIEND? DO NOT DESPAIR.
WE WILL HAVE YOU FATTENED UP IN NO TIME. YOU WILL SEE!
OUR SPECIALTY HERE--SALUMI! AND CHEESE FROM MY OWN GOATS.
OSSO BUCCO MILANESE! YOU LIKE? WITH SOME RISOTTO, OF COURSE.
I AM SO GRATEFUL, SIGNORE. GRAZIE!
GREETINGS, CHEF.
SALUTO, RAGAZZI.
WE'VE BEEN EAGERLY AWAITING YOUR RETURN, CHEF!
JUST IN TIME FOR DINNER, CHEF.
CLACK-CLACK-CL
SO. WHAT BROUGHT YOU TO US, YOUNG COOK? WE SEE TOO FEW NEW FACES.
NOT MUCH TO SAY. I AM A SIMPLE COOK. AN APPRENTICE. I WORKED IN A LITTLE VILLAGE SOUTH OF HERE--NEAR SALO.
UNTIL MY MASTER DIED SUDDENLY. NOW I AM ON MY OWN.

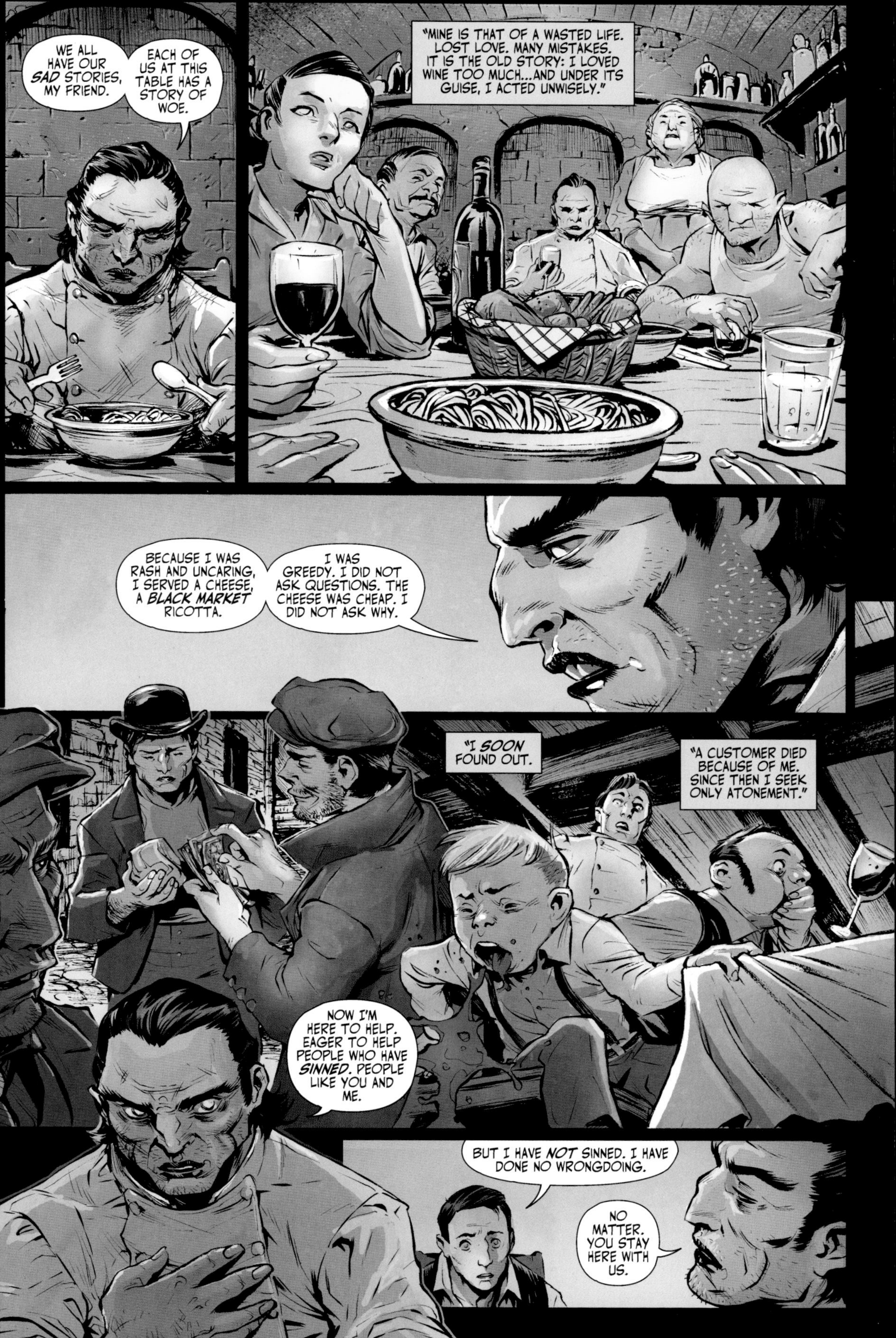
WE ALL HAVE OUR SAD STORIES, MY FRIEND.
EACH OF US AT THIS TABLE HAS A STORY OF WOE.
"MINE IS THAT OF A WASTED LIFE. LOST LOVE. MANY MISTAKES. IT IS THE OLD STORY: I LOVED WINE TOO MUCH...AND UNDER ITS GUISE, I ACTED UNWISELY."
BECAUSE I WAS RASH AND UNCARING, I SERVED A CHEESE, A BLACK MARKET RICOTTA.
I WAS GREEDY. I DID NOT ASK QUESTIONS. THE CHEESE WAS CHEAP. I DID NOT ASK WHY.
"I SOON FOUND OUT.
"A CUSTOMER DIED BECAUSE OF ME. SINCE THEN I SEEK ONLY ATONEMENT."
NOW I'M HERE TO HELP. EAGER TO HELP PEOPLE WHO HAVE SINNED. PEOPLE LIKE YOU AND ME.
BUT I HAVE NOT SINNED. I HAVE DONE NO WRONGDOING.
NO MATTER. YOU STAY HERE WITH US.

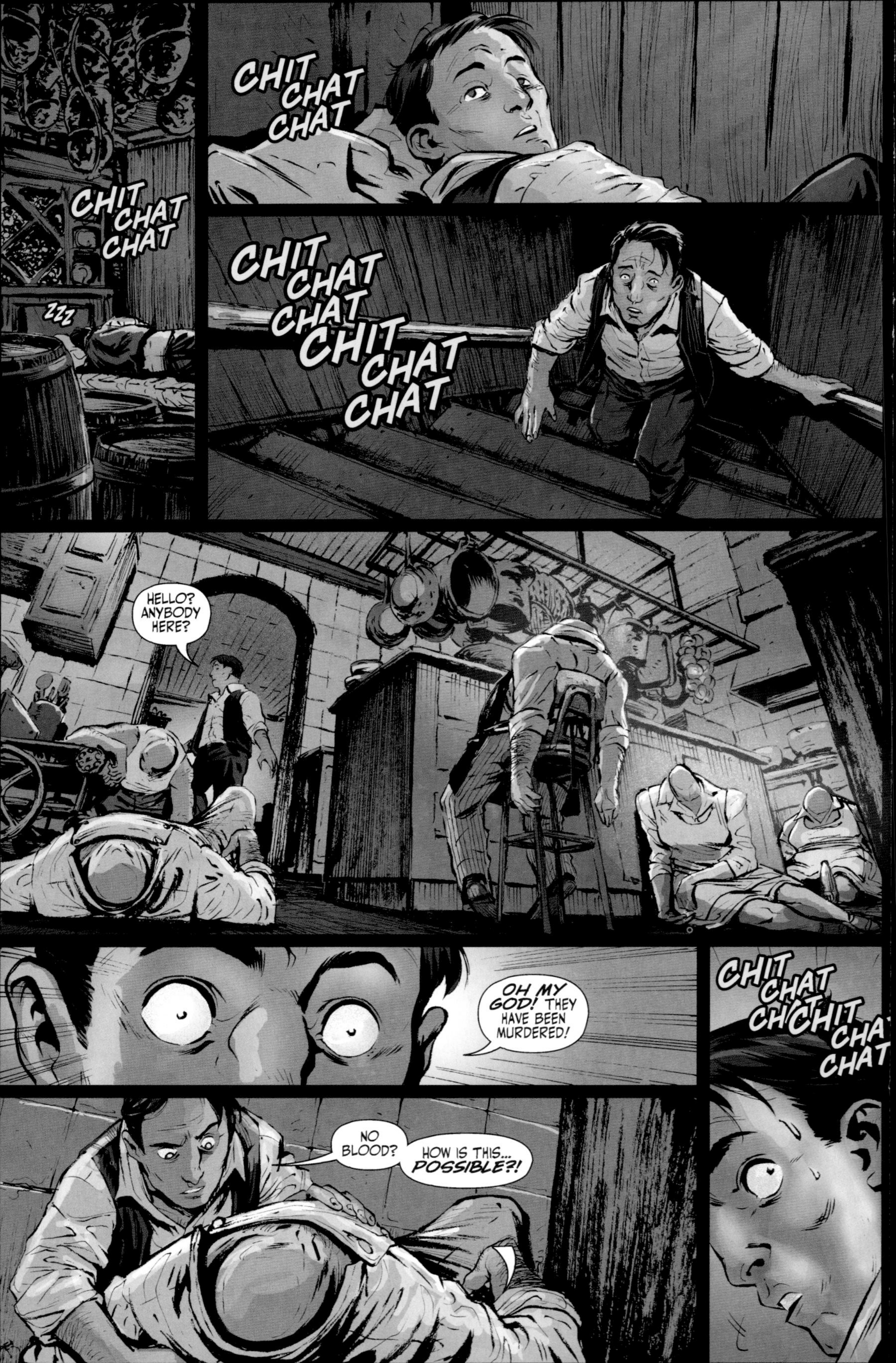
CHIT CHAT CHAT
CHIT CHAT CHAT
ZZZ
CHIT CHAT CHAT CHIT CHAT CHAT
HELLO? ANYBODY HERE?
OH MY GOD! THEY HAVE BEEN MURDERED!
CHIT CHAT CH CHIT CHAT CHAT
NO BLOOD?
HOW IS THIS... POSSIBLE?!

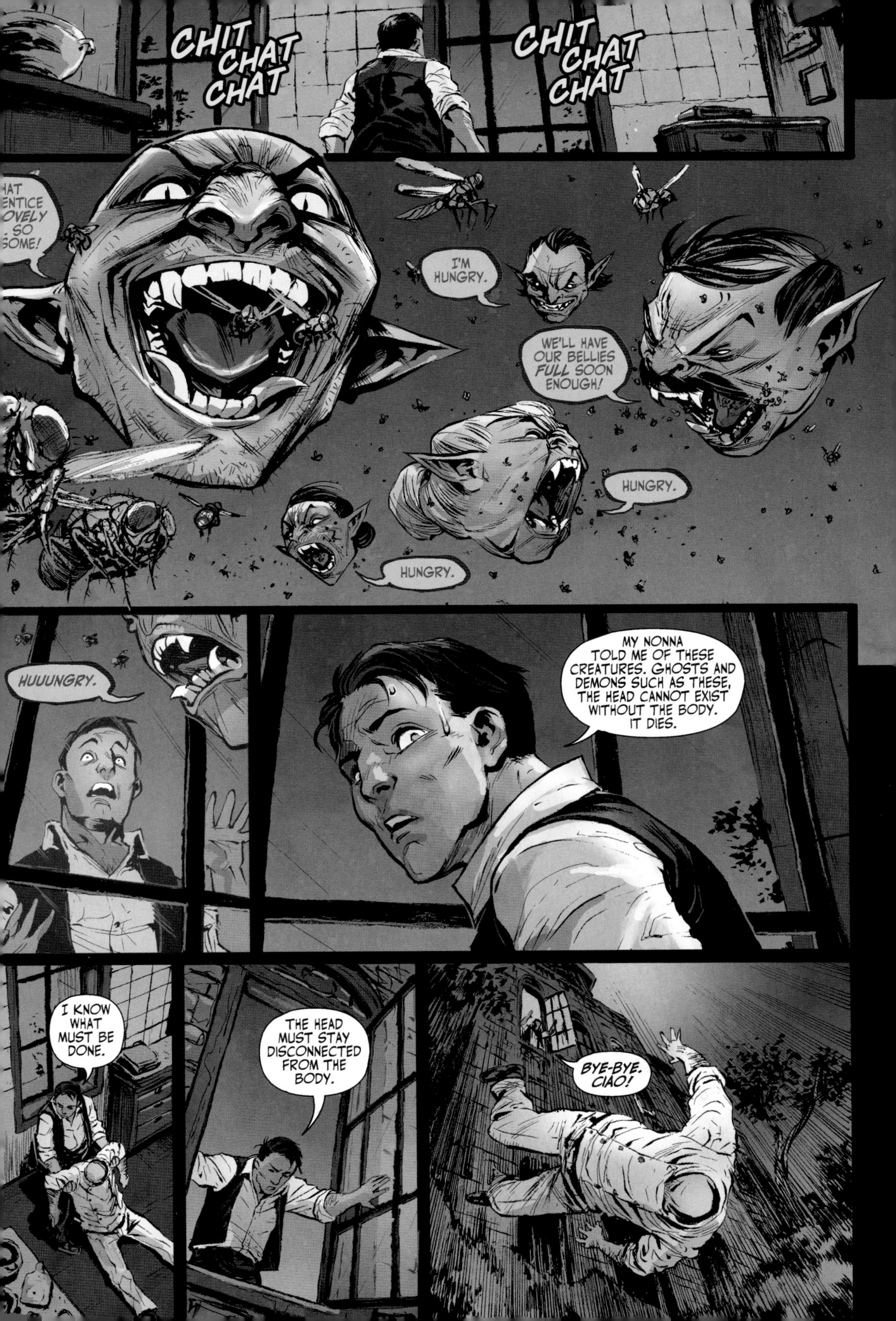
CHIT CHAT CHAT
CHIT CHAT CHAT
I'M HUNGRY.
WE'LL HAVE OUR BELLIES *FULL* SOON ENOUGH!
HUNGRY.
HUNGRY.
HUUUNGRY.
MY NONNA TOLD ME OF THESE CREATURES. GHOSTS AND DEMONS SUCH AS THESE, THE HEAD CANNOT EXIST WITHOUT THE BODY. IT DIES.
I KNOW WHAT MUST BE DONE.
THE HEAD MUST STAY DISCONNECTED FROM THE BODY.
BYE-BYE. CIAO!

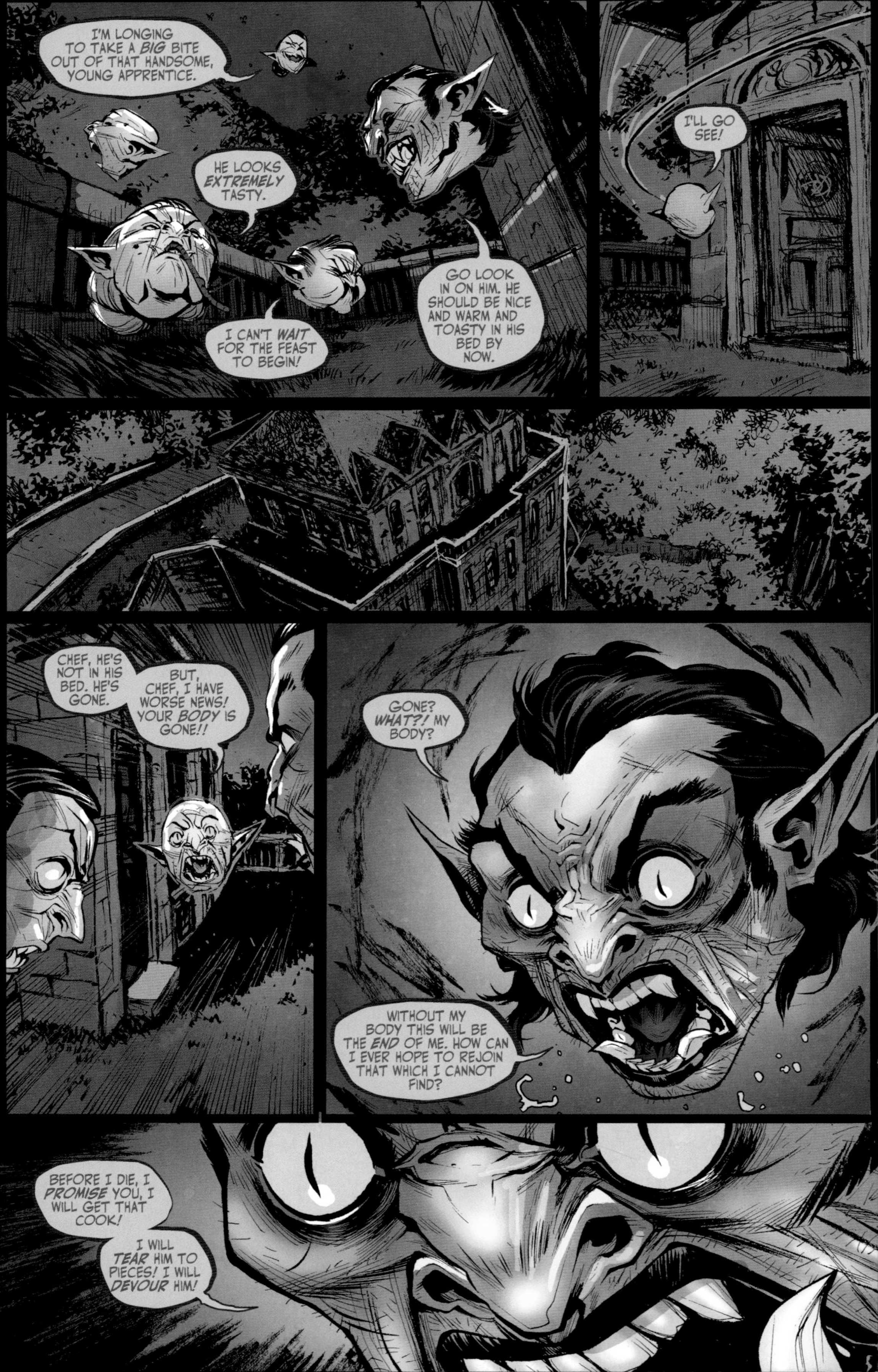
I'M LONGING TO TAKE A BIG BITE OUT OF THAT HANDSOME, YOUNG APPRENTICE.
HE LOOKS EXTREMELY TASTY.
I CAN'T WAIT FOR THE FEAST TO BEGIN!
GO LOOK IN ON HIM. HE SHOULD BE NICE AND WARM AND TOASTY IN HIS BED BY NOW.
I'LL GO SEE!
CHEF, HE'S NOT IN HIS BED. HE'S GONE.
BUT, CHEF, I HAVE WORSE NEWS! YOUR BODY IS GONE!!
GONE? WHAT?! MY BODY?
WITHOUT MY BODY THIS WILL BE THE END OF ME. HOW CAN I EVER HOPE TO REJOIN THAT WHICH I CANNOT FIND?
BEFORE I DIE, I PROMISE YOU, I WILL GET THAT COOK!
I WILL TEAR HIM TO PIECES! I WILL DEVOUR HIM!

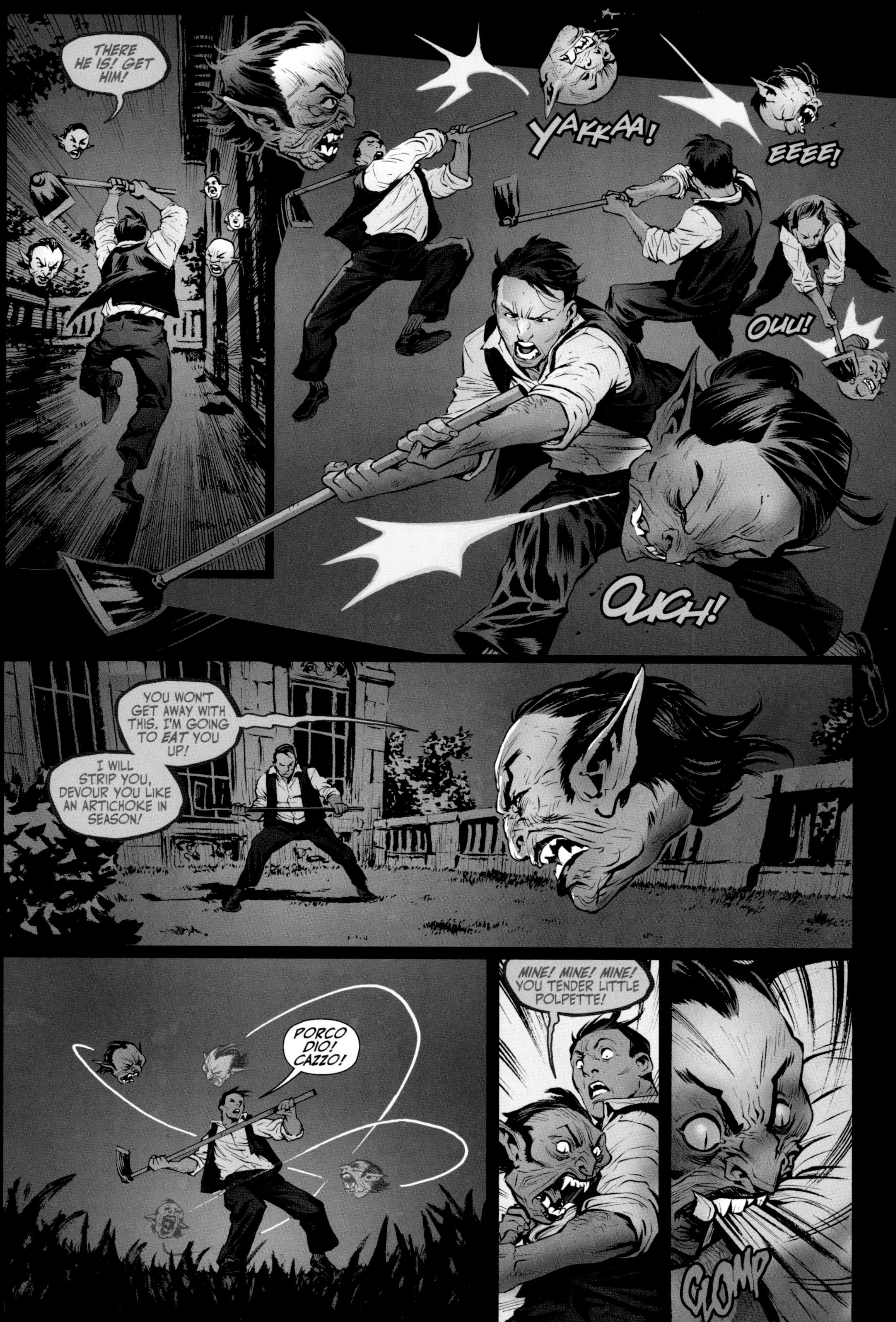
THERE HE IS! GET HIM!
YAKKAA!
EEEE!
OUU!
OUCH!
YOU WON'T GET AWAY WITH THIS. I'M GOING TO EAT YOU UP!
I WILL STRIP YOU, DEVOUR YOU LIKE AN ARTICHOKE IN SEASON!
PORCO DIO! CAZZO!
MINE! MINE! MINE! YOU TENDER LITTLE POLPETTE!
CLOMP

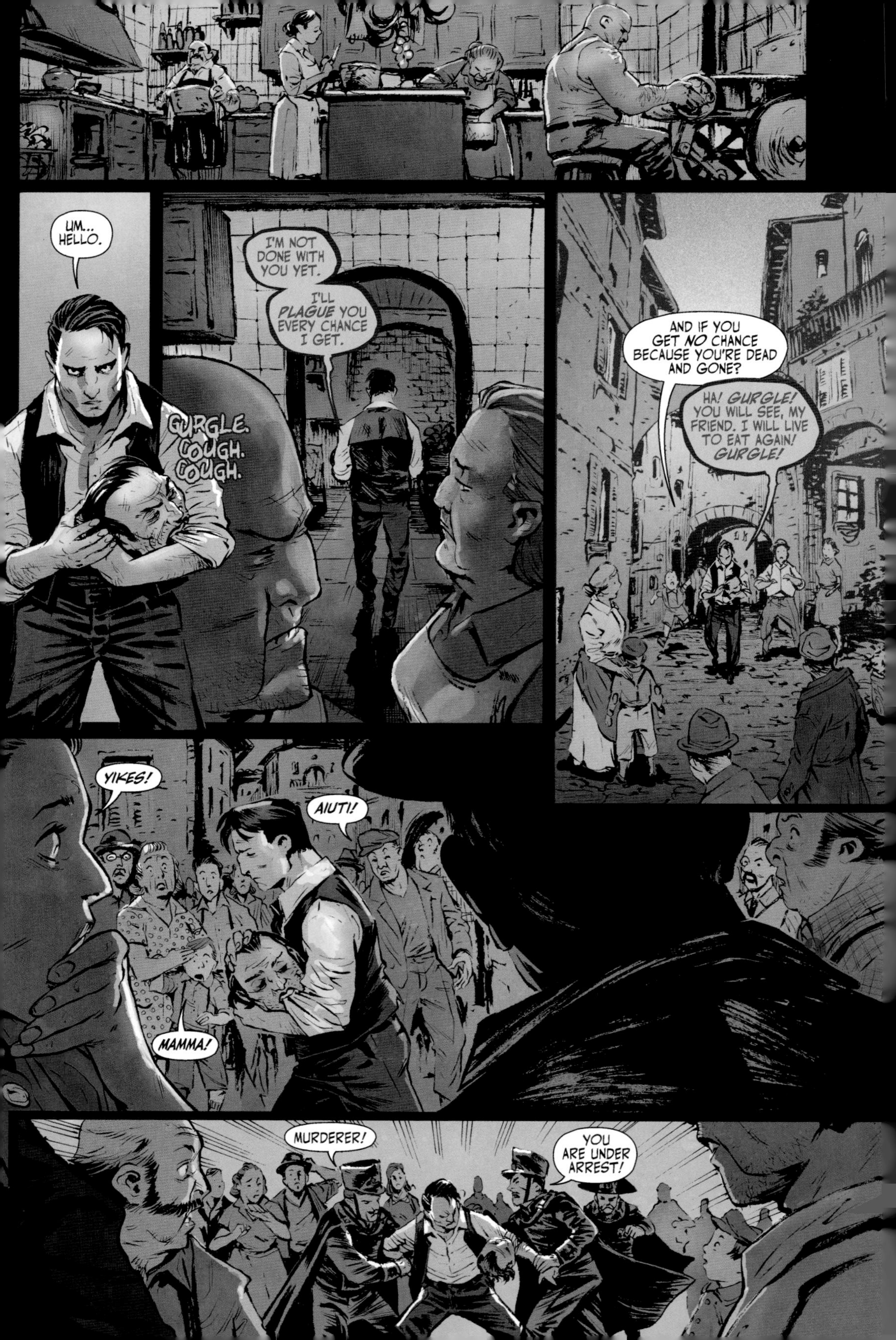
UM... HELLO.
I'M NOT DONE WITH YOU YET.
I'LL *PLAGUE* YOU EVERY CHANCE I GET.
GURGLE. COUGH. COUGH.
AND IF YOU GET *NO* CHANCE BECAUSE YOU'RE DEAD AND GONE?
HA! *GURGLE!* YOU WILL SEE, MY FRIEND. I WILL LIVE TO EAT AGAIN! *GURGLE!*
YIKES!
AIUTI!
MAMMA!
MURDERER!
YOU ARE UNDER ARREST!

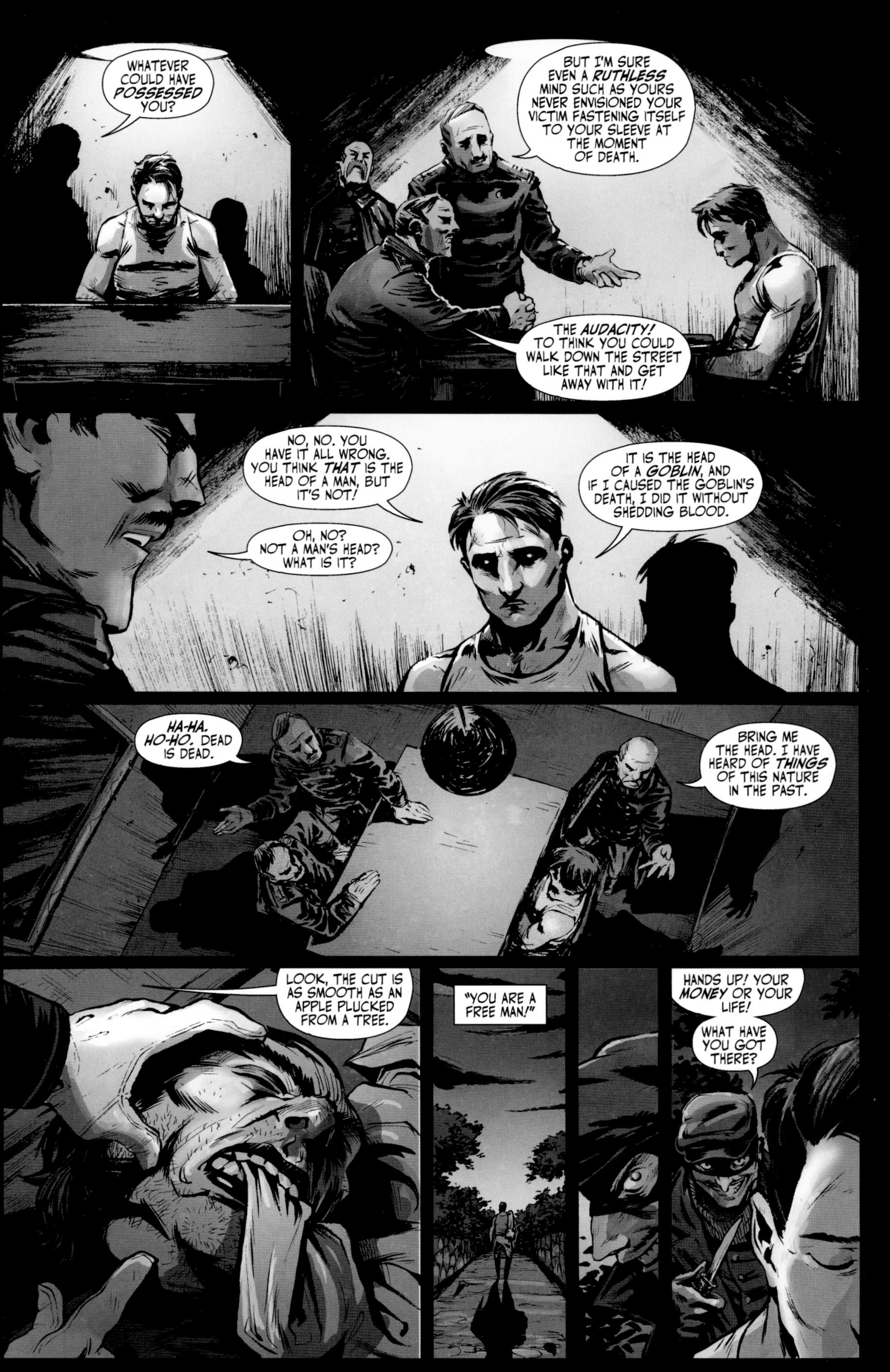
WHATEVER COULD HAVE POSSESSED YOU?
BUT I'M SURE EVEN A RUTHLESS MIND SUCH AS YOURS NEVER ENVISIONED YOUR VICTIM FASTENING ITSELF TO YOUR SLEEVE AT THE MOMENT OF DEATH.
THE AUDACITY! TO THINK YOU COULD WALK DOWN THE STREET LIKE THAT AND GET AWAY WITH IT!
NO, NO. YOU HAVE IT ALL WRONG. YOU THINK THAT IS THE HEAD OF A MAN, BUT IT'S NOT!
OH, NO? NOT A MAN'S HEAD? WHAT IS IT?
IT IS THE HEAD OF A GOBLIN, AND IF I CAUSED THE GOBLIN'S DEATH, I DID IT WITHOUT SHEDDING BLOOD.
HA-HA. HO-HO. DEAD IS DEAD.
BRING ME THE HEAD. I HAVE HEARD OF THINGS OF THIS NATURE IN THE PAST.
LOOK, THE CUT IS AS SMOOTH AS AN APPLE PLUCKED FROM A TREE.
"YOU ARE A FREE MAN!"
HANDS UP! YOUR MONEY OR YOUR LIFE!
WHAT HAVE YOU GOT THERE?

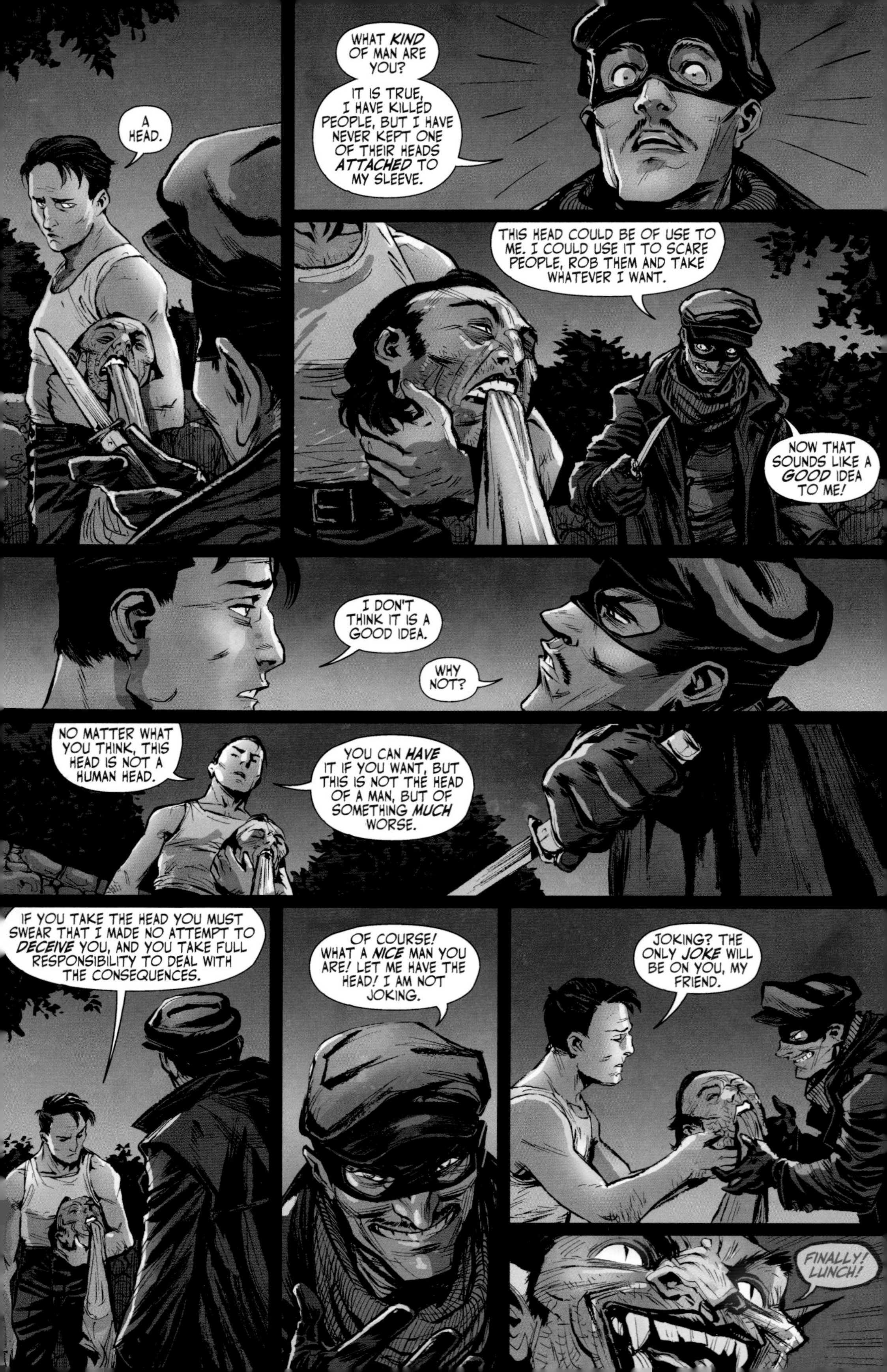
A HEAD.
WHAT KIND OF MAN ARE YOU?
IT IS TRUE, I HAVE KILLED PEOPLE, BUT I HAVE NEVER KEPT ONE OF THEIR HEADS ATTACHED TO MY SLEEVE.
THIS HEAD COULD BE OF USE TO ME. I COULD USE IT TO SCARE PEOPLE, ROB THEM AND TAKE WHATEVER I WANT.
NOW THAT SOUNDS LIKE A GOOD IDEA TO ME!
I DON'T THINK IT IS A GOOD IDEA.
WHY NOT?
NO MATTER WHAT YOU THINK, THIS HEAD IS NOT A HUMAN HEAD.
YOU CAN HAVE IT IF YOU WANT, BUT THIS IS NOT THE HEAD OF A MAN, BUT OF SOMETHING MUCH WORSE.
IF YOU TAKE THE HEAD YOU MUST SWEAR THAT I MADE NO ATTEMPT TO DECEIVE YOU, AND YOU TAKE FULL RESPONSIBILITY TO DEAL WITH THE CONSEQUENCES.
OF COURSE! WHAT A NICE MAN YOU ARE! LET ME HAVE THE HEAD! I AM NOT JOKING.
JOKING? THE ONLY JOKE WILL BE ON YOU, MY FRIEND.
FINALLY! LUNCH!

DEEP

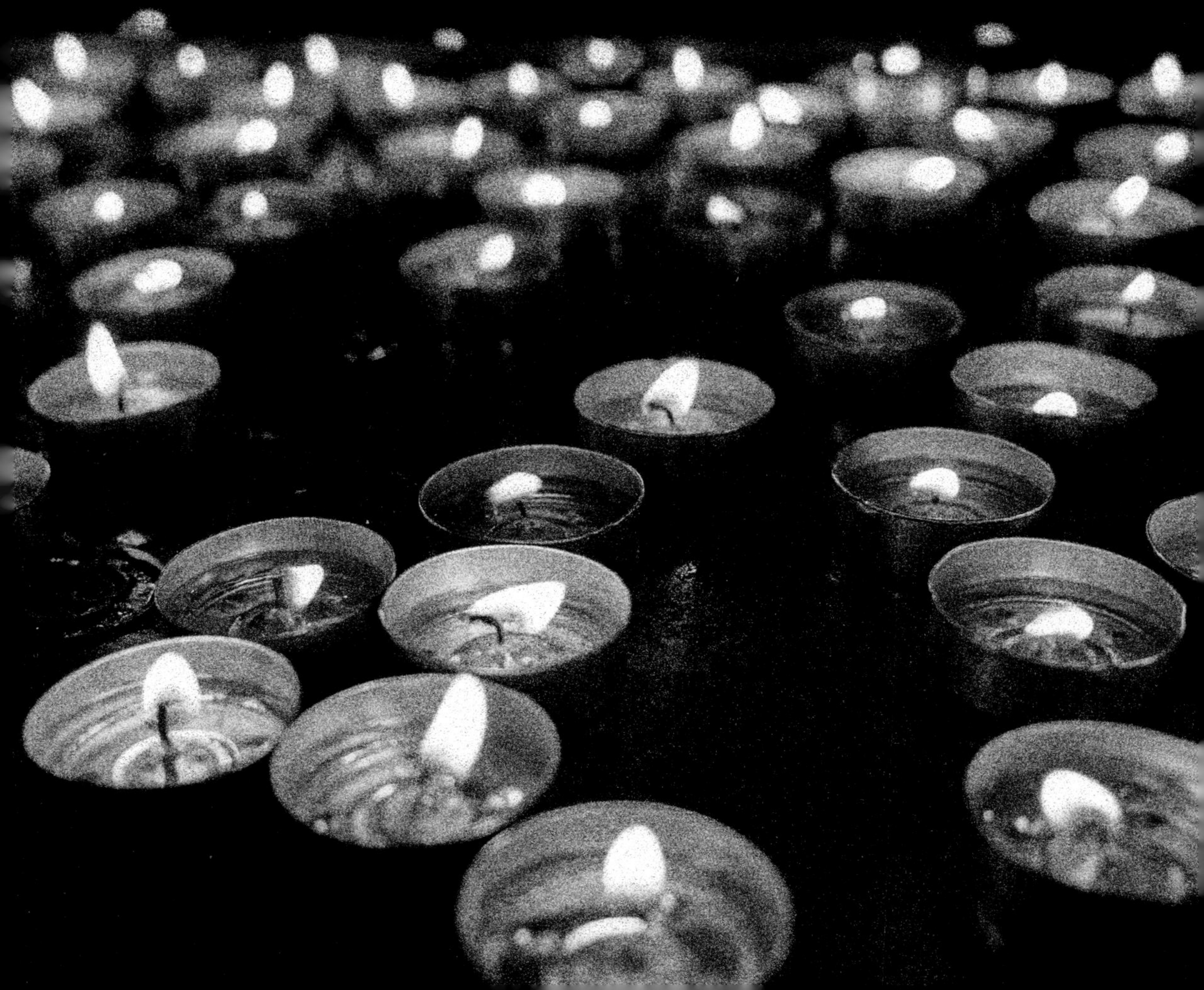

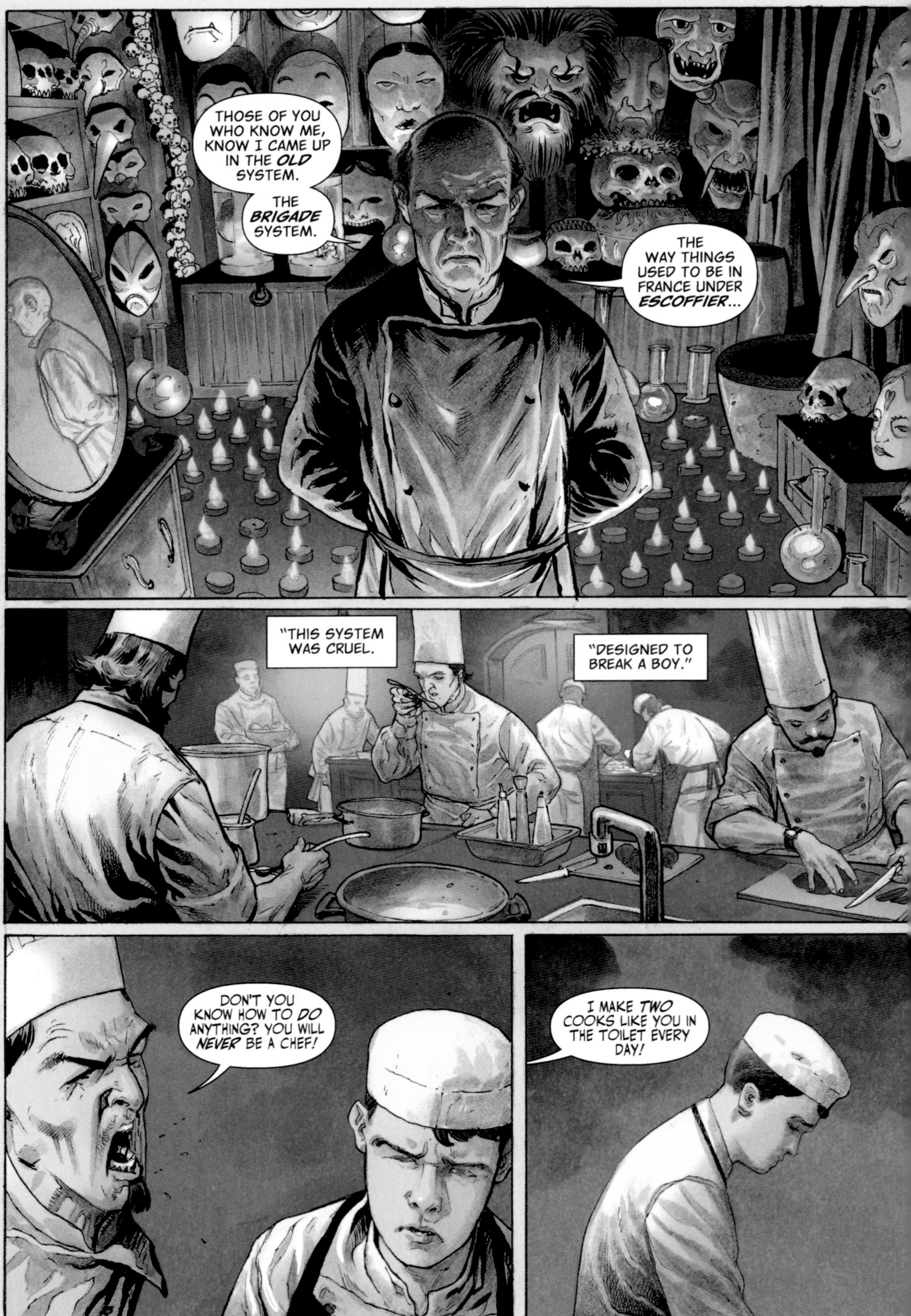
THOSE OF YOU WHO KNOW ME, KNOW I CAME UP IN THE OLD SYSTEM.
THE BRIGADE SYSTEM.
THE WAY THINGS USED TO BE IN FRANCE UNDER ESCOFFIER...
"THIS SYSTEM WAS CRUEL.
"DESIGNED TO BREAK A BOY."
DON'T YOU KNOW HOW TO DO ANYTHING? YOU WILL NEVER BE A CHEF!
I MAKE TWO COOKS LIKE YOU IN THE TOILET EVERY DAY!

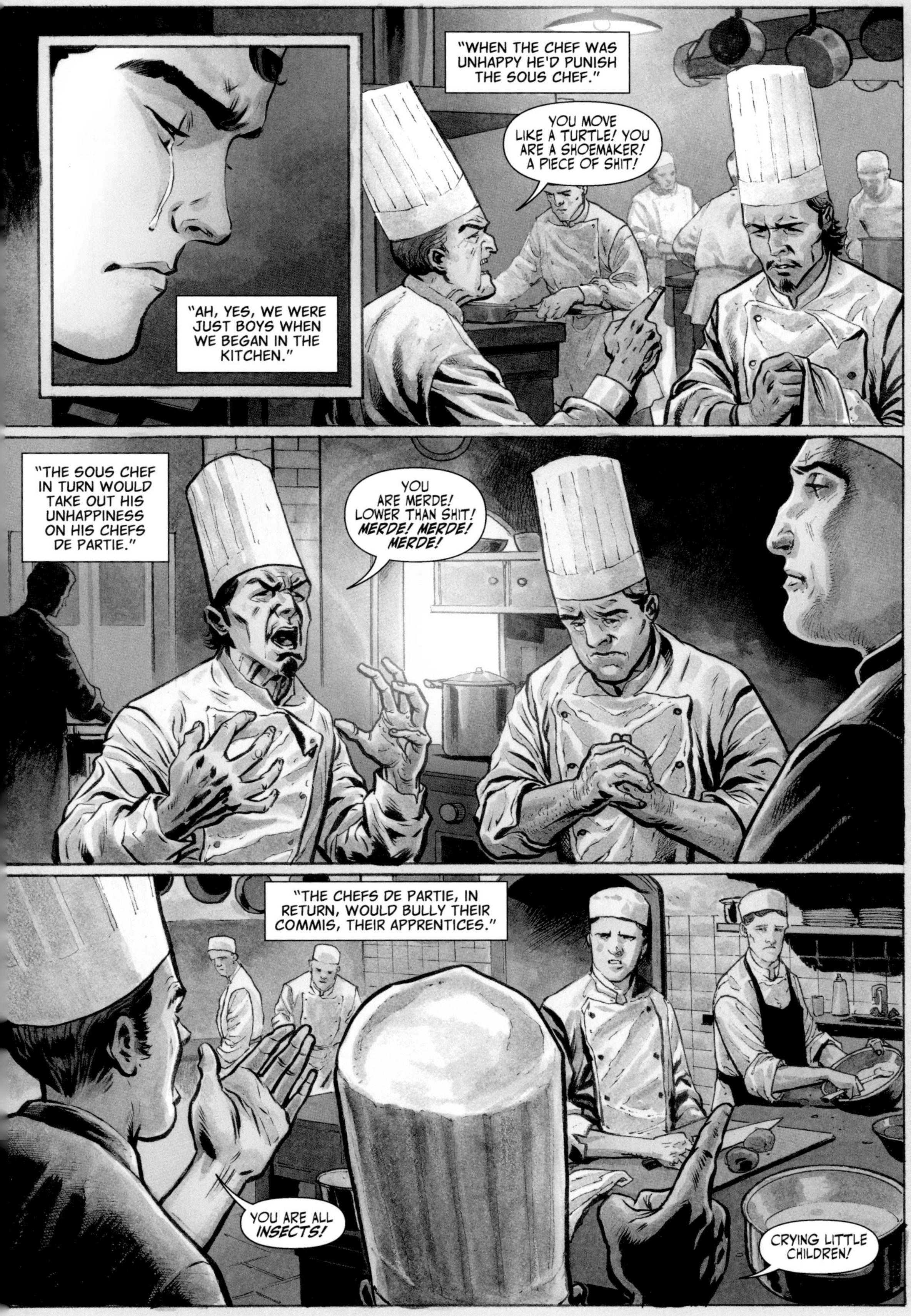
"AH, YES, WE WERE JUST BOYS WHEN WE BEGAN IN THE KITCHEN."
"WHEN THE CHEF WAS UNHAPPY HE'D PUNISH THE SOUS CHEF."
YOU MOVE LIKE A TURTLE! YOU ARE A SHOEMAKER! A PIECE OF SHIT!
"THE SOUS CHEF IN TURN WOULD TAKE OUT HIS UNHAPPINESS ON HIS CHEFS DE PARTIE."
YOU ARE MERDE! LOWER THAN SHIT! *MERDE! MERDE! MERDE!*
"THE CHEFS DE PARTIE, IN RETURN, WOULD BULLY THEIR COMMIS, THEIR APPRENTICES."
YOU ARE ALL *INSECTS!*
CRYING LITTLE CHILDREN!

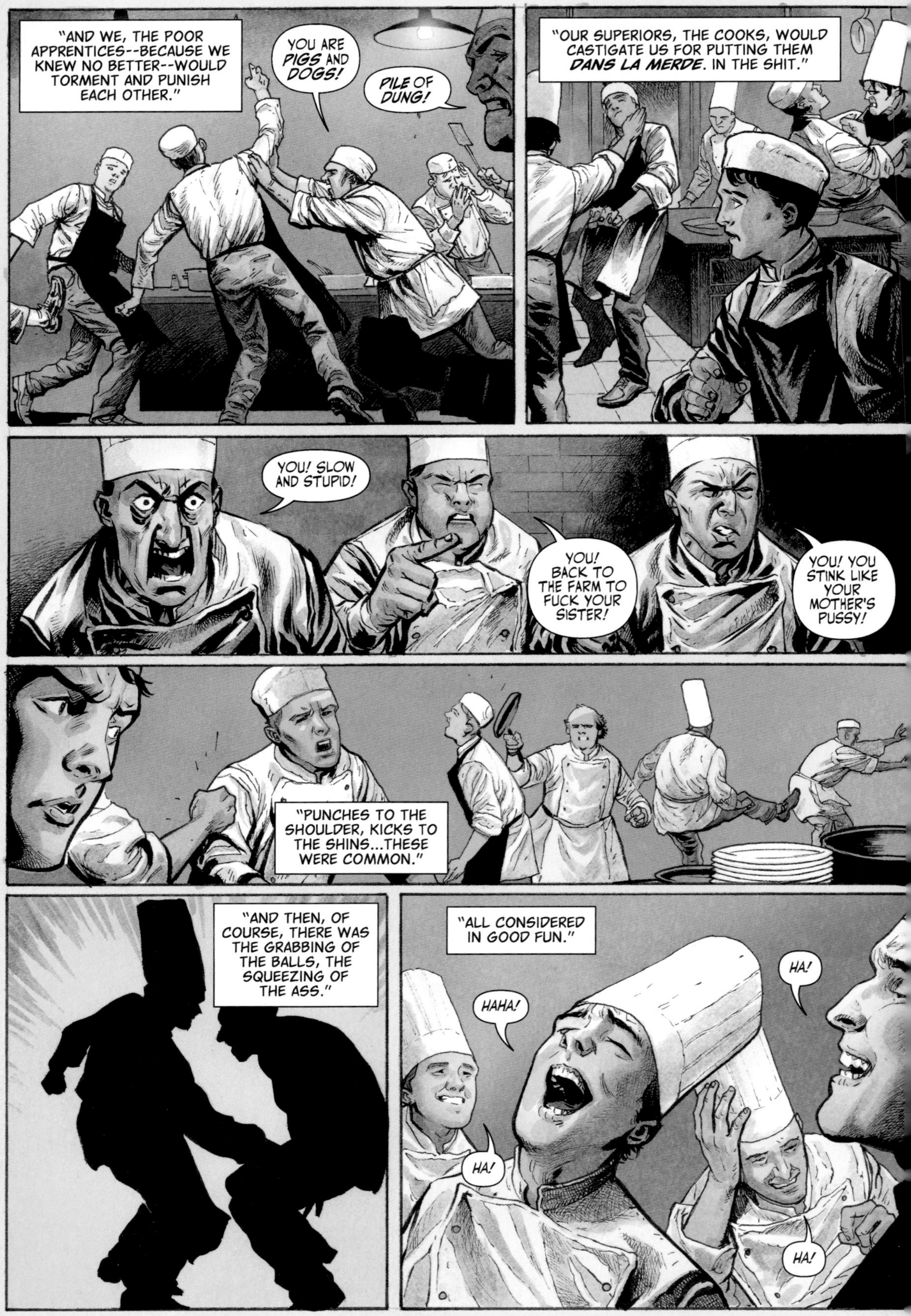
"AND WE, THE POOR APPRENTICES--BECAUSE WE KNEW NO BETTER--WOULD TORMENT AND PUNISH EACH OTHER."
YOU ARE *PIGS* AND *DOGS!*
PILE OF *DUNG!*
"OUR SUPERIORS, THE COOKS, WOULD CASTIGATE US FOR PUTTING THEM ***DANS LA MERDE***. IN THE SHIT."
YOU! SLOW AND STUPID!
YOU! BACK TO THE FARM TO FUCK YOUR SISTER!
YOU! YOU STINK LIKE YOUR MOTHER'S PUSSY!
"PUNCHES TO THE SHOULDER, KICKS TO THE SHINS...THESE WERE COMMON."
"AND THEN, OF COURSE, THERE WAS THE GRABBING OF THE BALLS, THE SQUEEZING OF THE ASS."
"ALL CONSIDERED IN GOOD FUN."
HAHA!
HA!
HA!
HA!

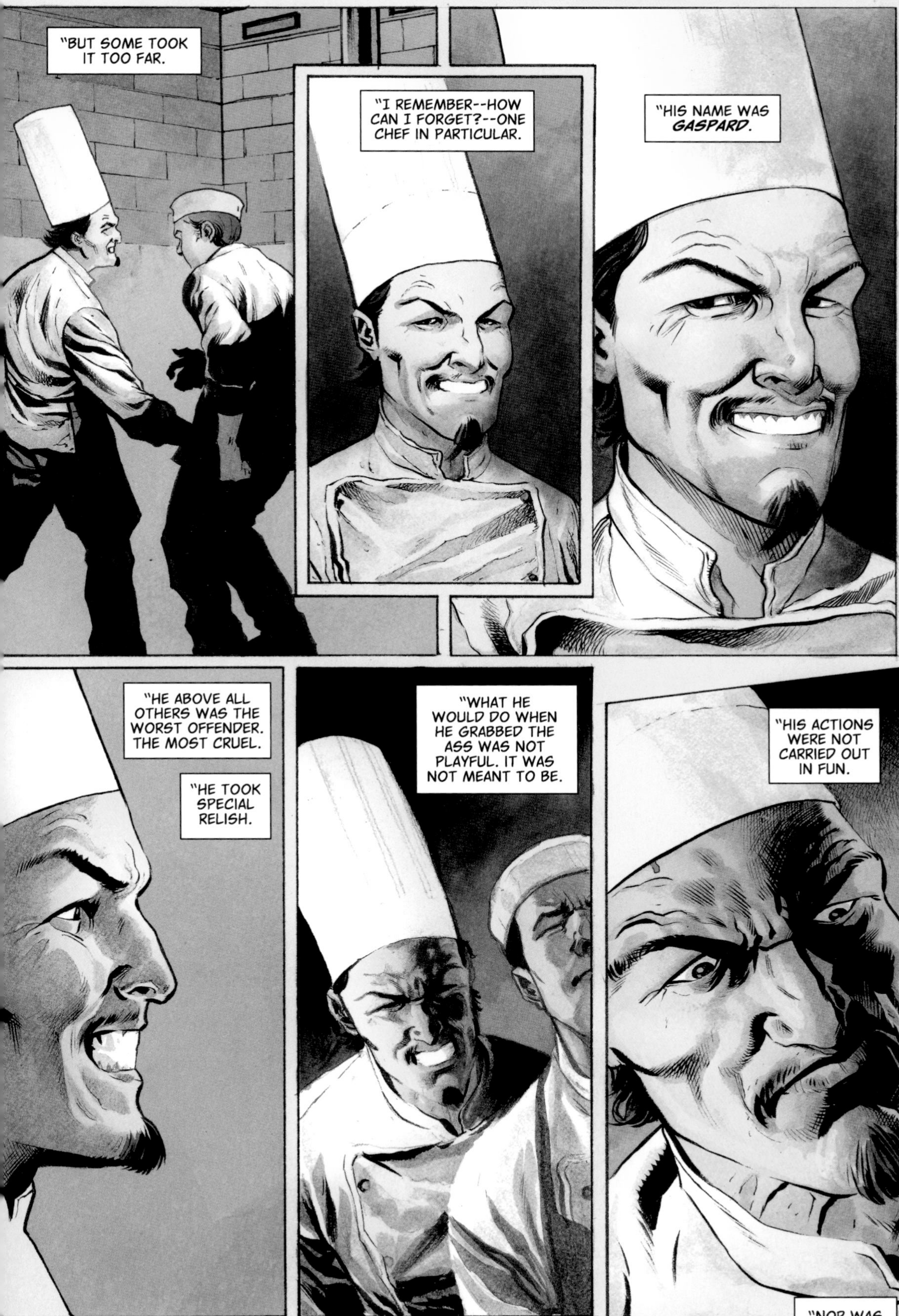
"BUT SOME TOOK IT TOO FAR.
"I REMEMBER--HOW CAN I FORGET?--ONE CHEF IN PARTICULAR.
"HIS NAME WAS *GASPARD*.
"HE ABOVE ALL OTHERS WAS THE WORST OFFENDER. THE MOST CRUEL.
"HE TOOK SPECIAL RELISH.
"WHAT HE WOULD DO WHEN HE GRABBED THE ASS WAS NOT PLAYFUL. IT WAS NOT MEANT TO BE.
"HIS ACTIONS WERE NOT CARRIED OUT IN FUN.
"NOR WAS IT DESIRE."

"THIS MAN, THIS GASPARD, HE GRABBED, HE POKED, HE SLAPPED WITH A CERTAIN RAGE. A DESIRE TO DESTROY.

"WHAT HE DID WAS A COMPULSION MEANT TO CAUSE PAIN. TO HUMILIATE.

"THESE WERE EXPRESSIONS OF POWER, A DESIRE TO DOMINATE AND OBLITERATE THE YOUNGER AND THE SMALLER COOKS.

"MOST ESPECIALLY, ME!

"SADLY, I WAS THE YOUNGEST. AND I COULD NOT COMPLAIN.

"WE ALL HAD TO ENDURE IT. THIS WAS THE SYSTEM.

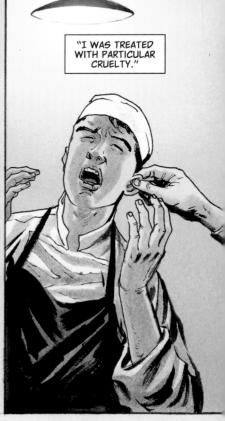

"I WAS TREATED WITH PARTICULAR CRUELTY."

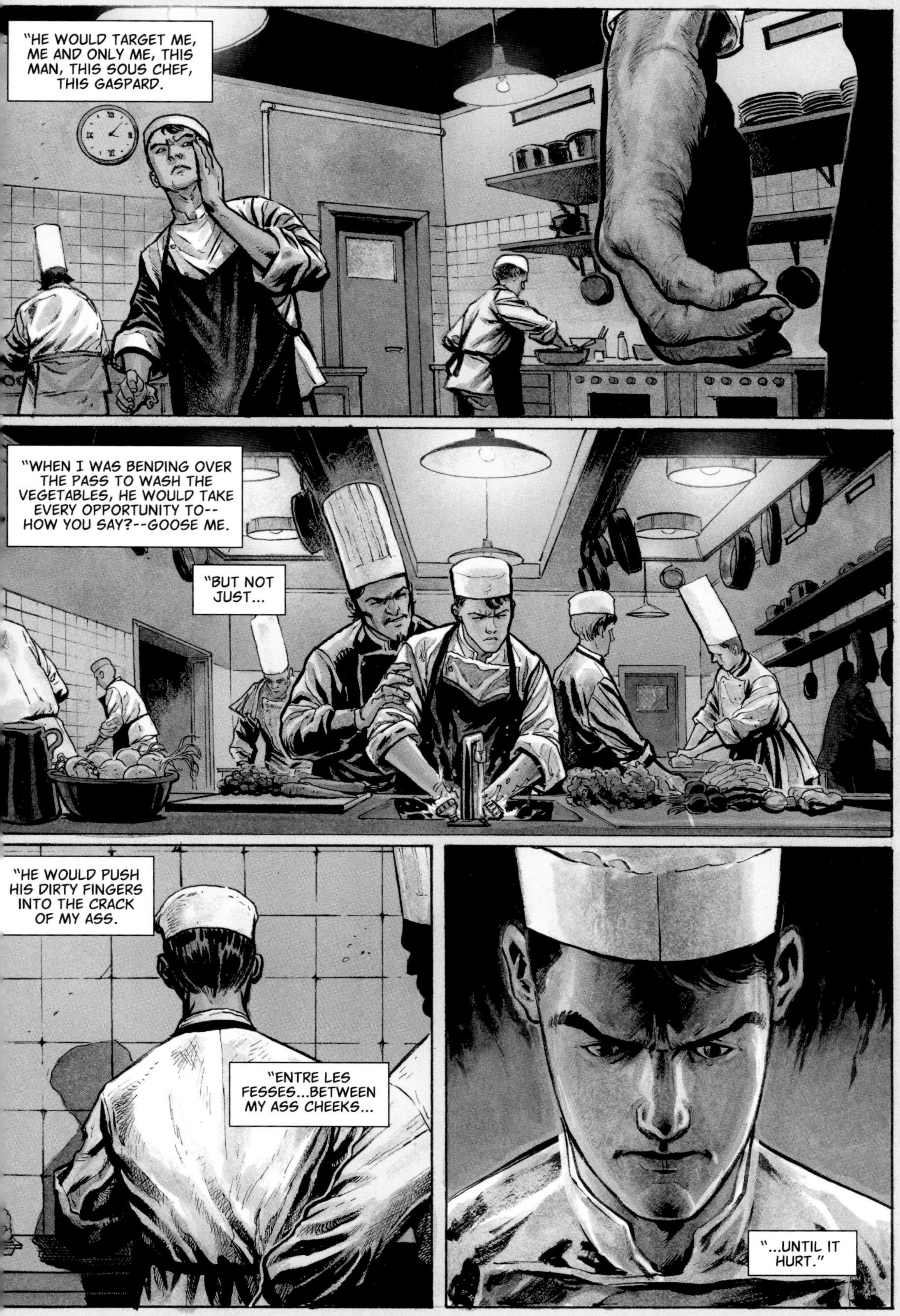
"HE WOULD TARGET ME, ME AND ONLY ME, THIS MAN, THIS SOUS CHEF, THIS GASPARD.
"WHEN I WAS BENDING OVER THE PASS TO WASH THE VEGETABLES, HE WOULD TAKE EVERY OPPORTUNITY TO--HOW YOU SAY?--GOOSE ME.
"BUT NOT JUST...
"HE WOULD PUSH HIS DIRTY FINGERS INTO THE CRACK OF MY ASS.
"ENTRE LES FESSES...BETWEEN MY ASS CHEEKS...
"...UNTIL IT HURT."

"ONE COOK TOOK PITY ON ME.

"THIS MAN WAS FROM A FRENCH-INDOCHINESE POSSESSION.

"HE GREW UP ON A PLANTATION IN VIETNAM OR LAOS OR CAMBODIA. I FORGET.

"FOR SOME TIME, HE WATCHED MY STRUGGLE.

"HE SAID NOTHING, BUT SOMETIMES I SAW HIM AS I SUFFERED, AND HE HAD THE STRANGEST EXPRESSION ON HIS FACE, LIKE HE KNEW...

"...LIKE WE SUFFERED TOGETHER. THE SAME THING."

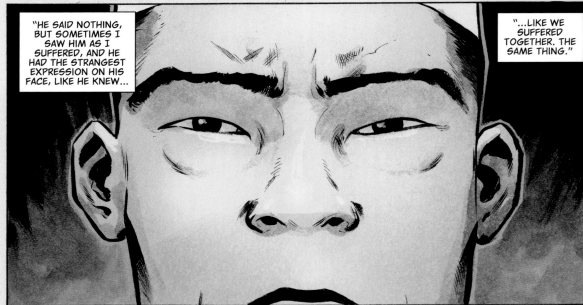

"ONE DAY HE TOOK ME ASIDE.

"'LITTLE ONE,' HE SAID."

LITTLE ONE. LOOK AT ME.

THIS MAN IS A BULLY. IN MY LIFE, I HAVE SEEN MEN LIKE THIS. THEY ALL SUFFER THE SAME CURSE. MEN LIKE THIS, THEY HAVE A SMALL *BALL* UP THEIR ASSES. TRULY! DON'T LAUGH! IT MAKES THEM VERY DISAGREEABLE.

BUT THERE ARE SPIRITS THAT *CRAVE* THESE SMALL BALLS. IN JAPAN THEY ARE CALLED KAPPA.

THESE KAPPA, THEY CONSIDER THE BALL A GREAT *DELICACY*.

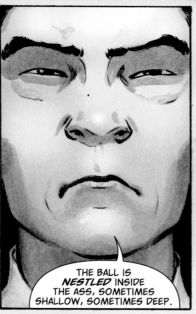

THE BALL IS *NESTLED* INSIDE THE ASS, SOMETIMES SHALLOW, SOMETIMES DEEP.

NO MATTER TO YOU, YOUNG ONE, THE KAPPA IS EAGER TO GET THE *SHIRIKODAMA*, THE SMALL BALL, OUT OF THE ASS AND EAT IT.

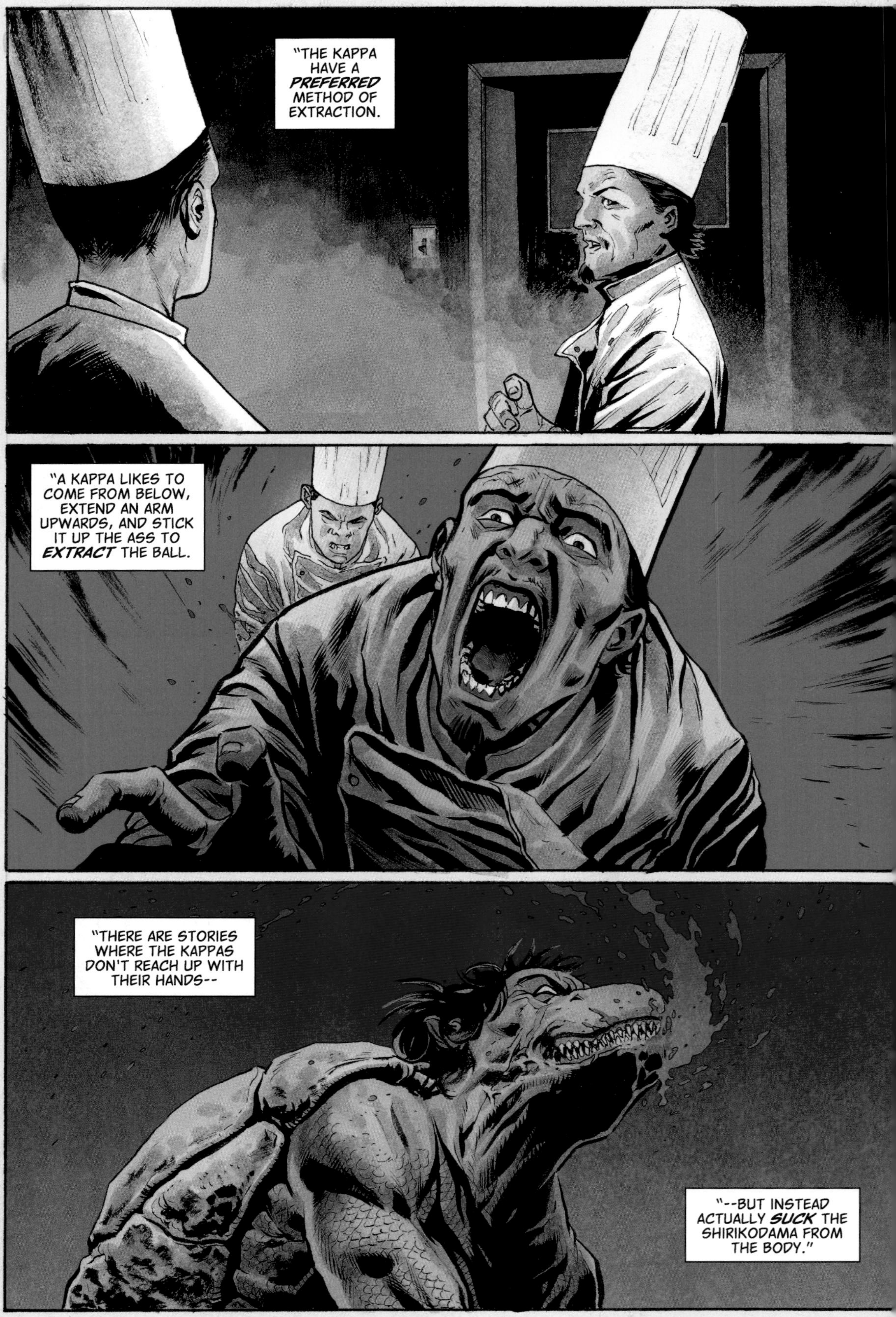
"THE KAPPA HAVE A PREFERRED METHOD OF EXTRACTION.
"A KAPPA LIKES TO COME FROM BELOW, EXTEND AN ARM UPWARDS, AND STICK IT UP THE ASS TO EXTRACT THE BALL.
"THERE ARE STORIES WHERE THE KAPPAS DON'T REACH UP WITH THEIR HANDS--
"--BUT INSTEAD ACTUALLY SUCK THE SHIRIKODAMA FROM THE BODY."

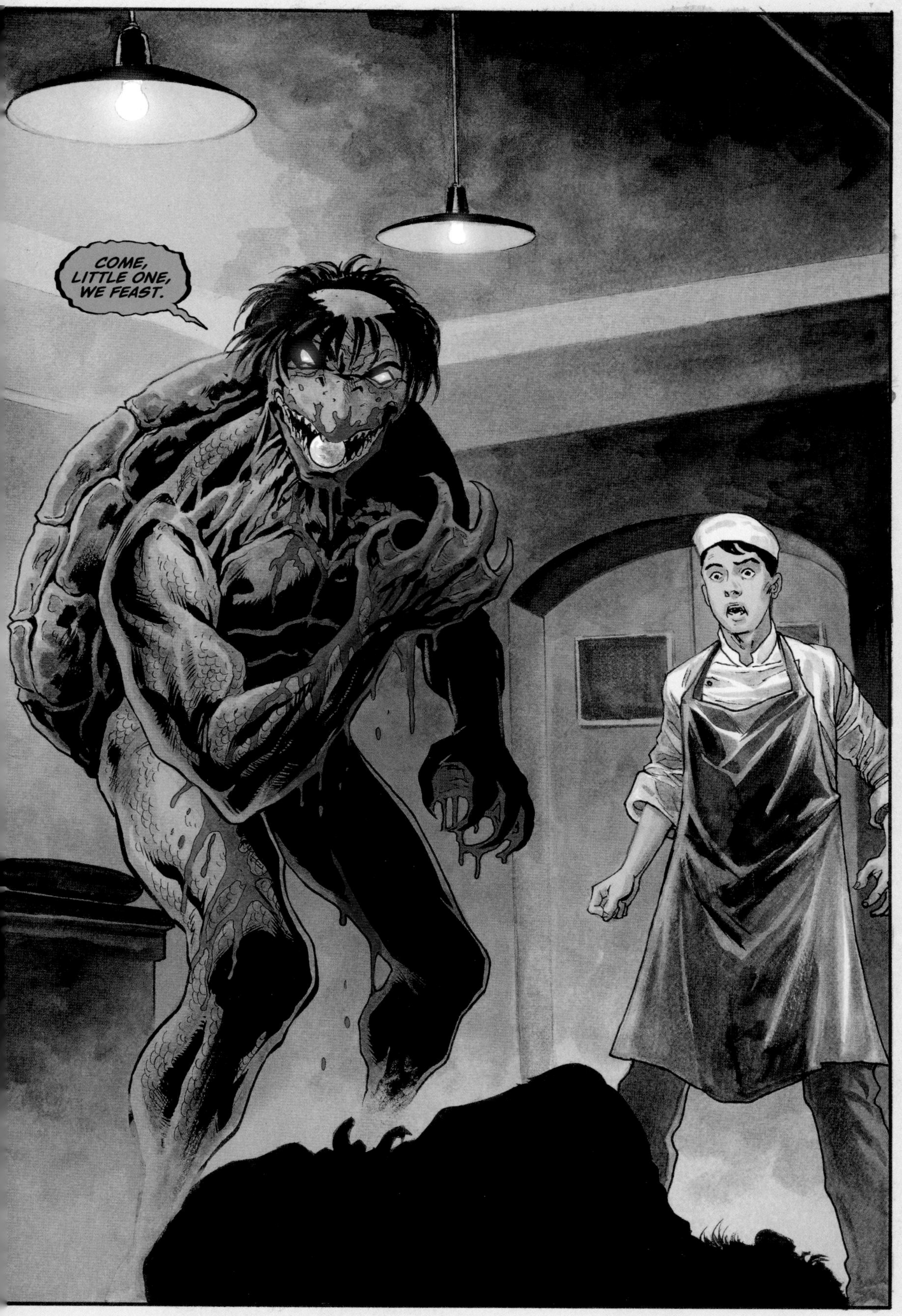
COME, LITTLE ONE, WE FEAST.

BOIL IN THE BELLY

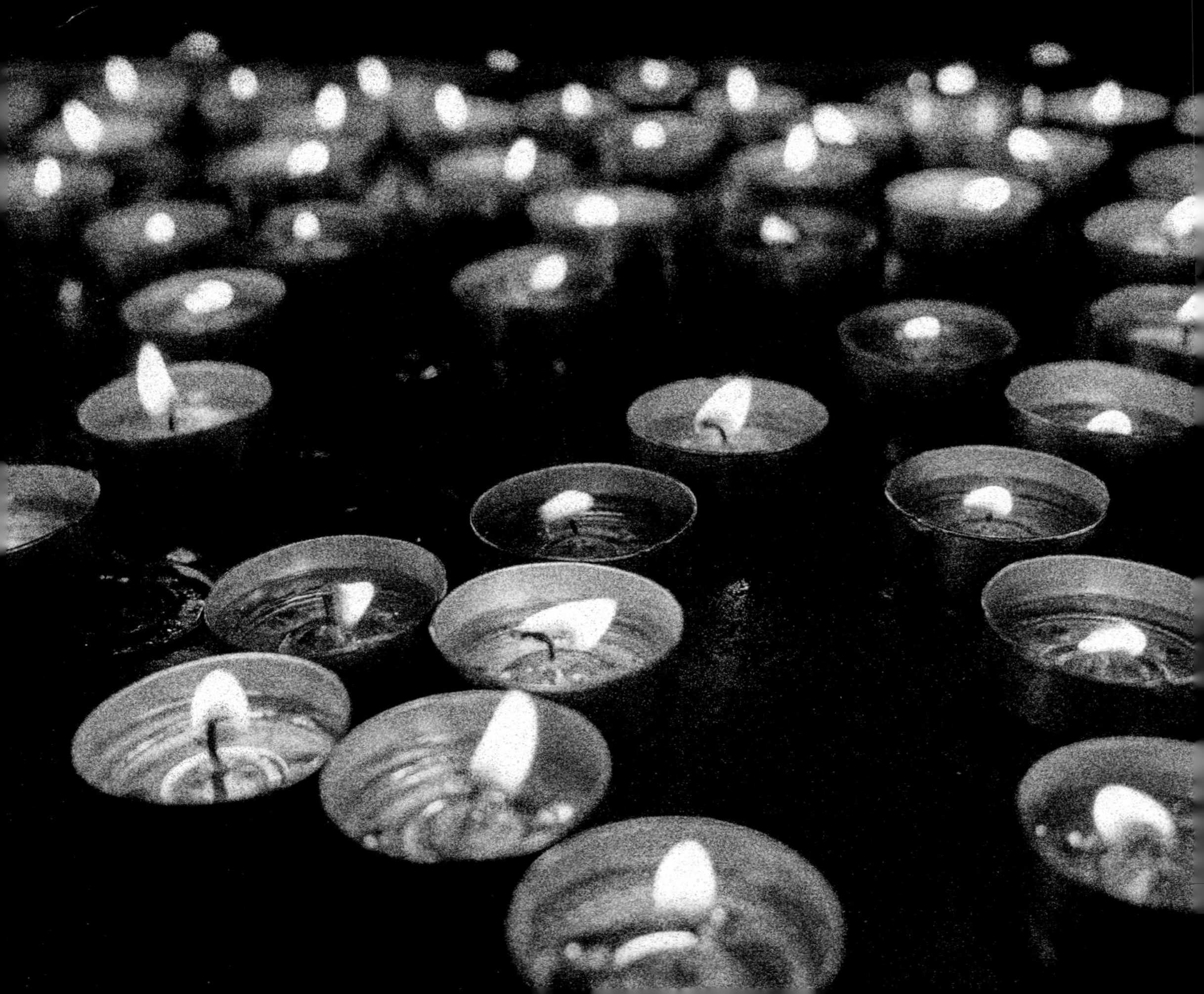

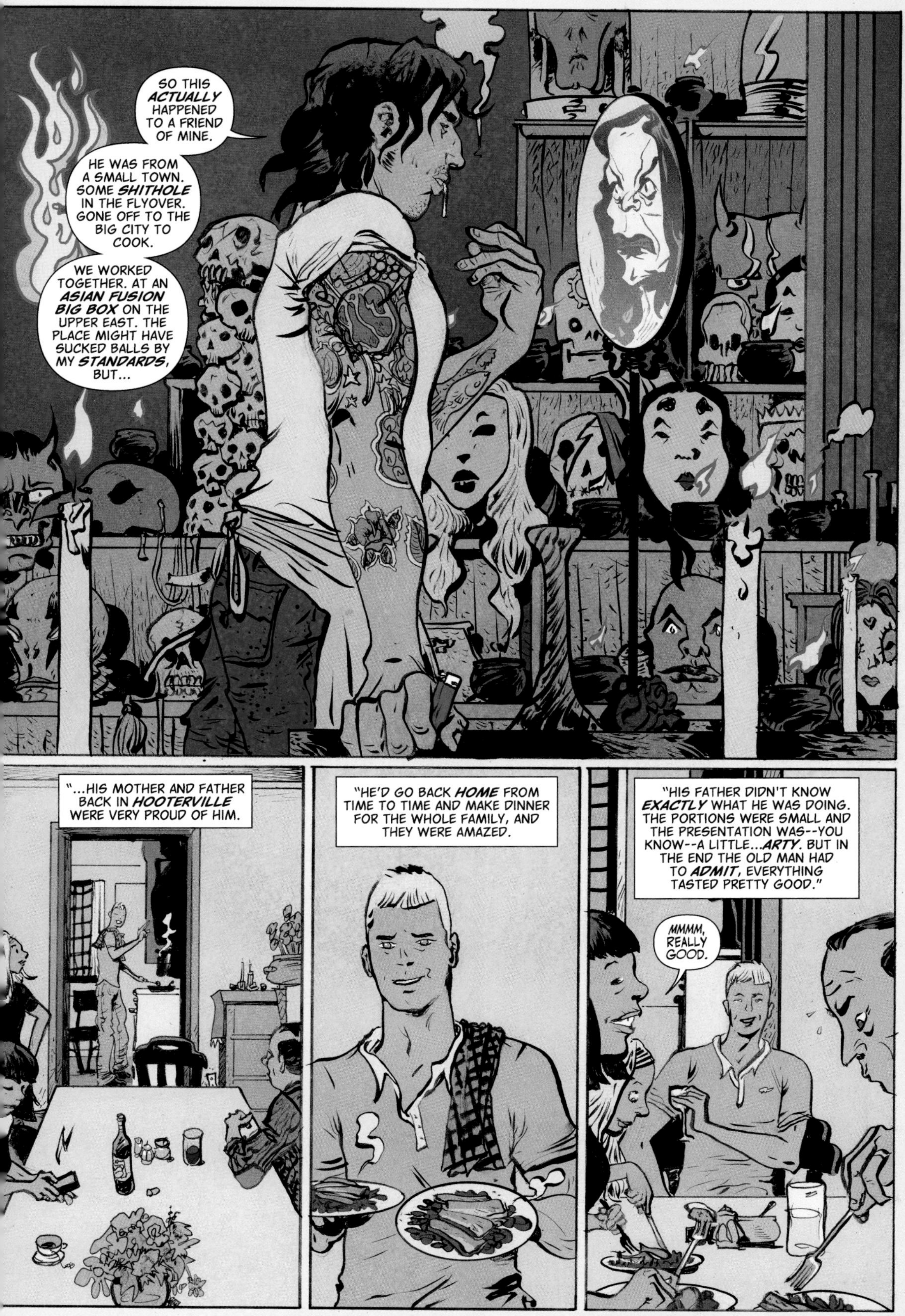

SO THIS ACTUALLY HAPPENED TO A FRIEND OF MINE.
HE WAS FROM A SMALL TOWN. SOME SHITHOLE IN THE FLYOVER. GONE OFF TO THE BIG CITY TO COOK.
WE WORKED TOGETHER. AT AN ASIAN FUSION BIG BOX ON THE UPPER EAST. THE PLACE MIGHT HAVE SUCKED BALLS BY MY STANDARDS, BUT...
"...HIS MOTHER AND FATHER BACK IN HOOTERVILLE WERE VERY PROUD OF HIM.
"HE'D GO BACK HOME FROM TIME TO TIME AND MAKE DINNER FOR THE WHOLE FAMILY, AND THEY WERE AMAZED.
"HIS FATHER DIDN'T KNOW EXACTLY WHAT HE WAS DOING. THE PORTIONS WERE SMALL AND THE PRESENTATION WAS--YOU KNOW--A LITTLE...ARTY. BUT IN THE END THE OLD MAN HAD TO ADMIT, EVERYTHING TASTED PRETTY GOOD."
MMMM, REALLY GOOD.

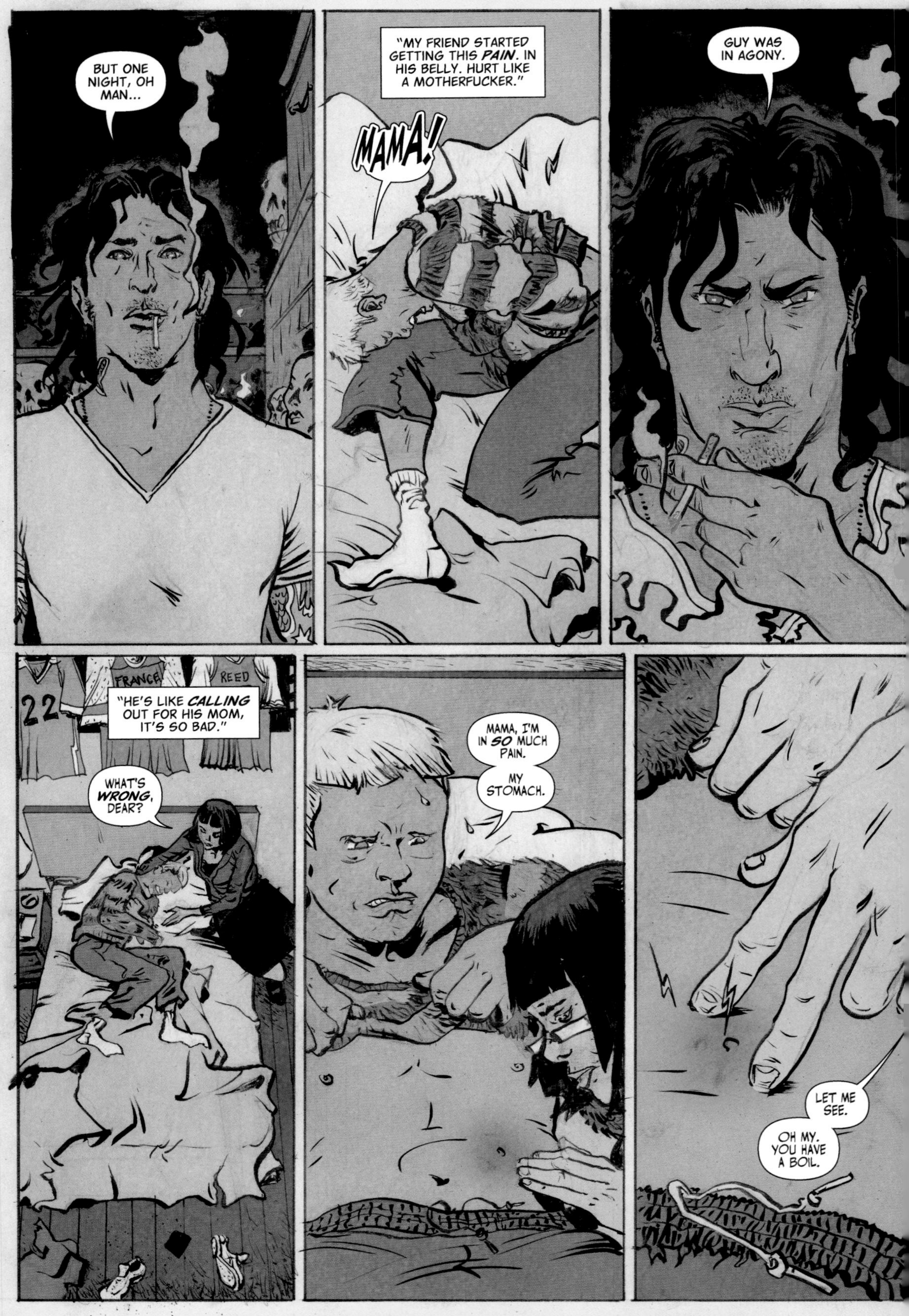
BUT ONE NIGHT, OH MAN...
"MY FRIEND STARTED GETTING THIS PAIN. IN HIS BELLY. HURT LIKE A MOTHERFUCKER."
MAMA!
GUY WAS IN AGONY.
FRANCE
REED
22
"HE'S LIKE CALLING OUT FOR HIS MOM, IT'S SO BAD."
WHAT'S WRONG, DEAR?
MAMA, I'M IN SO MUCH PAIN.
MY STOMACH.
LET ME SEE.
OH MY. YOU HAVE A BOIL.

THIS SHOULD TAKE CARE OF IT.

IT'S NOTHING.

OH MY!

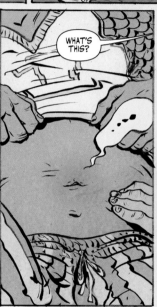

WHAT'S THIS?

THIS IS SOMETHING.

FEED ME...

"SO OFF MAMA GOES TO THE KITCHEN...

"...TO COOK FOR THE MOUTH.

"THE THING WAS INSATIABLE."

SMACK.. SMACK...

"MY FRIEND COULDN'T EAT, HIMSELF. I MEAN... WHO COULD *BLAME* HIM? THIS THING CHOMPING AWAY DOWN THERE.

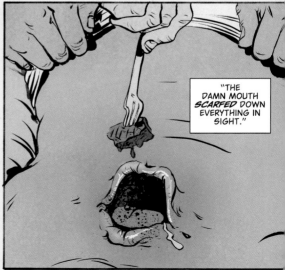

"THE DAMN MOUTH *SCARFED* DOWN EVERYTHING IN SIGHT."

"ALWAYS HUNGRY, ALWAYS WANTING MORE.

"ALWAYS-- DEMANDING-- MORE..."

MUNCH MUNCH GULP

MORE--

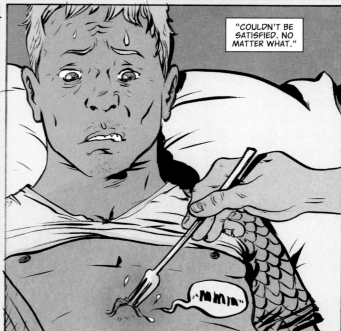

"COULDN'T BE SATISFIED. NO MATTER WHAT."

MMM

"SLURP.."

"SLURP.."

"WHAT COULD SHE DO?"

MORE...

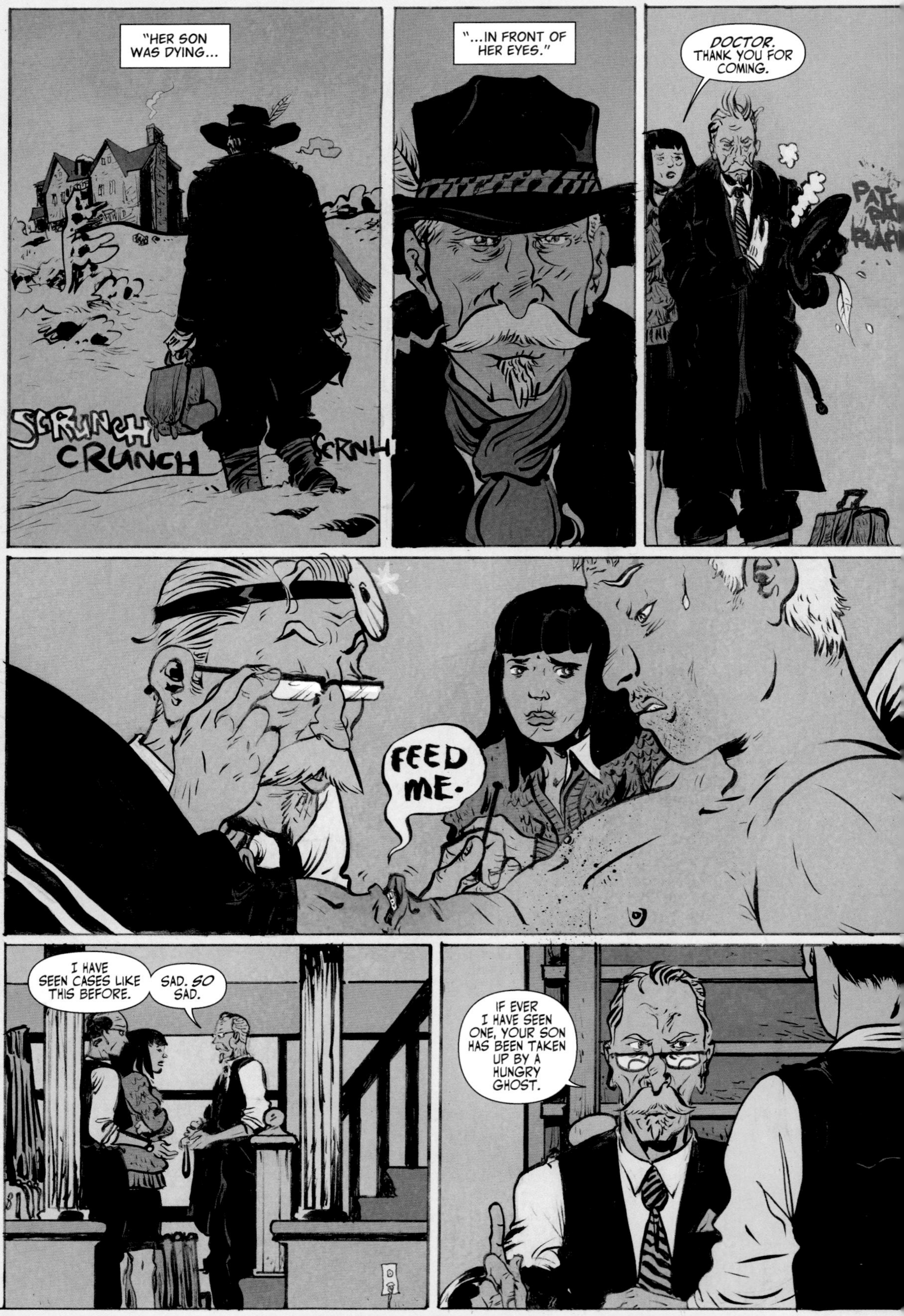

"HER SON WAS DYING...
SCRUNCH
CRUNCH
SCRNH
"...IN FRONT OF HER EYES."
DOCTOR. THANK YOU FOR COMING.
FEED ME.
I HAVE SEEN CASES LIKE THIS BEFORE.
SAD. SO SAD.
IF EVER I HAVE SEEN ONE, YOUR SON HAS BEEN TAKEN UP BY A HUNGRY GHOST.

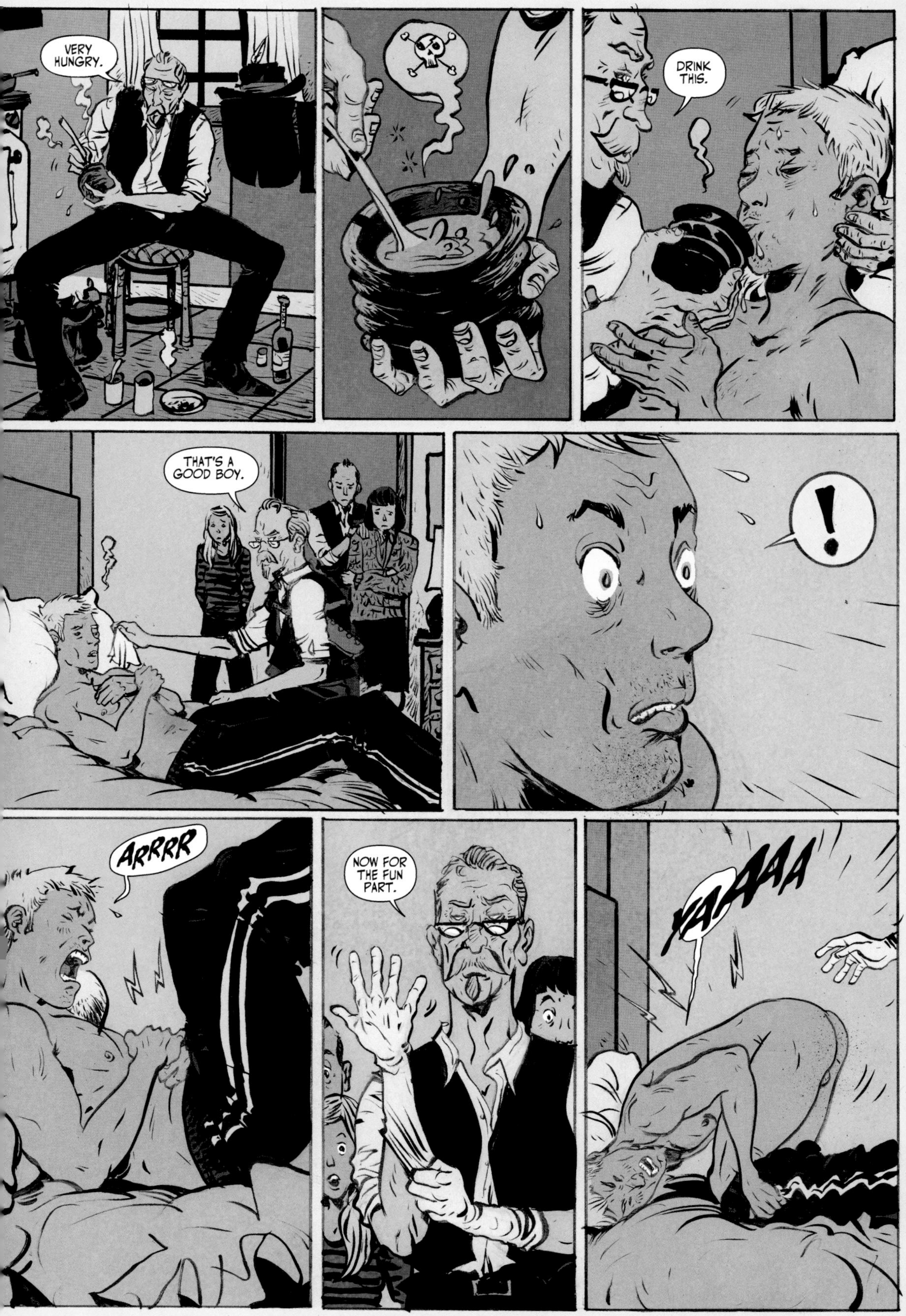
VERY HUNGRY.
DRINK THIS.
THAT'S A GOOD BOY.
!
ARRRR
NOW FOR THE FUN PART.
YAAAAA

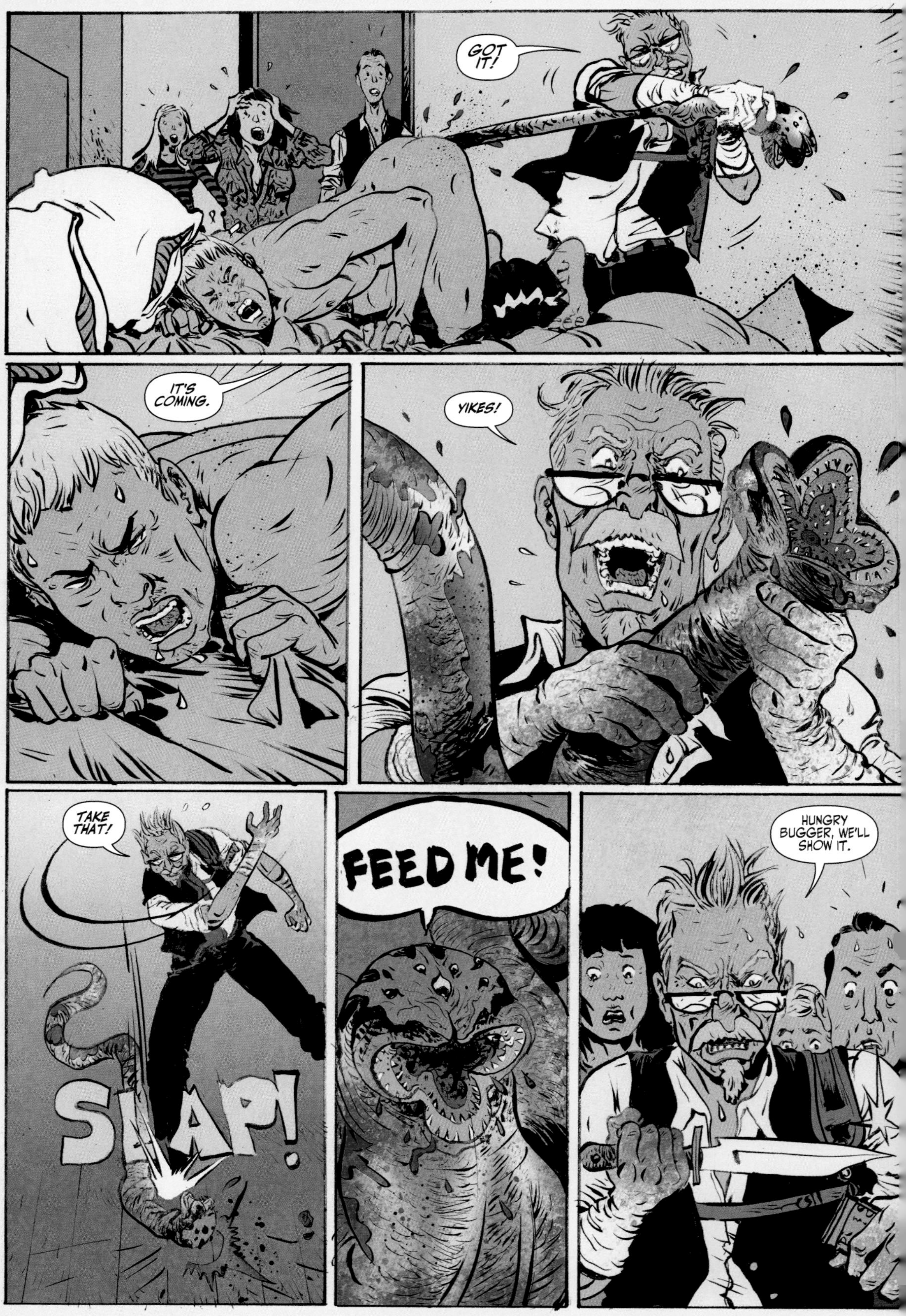
GOT IT!
IT'S COMING.
YIKES!
TAKE THAT!
SLAP!
FEED ME!
HUNGRY BUGGER, WE'LL SHOW IT.

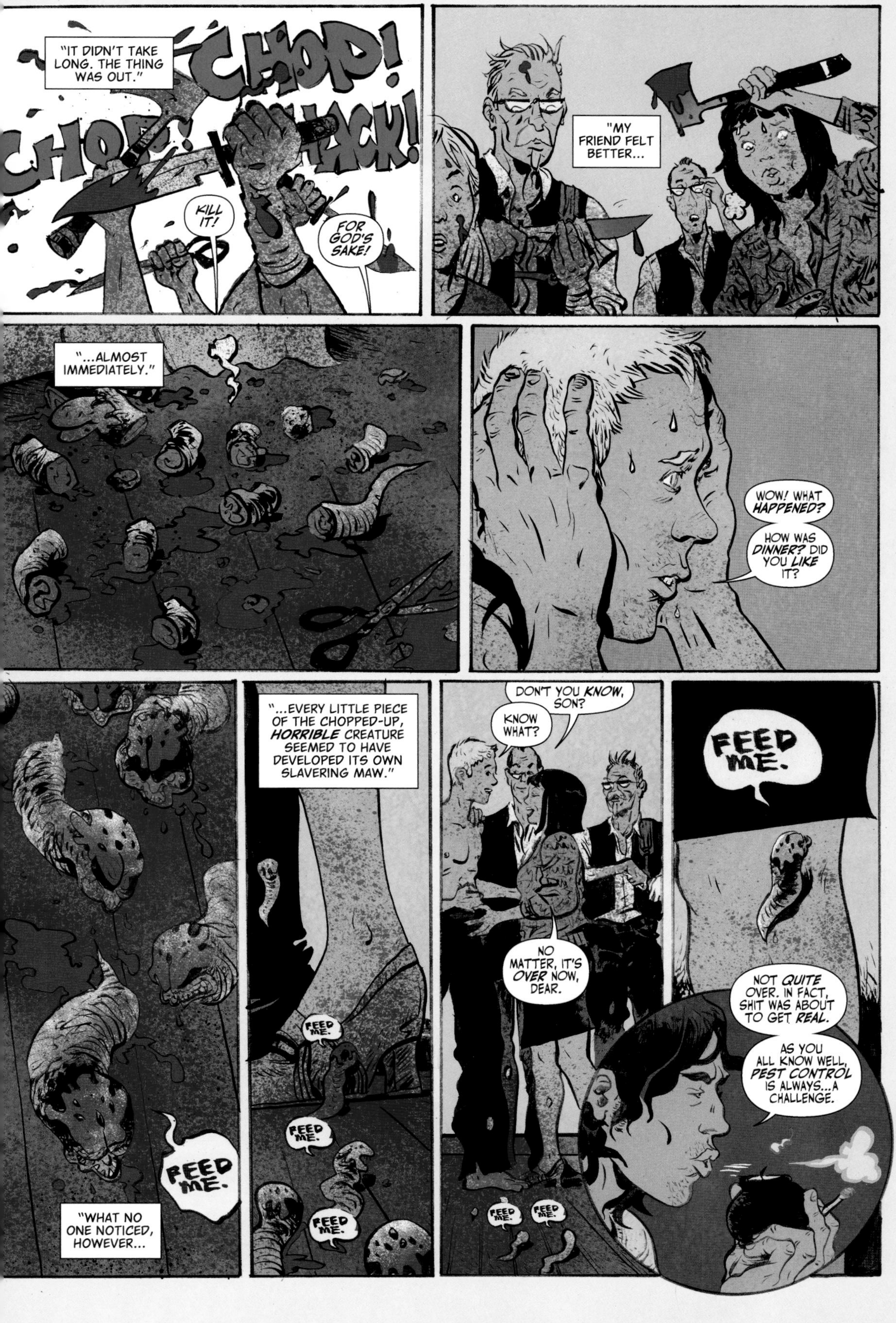
"IT DIDN'T TAKE LONG. THE THING WAS OUT."
CHOP!
CHOP!
HACK!
KILL IT!
FOR GOD'S SAKE!
"MY FRIEND FELT BETTER...
"...ALMOST IMMEDIATELY."
WOW! WHAT HAPPENED?
HOW WAS DINNER? DID YOU LIKE IT?
"WHAT NO ONE NOTICED, HOWEVER...
FEED ME.
"...EVERY LITTLE PIECE OF THE CHOPPED-UP, HORRIBLE CREATURE SEEMED TO HAVE DEVELOPED ITS OWN SLAVERING MAW."
FEED ME.
FEED ME.
FEED ME.
DON'T YOU KNOW, SON?
KNOW WHAT?
NO MATTER, IT'S OVER NOW, DEAR.
FEED ME.
FEED ME.
FEED ME.
NOT QUITE OVER. IN FACT, SHIT WAS ABOUT TO GET REAL.
AS YOU ALL KNOW WELL, PEST CONTROL IS ALWAYS...A CHALLENGE.

THE SNOW WOMAN

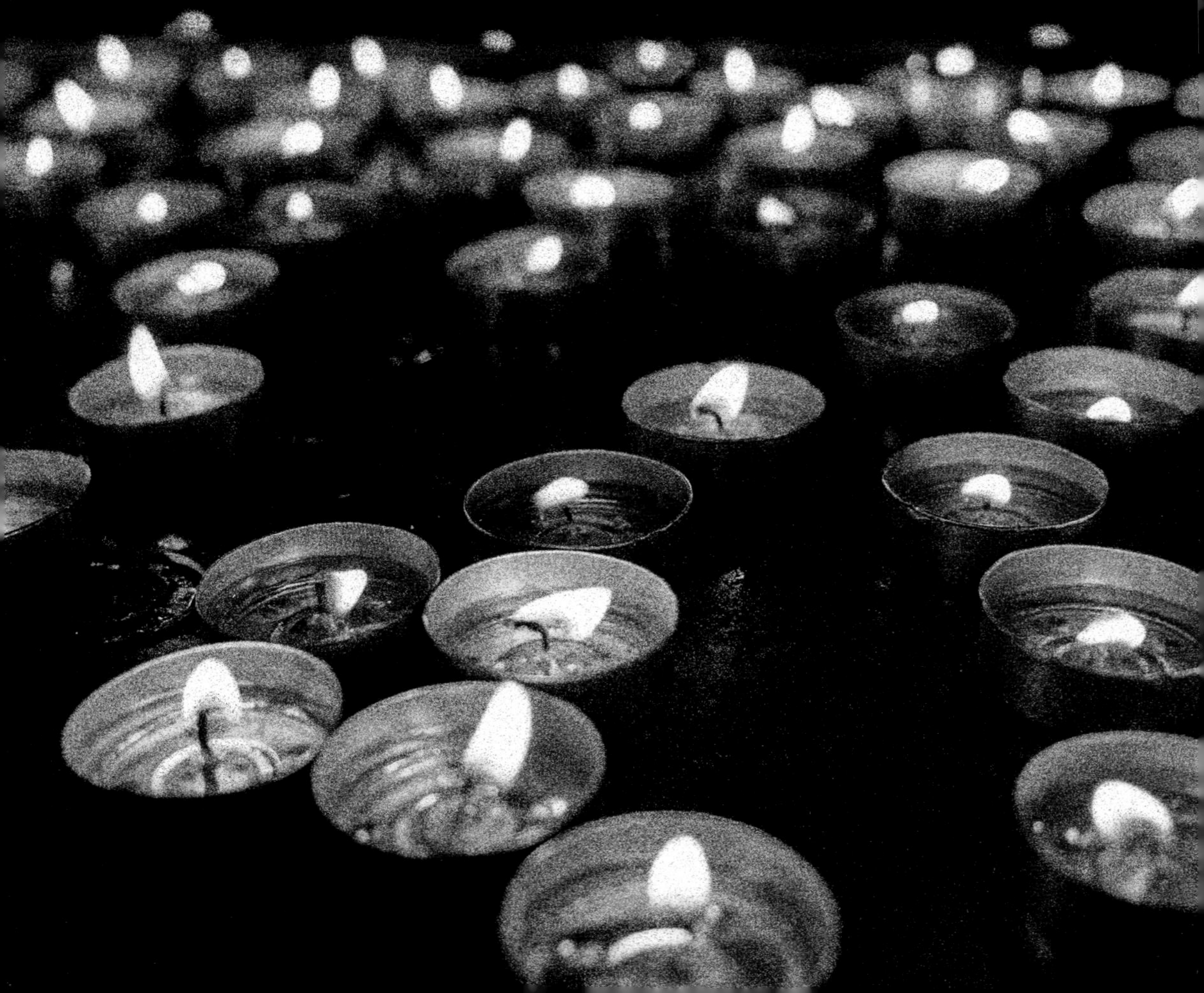

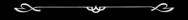

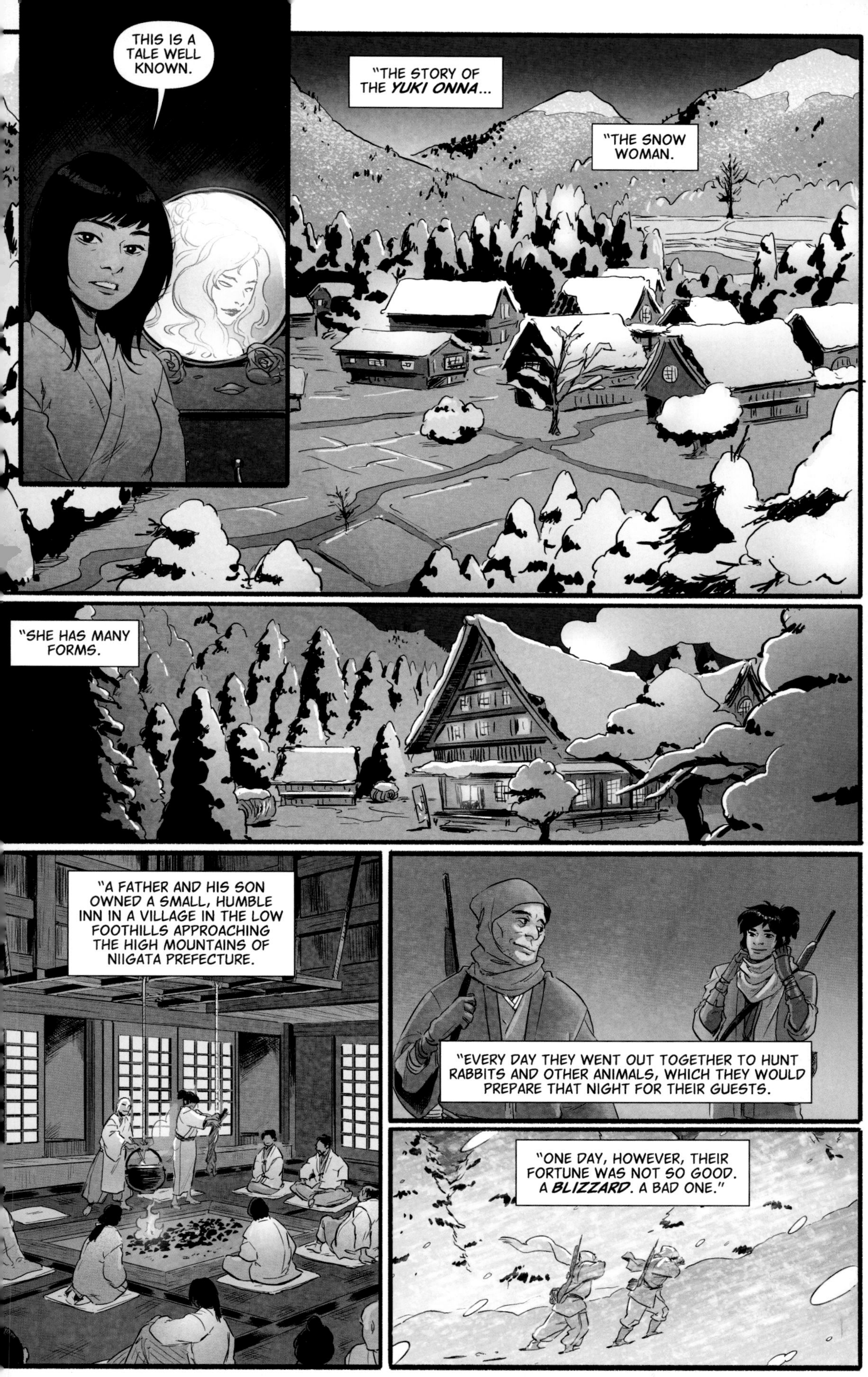
THIS IS A TALE WELL KNOWN.
"THE STORY OF THE YUKI ONNA...
"THE SNOW WOMAN.
"SHE HAS MANY FORMS.
"A FATHER AND HIS SON OWNED A SMALL, HUMBLE INN IN A VILLAGE IN THE LOW FOOTHILLS APPROACHING THE HIGH MOUNTAINS OF NIIGATA PREFECTURE.
"EVERY DAY THEY WENT OUT TOGETHER TO HUNT RABBITS AND OTHER ANIMALS, WHICH THEY WOULD PREPARE THAT NIGHT FOR THEIR GUESTS.
"ONE DAY, HOWEVER, THEIR FORTUNE WAS NOT SO GOOD. A BLIZZARD. A BAD ONE."

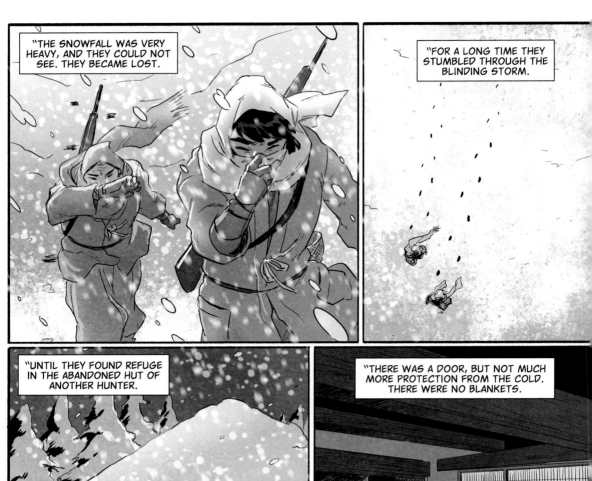

"THE SNOWFALL WAS VERY HEAVY, AND THEY COULD NOT SEE. THEY BECAME LOST.

"FOR A LONG TIME THEY STUMBLED THROUGH THE BLINDING STORM.

"UNTIL THEY FOUND REFUGE IN THE ABANDONED HUT OF ANOTHER HUNTER.

"THERE WAS A DOOR, BUT NOT MUCH MORE PROTECTION FROM THE COLD. THERE WERE NO BLANKETS.

"THE HUT HAD NO STOVE OR FIREPLACE. NOWHERE TO BUILD A FIRE, *NOTHING* TO KEEP WARM. BUT AT LEAST THEY WERE OUT OF THE SNOW."

"THEY FASTENED THE DOOR TO KEEP OUT THE WIND AND DRIVING SNOW AND LAID DOWN ON THE FLOOR, PULLING THEIR COATS TIGHTLY AROUND THEMSELVES AND HUDDLING TOGETHER.

"EVENTUALLY, THE SON FELL ASLEEP.

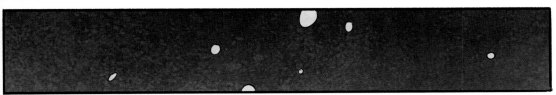

"IN THE MIDDLE OF THE NIGHT, THE SON WOKE TO FEEL SNOWFLAKES FALLING ON HIS FACE.

"ALTHOUGH HE HIMSELF HAD SHUT THE DOOR TO THE STORM, IT WAS NOW *OPEN*."

FATHER!

FATHER?

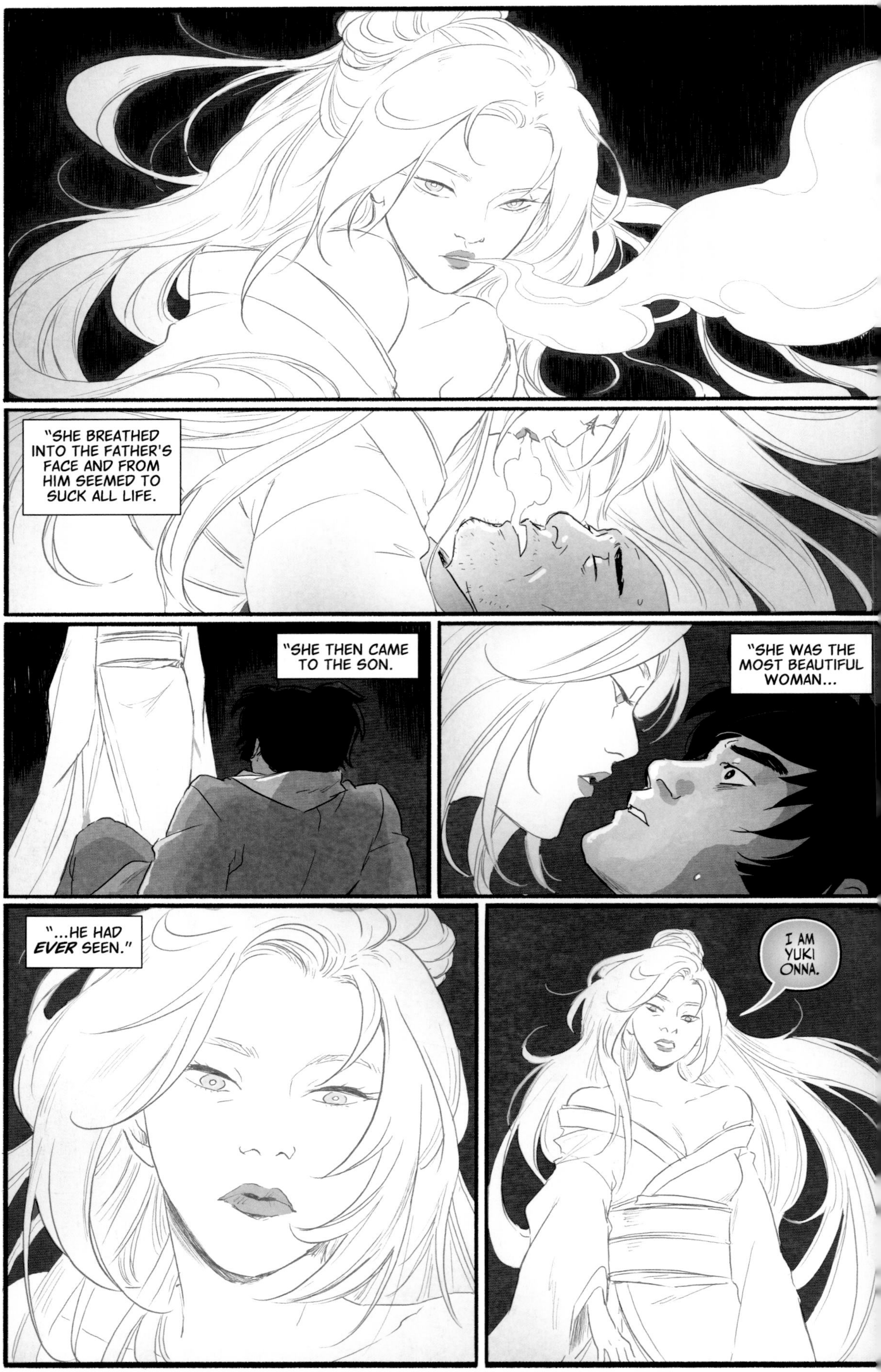
"SHE BREATHED INTO THE FATHER'S FACE AND FROM HIM SEEMED TO SUCK ALL LIFE.
"SHE THEN CAME TO THE SON.
"SHE WAS THE MOST BEAUTIFUL WOMAN...
"...HE HAD *EVER* SEEN."
I AM YUKI ONNA.

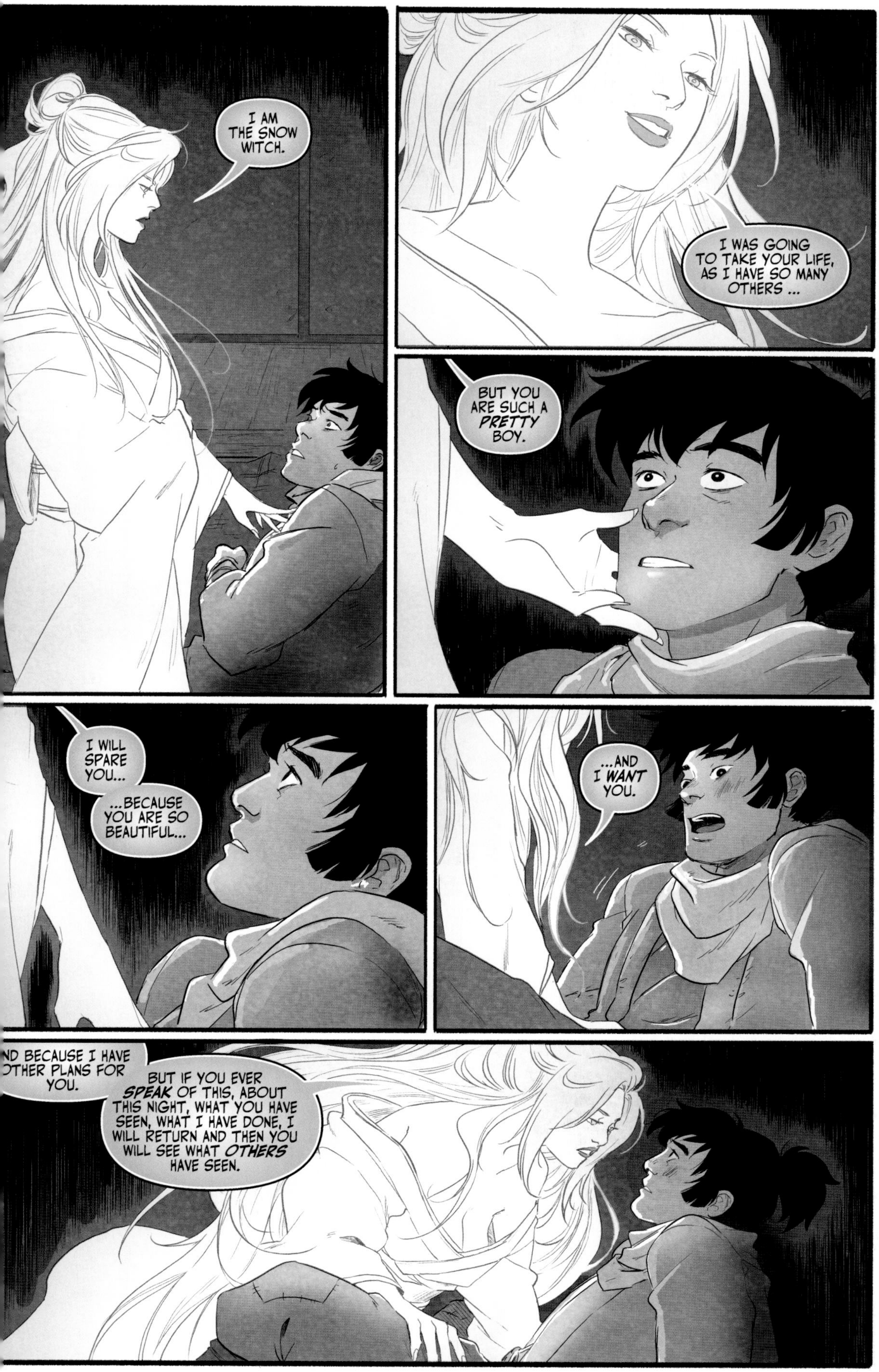
I AM THE SNOW WITCH.
I WAS GOING TO TAKE YOUR LIFE, AS I HAVE SO MANY OTHERS ...
BUT YOU ARE SUCH A *PRETTY* BOY.
I WILL SPARE YOU...
...BECAUSE YOU ARE SO BEAUTIFUL...
...AND I *WANT* YOU.
ND BECAUSE I HAVE OTHER PLANS FOR YOU.
BUT IF YOU EVER *SPEAK* OF THIS, ABOUT THIS NIGHT, WHAT YOU HAVE SEEN, WHAT I HAVE DONE, I WILL RETURN AND THEN YOU WILL SEE WHAT *OTHERS* HAVE SEEN.

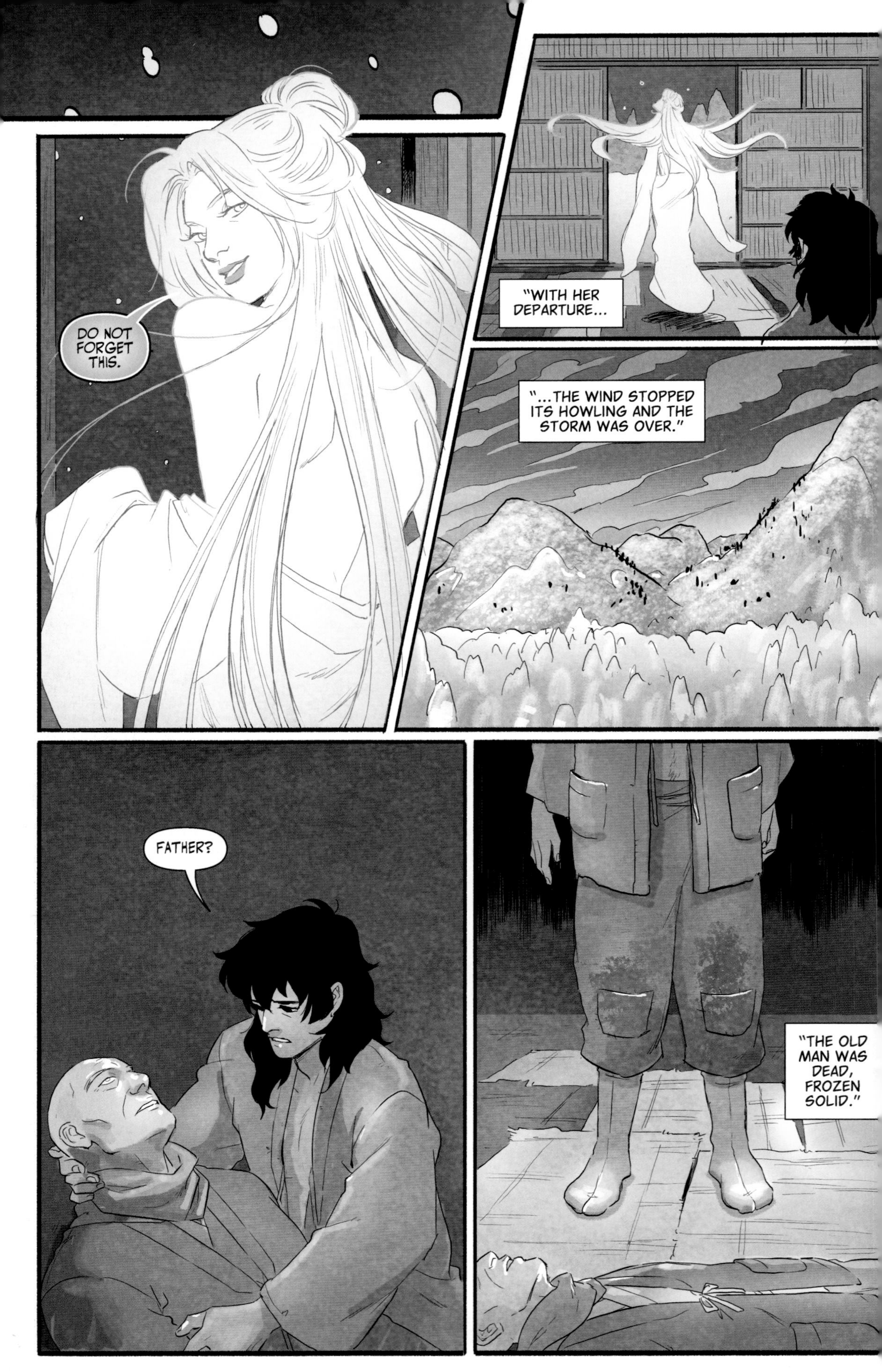
DO NOT FORGET THIS.
"WITH HER DEPARTURE...
"...THE WIND STOPPED ITS HOWLING AND THE STORM WAS OVER."
FATHER?
"THE OLD MAN WAS DEAD, FROZEN SOLID."

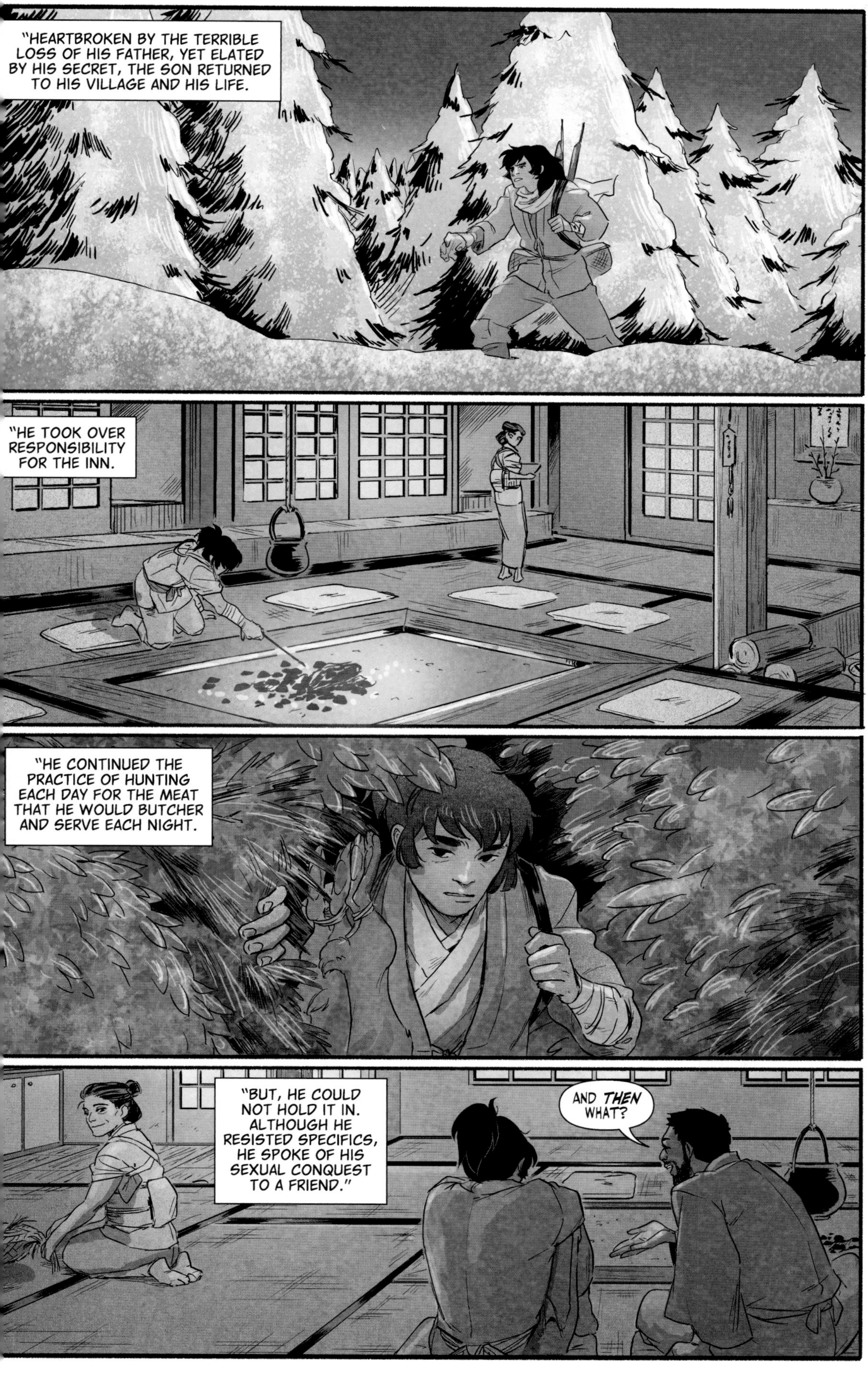
"HEARTBROKEN BY THE TERRIBLE LOSS OF HIS FATHER, YET ELATED BY HIS SECRET, THE SON RETURNED TO HIS VILLAGE AND HIS LIFE.
"HE TOOK OVER RESPONSIBILITY FOR THE INN.
"HE CONTINUED THE PRACTICE OF HUNTING EACH DAY FOR THE MEAT THAT HE WOULD BUTCHER AND SERVE EACH NIGHT.
"BUT, HE COULD NOT HOLD IT IN. ALTHOUGH HE RESISTED SPECIFICS, HE SPOKE OF HIS SEXUAL CONQUEST TO A FRIEND."
AND *THEN* WHAT?

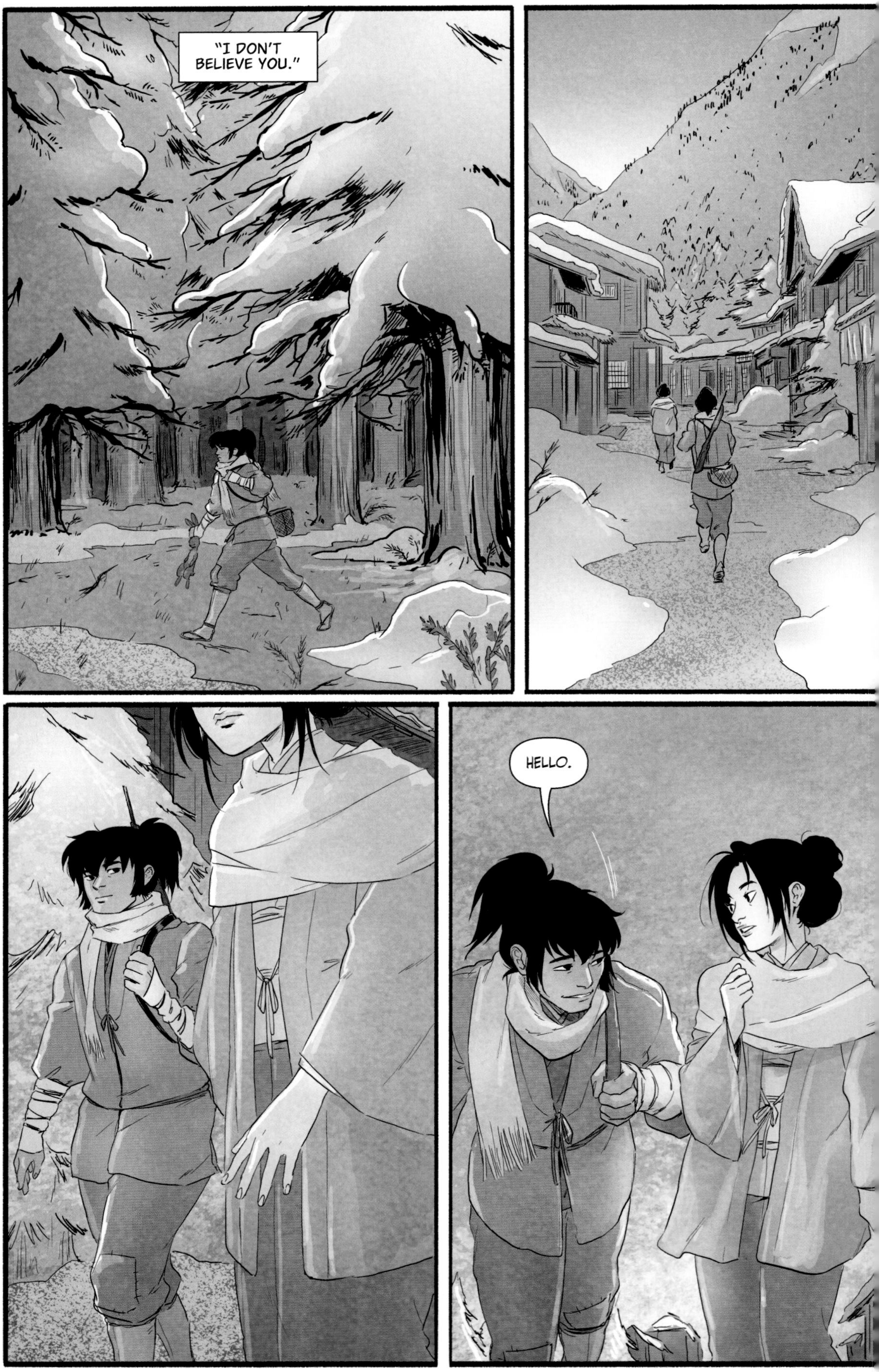
"I DON'T BELIEVE YOU."
HELLO.

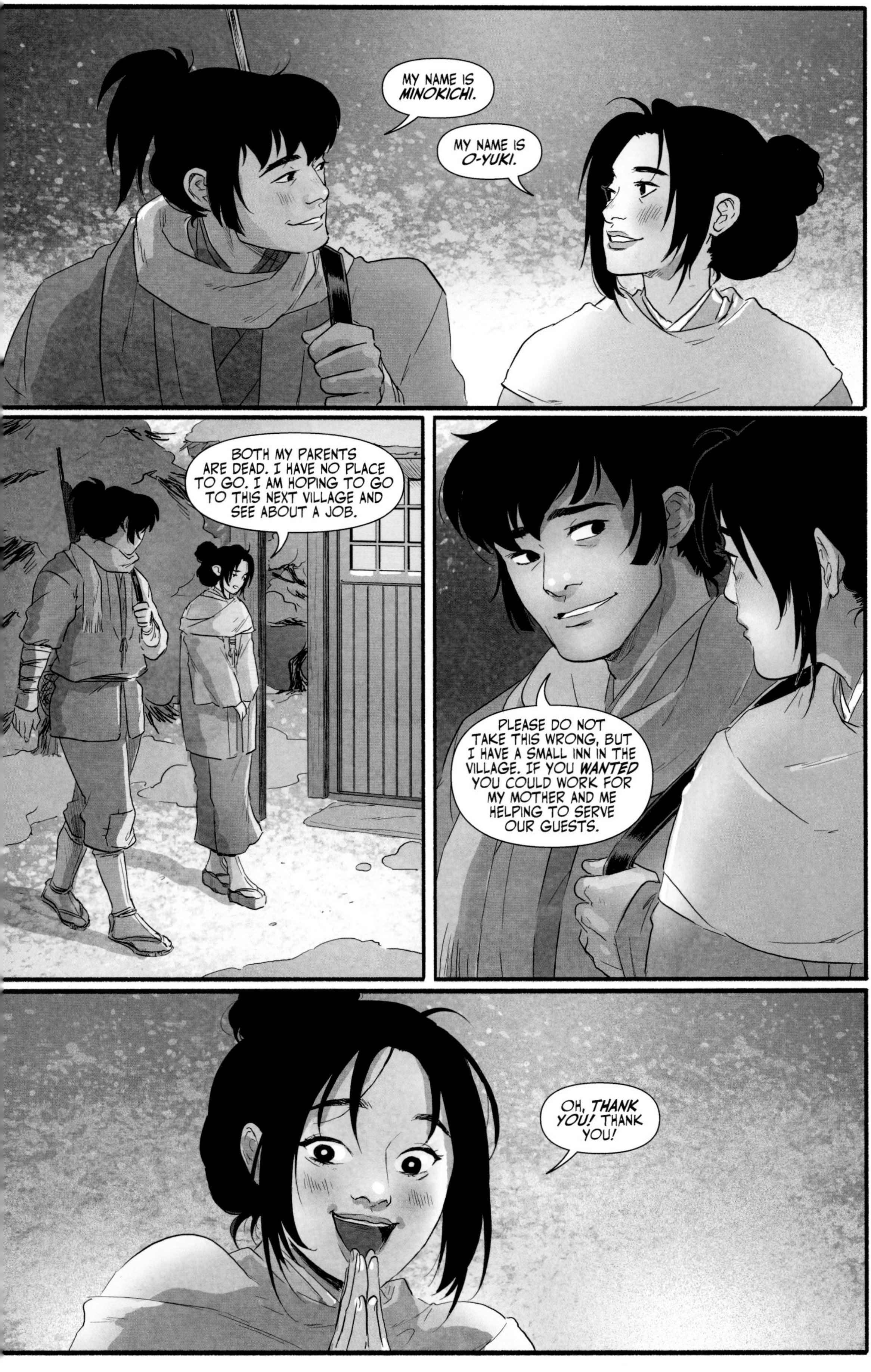
MY NAME IS MINOKICHI.
MY NAME IS O-YUKI.
BOTH MY PARENTS ARE DEAD. I HAVE NO PLACE TO GO. I AM HOPING TO GO TO THIS NEXT VILLAGE AND SEE ABOUT A JOB.
PLEASE DO NOT TAKE THIS WRONG, BUT I HAVE A SMALL INN IN THE VILLAGE. IF YOU WANTED YOU COULD WORK FOR MY MOTHER AND ME HELPING TO SERVE OUR GUESTS.
OH, THANK YOU! THANK YOU!

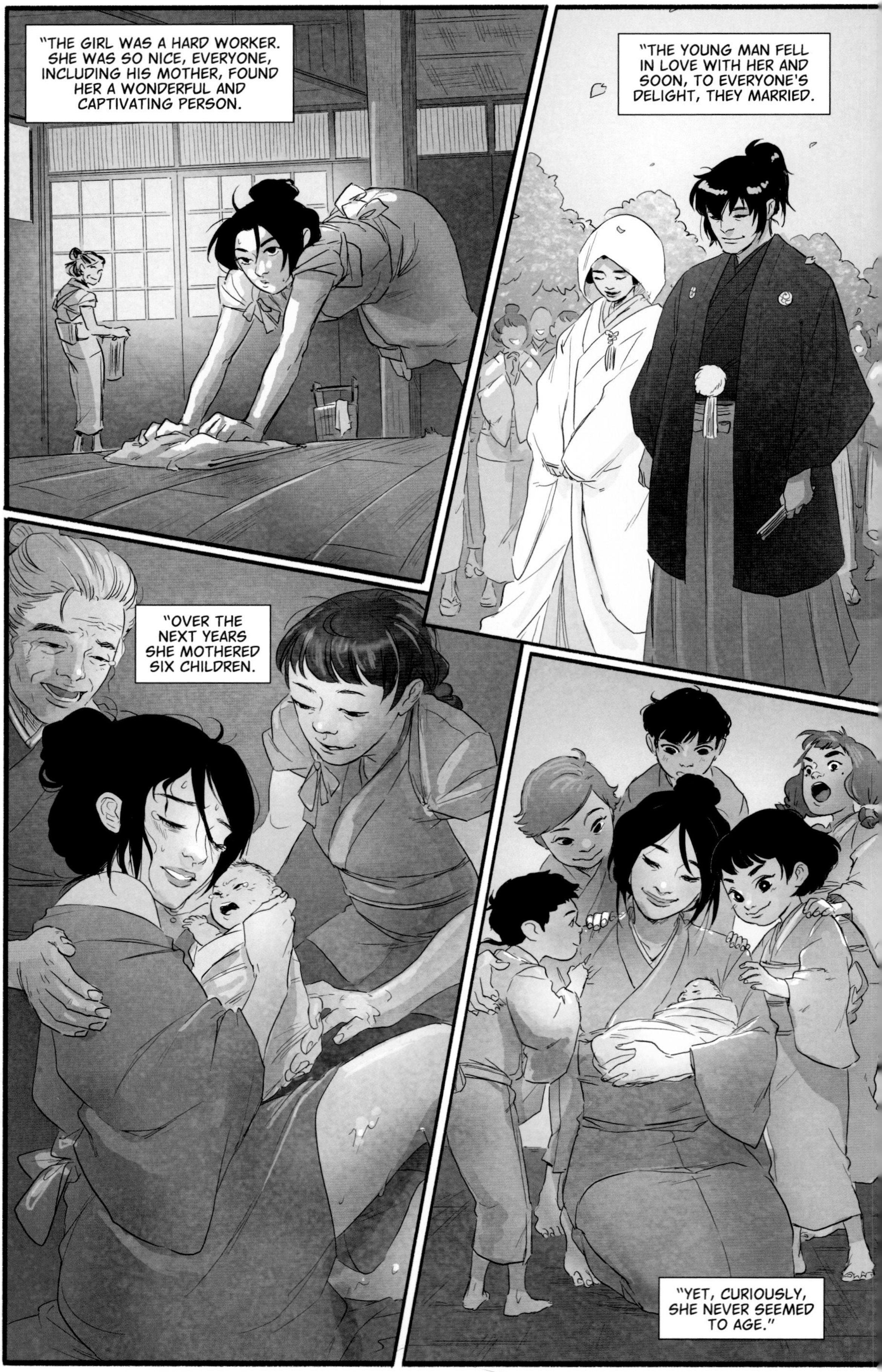
"THE GIRL WAS A HARD WORKER. SHE WAS SO NICE, EVERYONE, INCLUDING HIS MOTHER, FOUND HER A WONDERFUL AND CAPTIVATING PERSON.
"THE YOUNG MAN FELL IN LOVE WITH HER AND SOON, TO EVERYONE'S DELIGHT, THEY MARRIED.
"OVER THE NEXT YEARS SHE MOTHERED SIX CHILDREN.
"YET, CURIOUSLY, SHE NEVER SEEMED TO AGE."

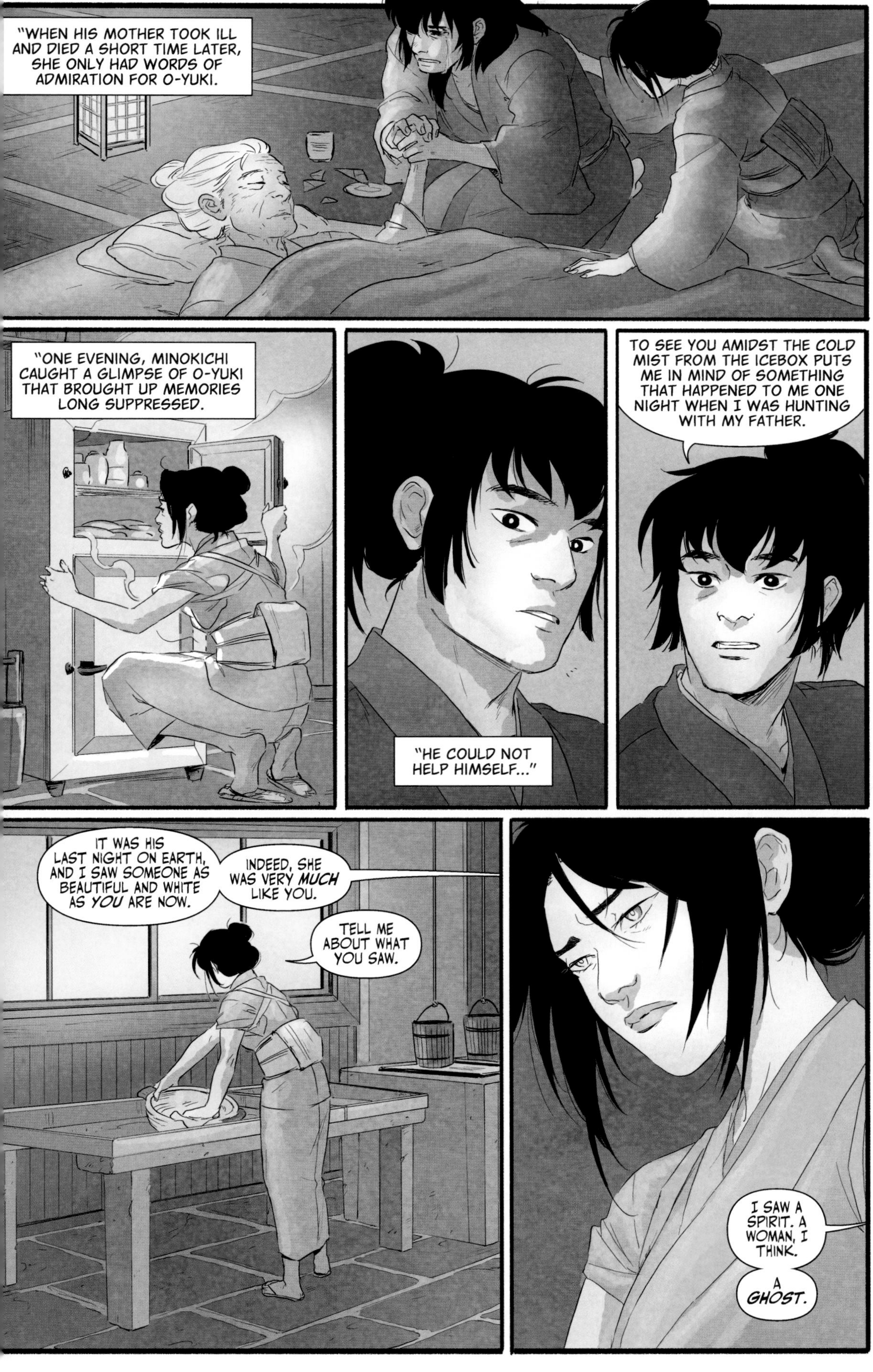
"WHEN HIS MOTHER TOOK ILL AND DIED A SHORT TIME LATER, SHE ONLY HAD WORDS OF ADMIRATION FOR O-YUKI.
"ONE EVENING, MINOKICHI CAUGHT A GLIMPSE OF O-YUKI THAT BROUGHT UP MEMORIES LONG SUPPRESSED.
"HE COULD NOT HELP HIMSELF..."
TO SEE YOU AMIDST THE COLD MIST FROM THE ICEBOX PUTS ME IN MIND OF SOMETHING THAT HAPPENED TO ME ONE NIGHT WHEN I WAS HUNTING WITH MY FATHER.
IT WAS HIS LAST NIGHT ON EARTH, AND I SAW SOMEONE AS BEAUTIFUL AND WHITE AS YOU ARE NOW.
INDEED, SHE WAS VERY MUCH LIKE YOU.
TELL ME ABOUT WHAT YOU SAW.
I SAW A SPIRIT. A WOMAN, I THINK.
A GHOST.

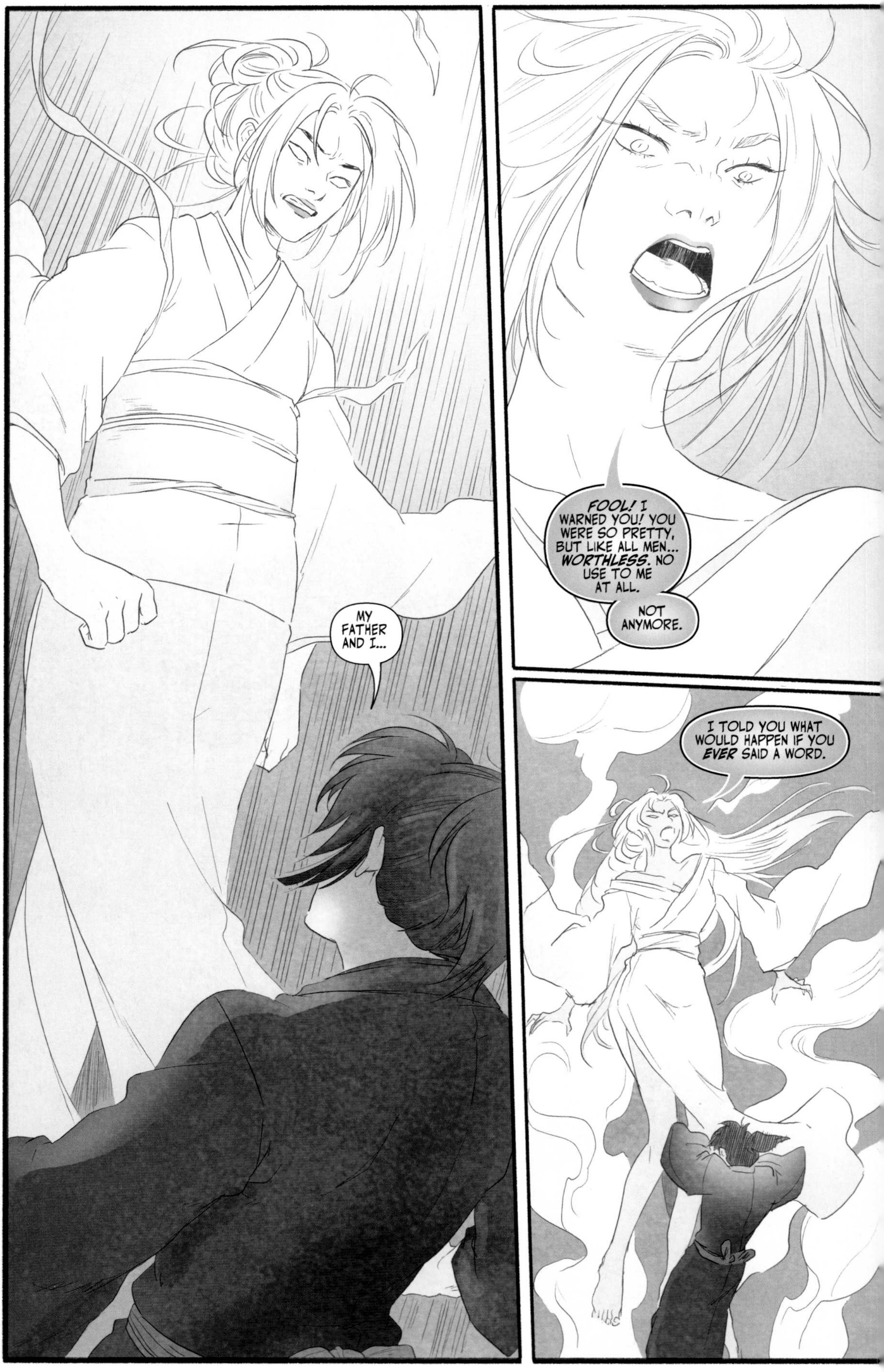
MY FATHER AND I...
FOOL! I WARNED YOU! YOU WERE SO PRETTY, BUT LIKE ALL MEN... WORTHLESS. NO USE TO ME AT ALL.
NOT ANYMORE.
I TOLD YOU WHAT WOULD HAPPEN IF YOU EVER SAID A WORD.

THIS TIME I WILL NOT SPARE YOU...

...THOUGH PERHAPS YOU CAN BE OF ONE SMALL, *FINAL* SERVICE.

OH, IT IS A *BRIGHT* DAY!

MAMA? PAPA? I'M *HUNGRY*.

WHAT'S FOR BREAKFAST?

MAAAAAMA!

PAAAAAPA!

WAAAAAAAA!

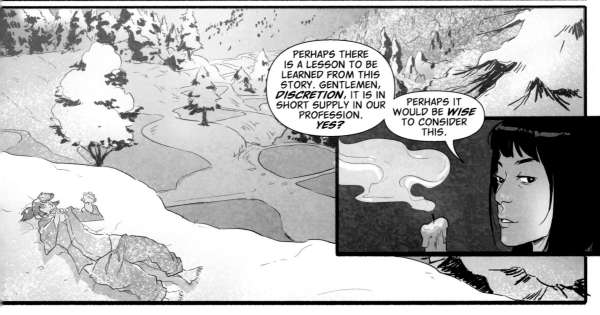

PERHAPS THERE IS A LESSON TO BE LEARNED FROM THIS STORY. GENTLEMEN, *DISCRETION*, IT IS IN SHORT SUPPLY IN OUR PROFESSION. *YES?*

PERHAPS IT WOULD BE *WISE* TO CONSIDER THIS.

And finally…

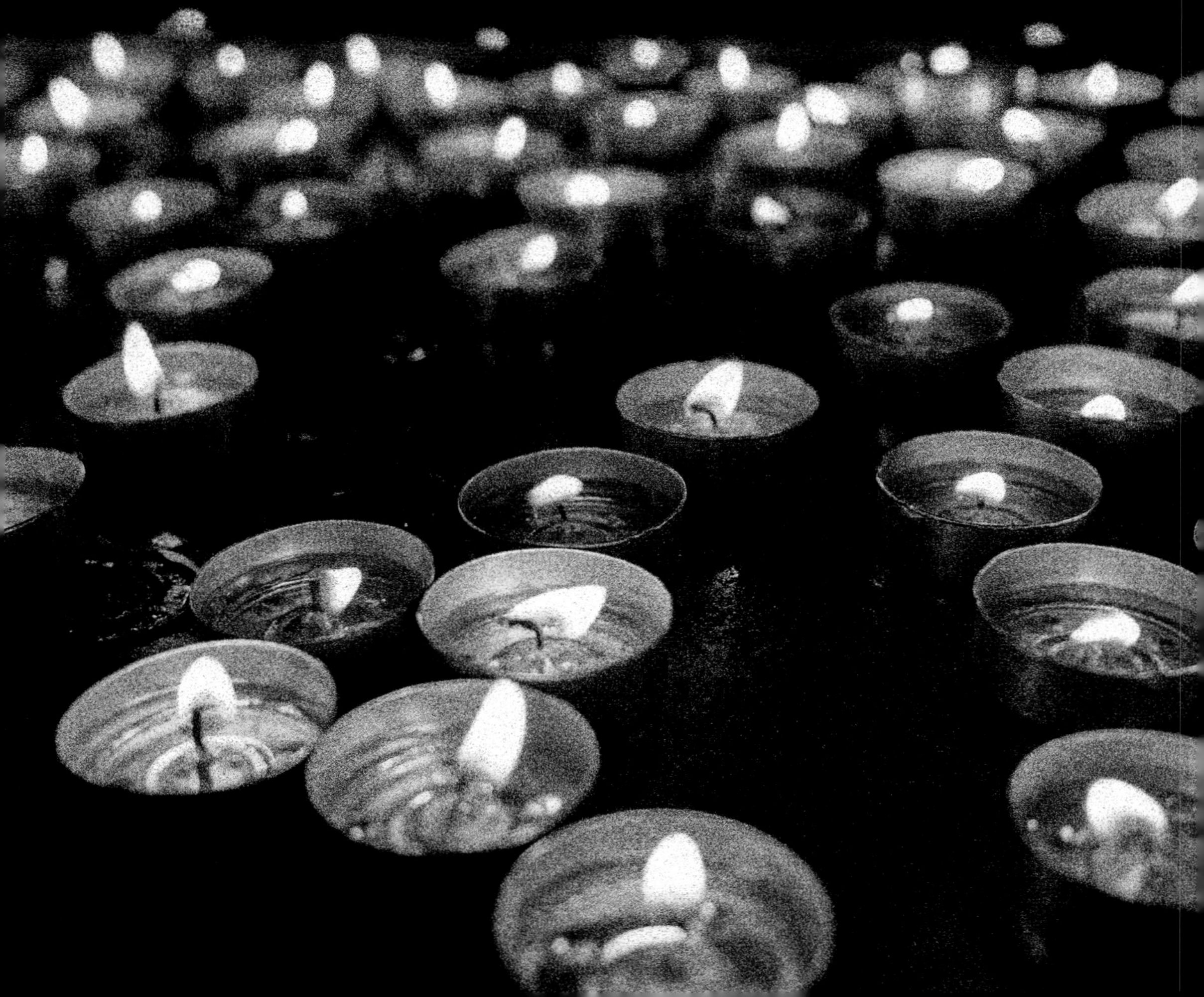

THE COW HEAD

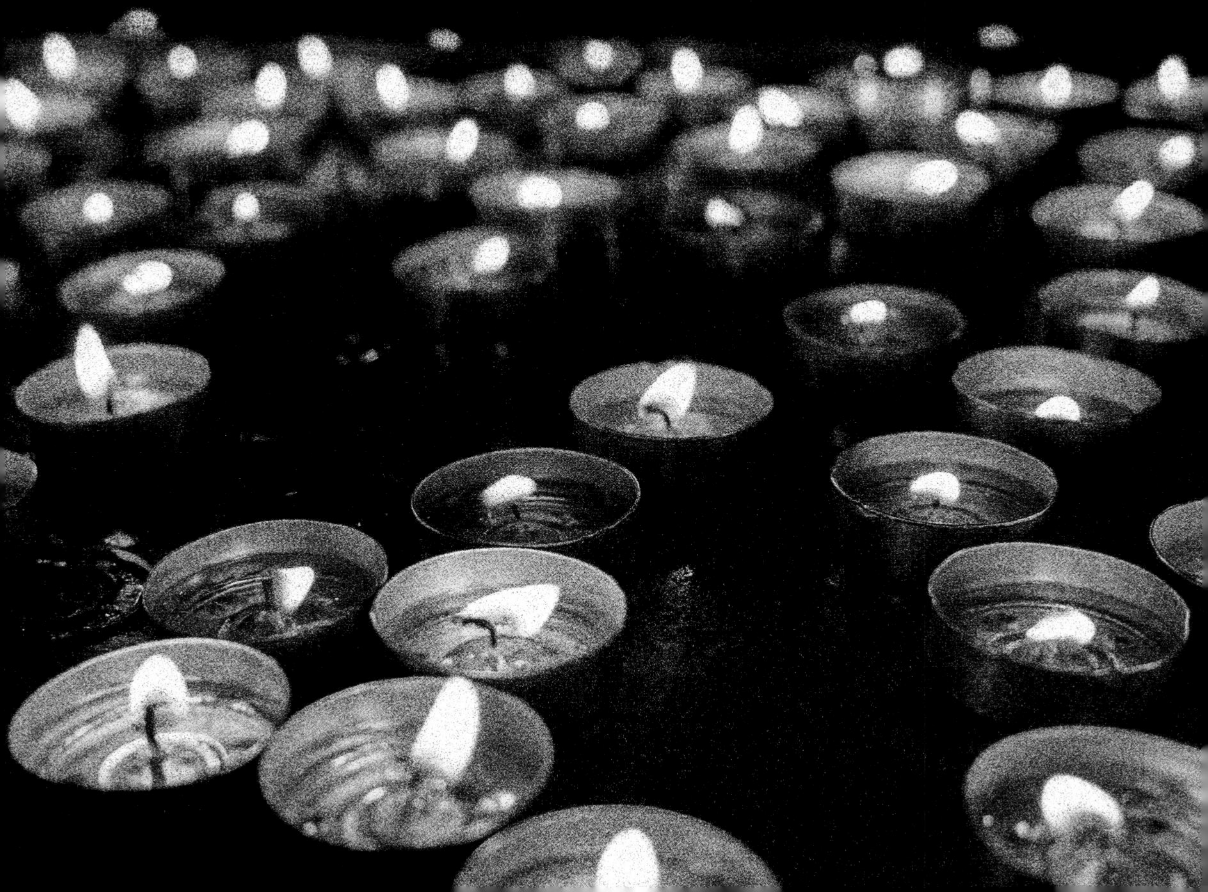

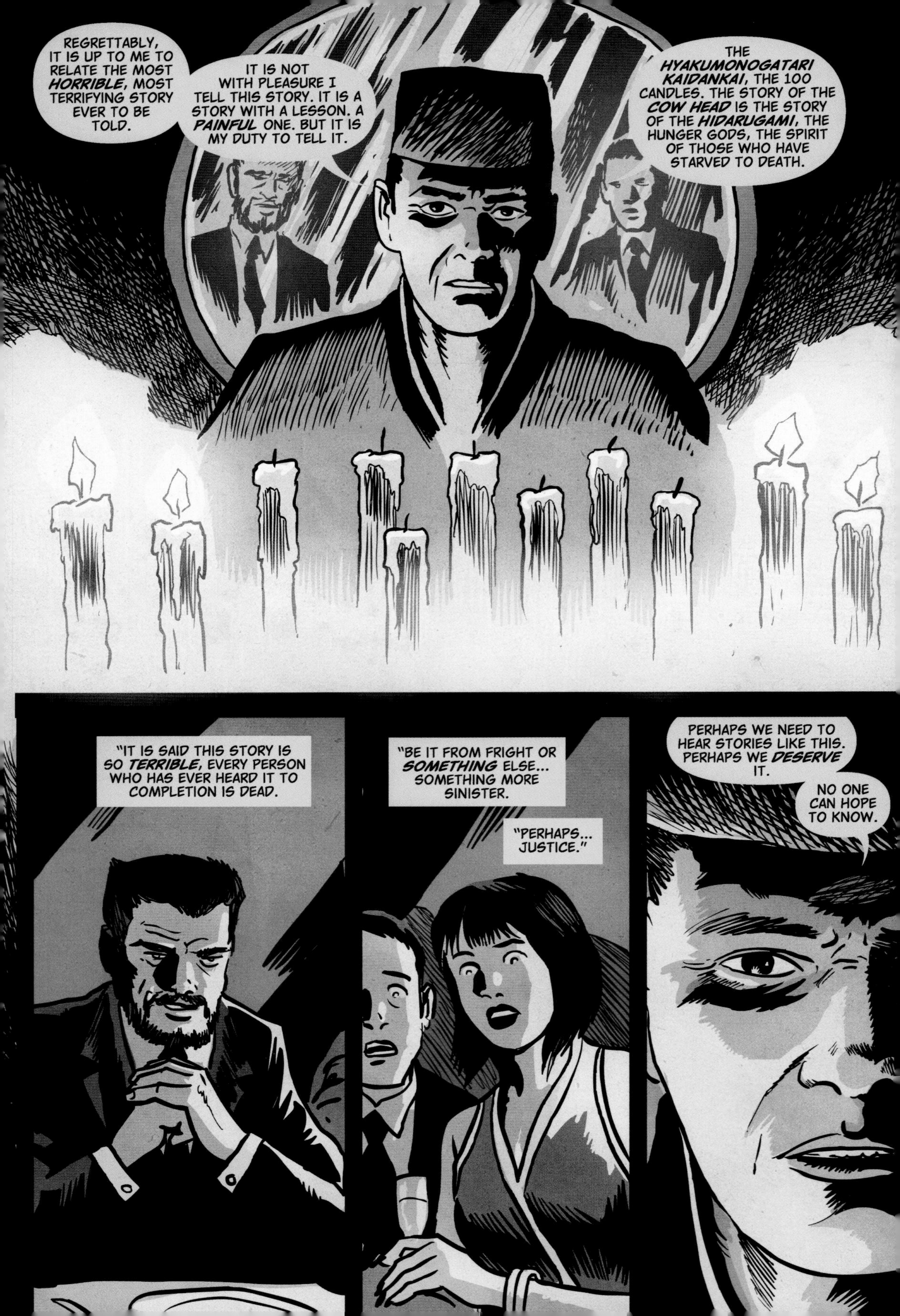
REGRETTABLY, IT IS UP TO ME TO RELATE THE MOST HORRIBLE, MOST TERRIFYING STORY EVER TO BE TOLD.
IT IS NOT WITH PLEASURE I TELL THIS STORY. IT IS A STORY WITH A LESSON. A PAINFUL ONE. BUT IT IS MY DUTY TO TELL IT.
THE HYAKUMONOGATARI KAIDANKAI, THE 100 CANDLES. THE STORY OF THE COW HEAD IS THE STORY OF THE HIDARUGAMI, THE HUNGER GODS, THE SPIRIT OF THOSE WHO HAVE STARVED TO DEATH.
"IT IS SAID THIS STORY IS SO TERRIBLE, EVERY PERSON WHO HAS EVER HEARD IT TO COMPLETION IS DEAD.
"BE IT FROM FRIGHT OR SOMETHING ELSE... SOMETHING MORE SINISTER.
"PERHAPS... JUSTICE."
PERHAPS WE NEED TO HEAR STORIES LIKE THIS. PERHAPS WE DESERVE IT.
NO ONE CAN HOPE TO KNOW.

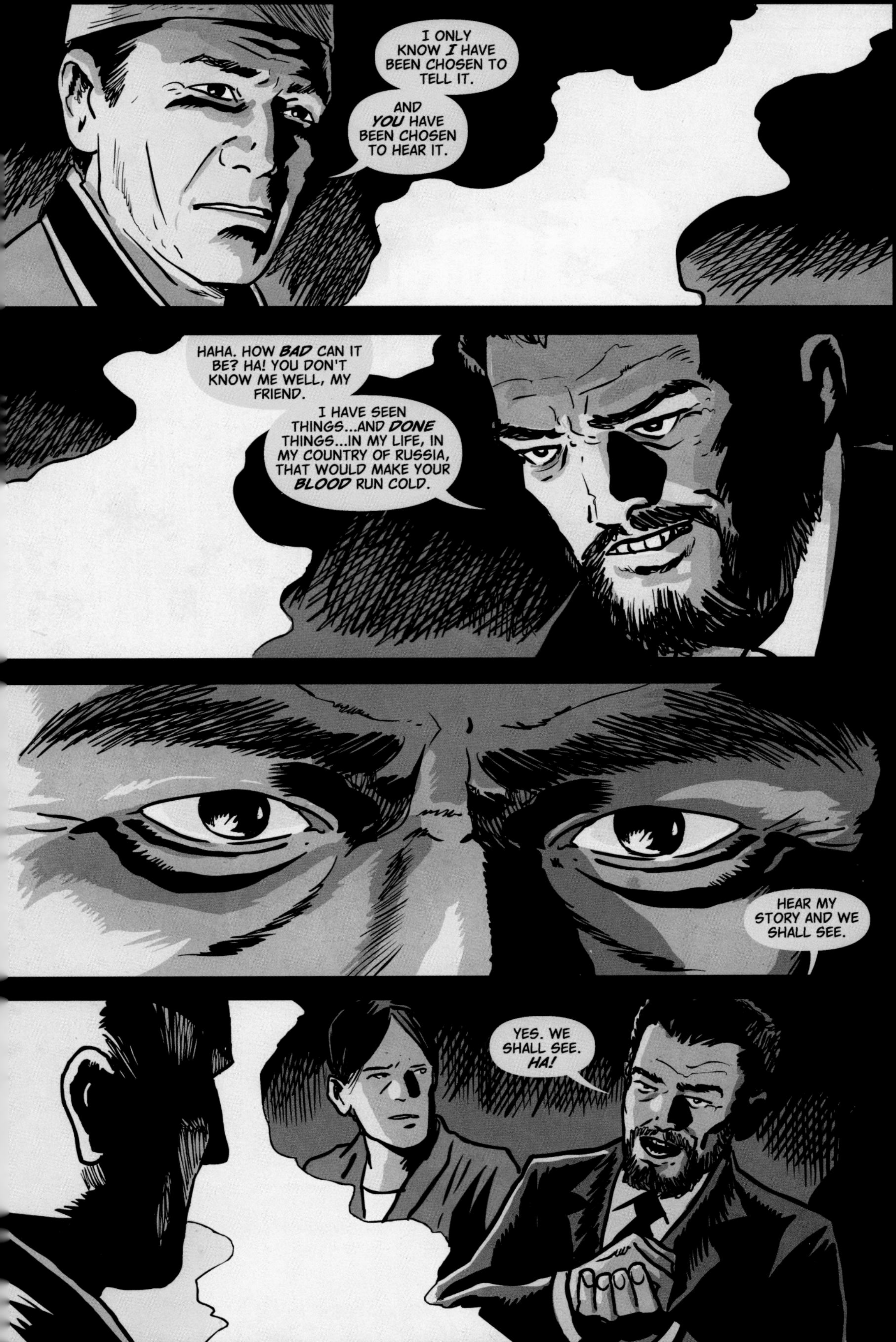
I ONLY KNOW *I* HAVE BEEN CHOSEN TO TELL IT.
AND *YOU* HAVE BEEN CHOSEN TO HEAR IT.
HAHA. HOW *BAD* CAN IT BE? HA! YOU DON'T KNOW ME WELL, MY FRIEND.
I HAVE SEEN THINGS...AND *DONE* THINGS...IN MY LIFE, IN MY COUNTRY OF RUSSIA, THAT WOULD MAKE YOUR *BLOOD* RUN COLD.
HEAR MY STORY AND WE SHALL SEE.
YES. WE SHALL SEE. *HA!*

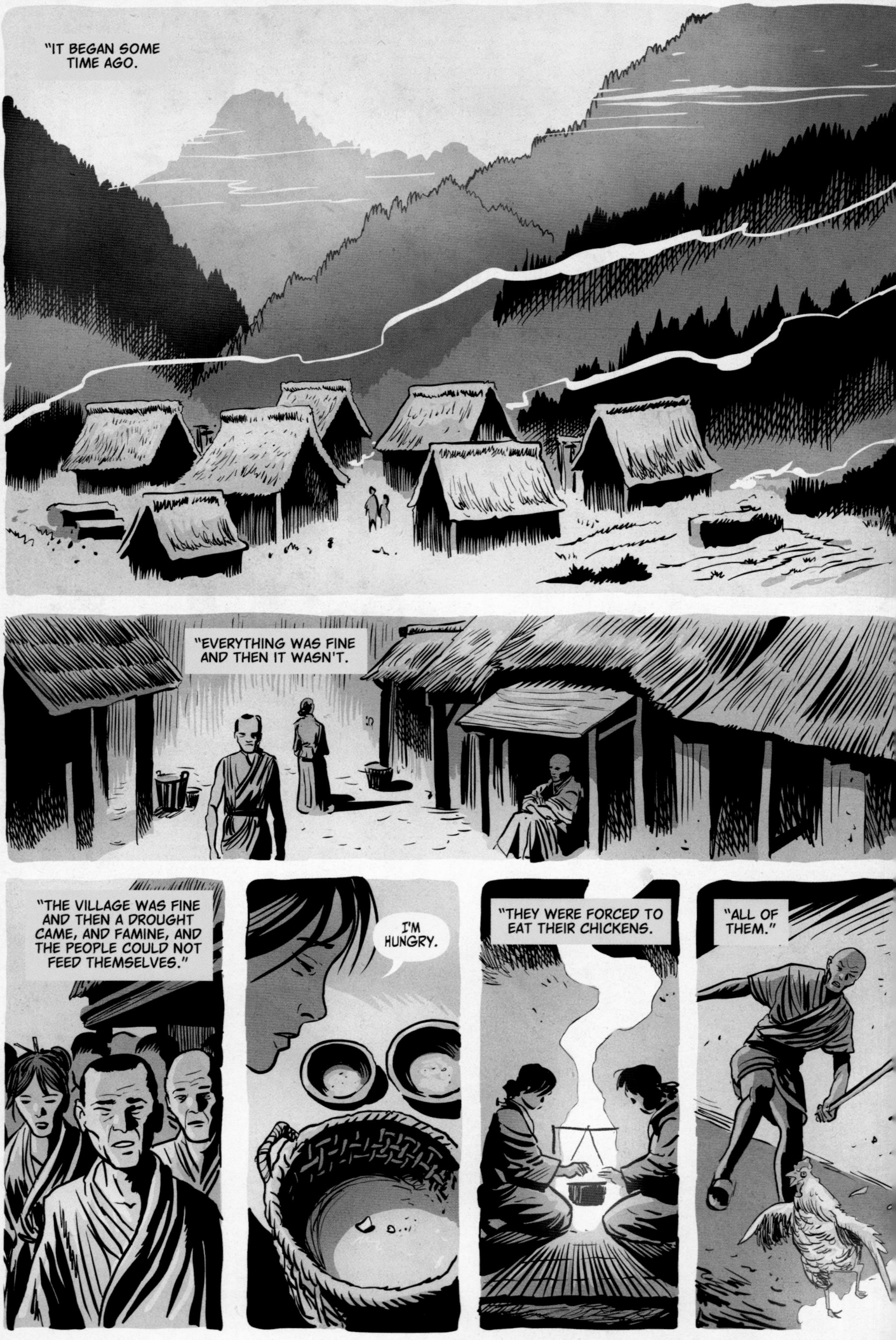
"IT BEGAN SOME TIME AGO.
"EVERYTHING WAS FINE AND THEN IT WASN'T.
"THE VILLAGE WAS FINE AND THEN A DROUGHT CAME, AND FAMINE, AND THE PEOPLE COULD NOT FEED THEMSELVES."
I'M HUNGRY.
"THEY WERE FORCED TO EAT THEIR CHICKENS.
"ALL OF THEM."

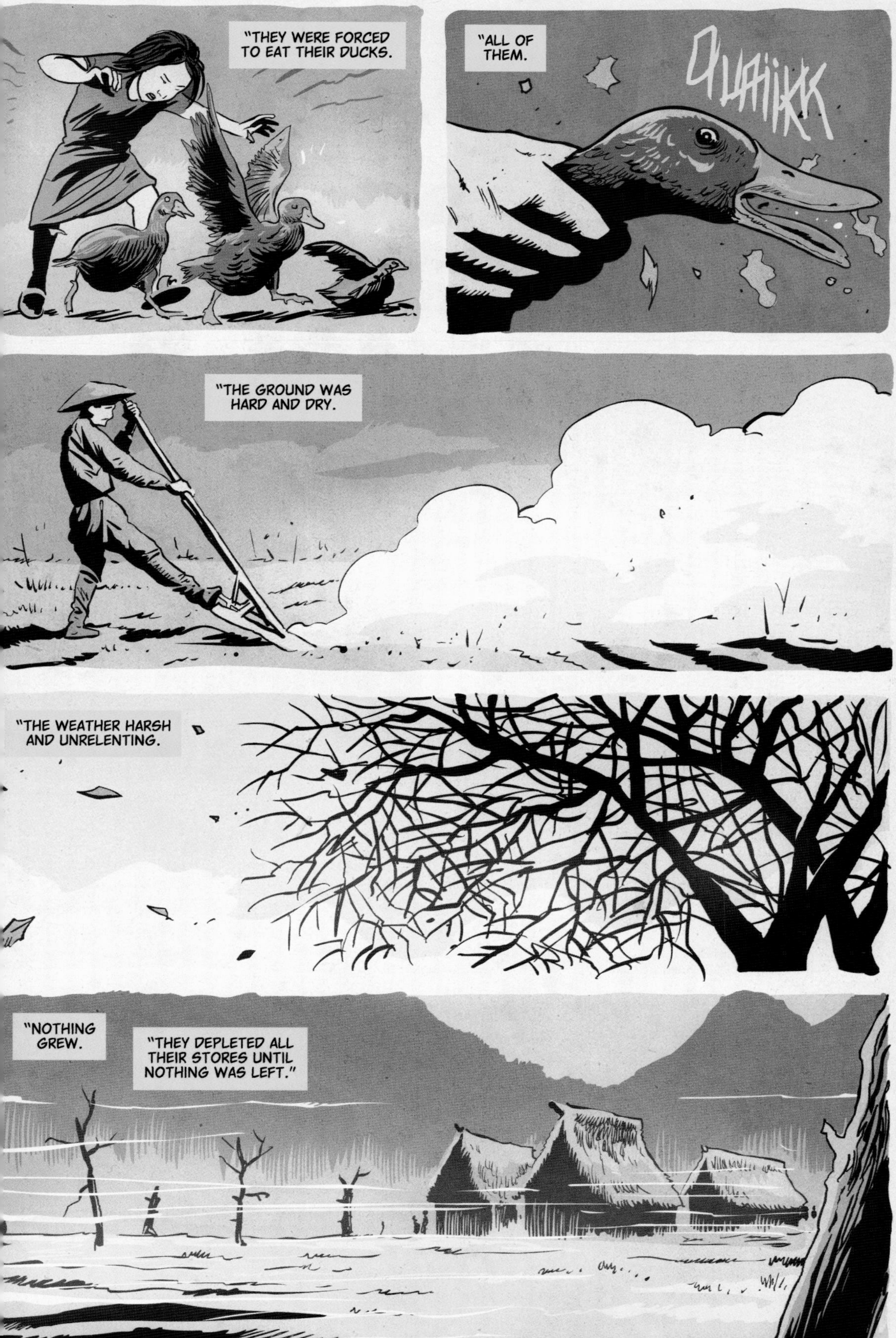
"THEY WERE FORCED TO EAT THEIR DUCKS.
"ALL OF THEM.
QUAIIKK
"THE GROUND WAS HARD AND DRY.
"THE WEATHER HARSH AND UNRELENTING.
"NOTHING GREW.
"THEY DEPLETED ALL THEIR STORES UNTIL NOTHING WAS LEFT."

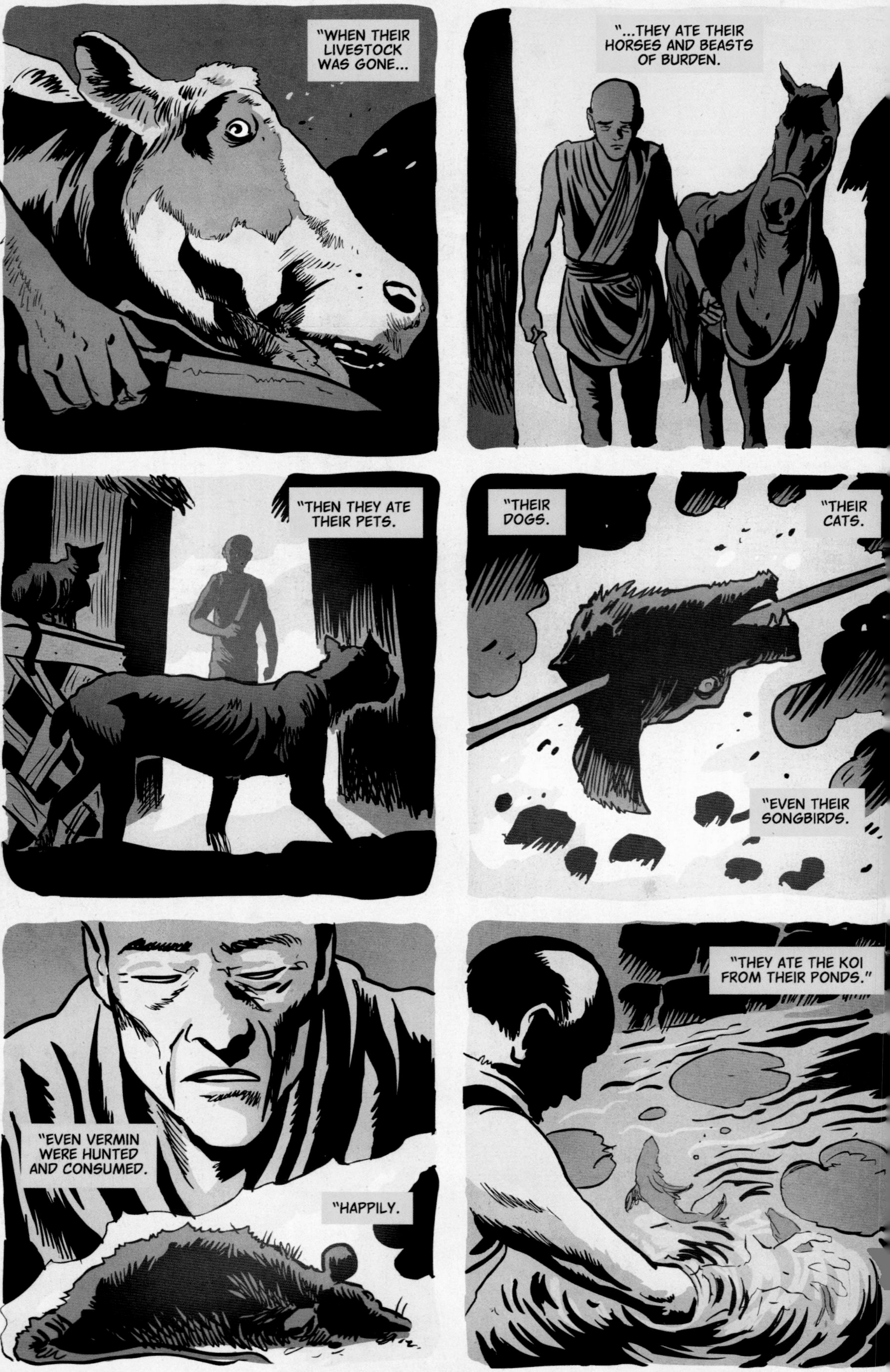
"WHEN THEIR LIVESTOCK WAS GONE...
"...THEY ATE THEIR HORSES AND BEASTS OF BURDEN.
"THEN THEY ATE THEIR PETS.
"THEIR DOGS.
"THEIR CATS.
"EVEN THEIR SONGBIRDS.
"EVEN VERMIN WERE HUNTED AND CONSUMED.
"HAPPILY.
"THEY ATE THE KOI FROM THEIR PONDS."

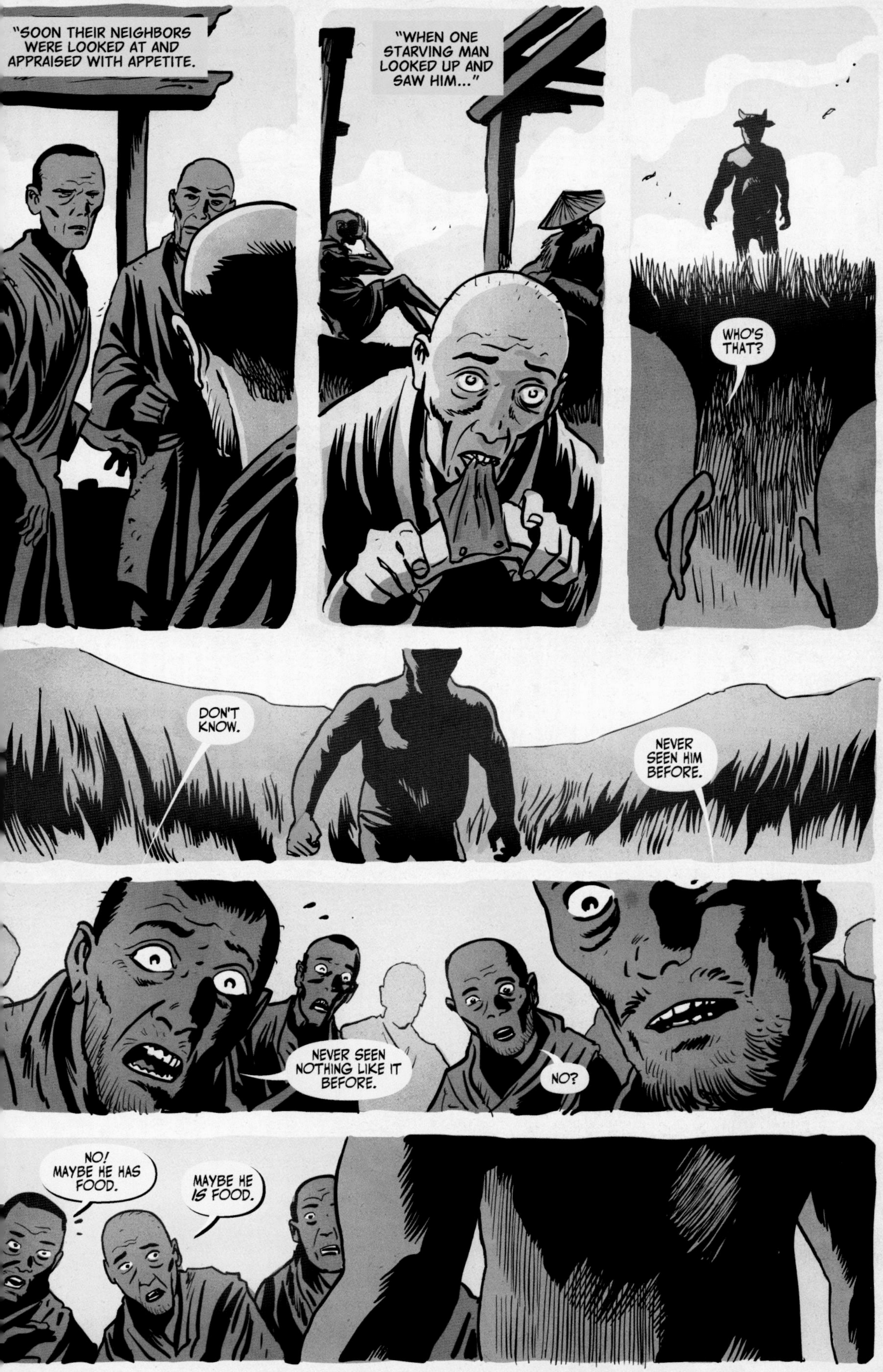
"SOON THEIR NEIGHBORS WERE LOOKED AT AND APPRAISED WITH APPETITE.
"WHEN ONE STARVING MAN LOOKED UP AND SAW HIM..."
WHO'S THAT?
DON'T KNOW.
NEVER SEEN HIM BEFORE.
NEVER SEEN NOTHING LIKE IT BEFORE.
NO?
NO! MAYBE HE HAS FOOD.
MAYBE HE IS FOOD.

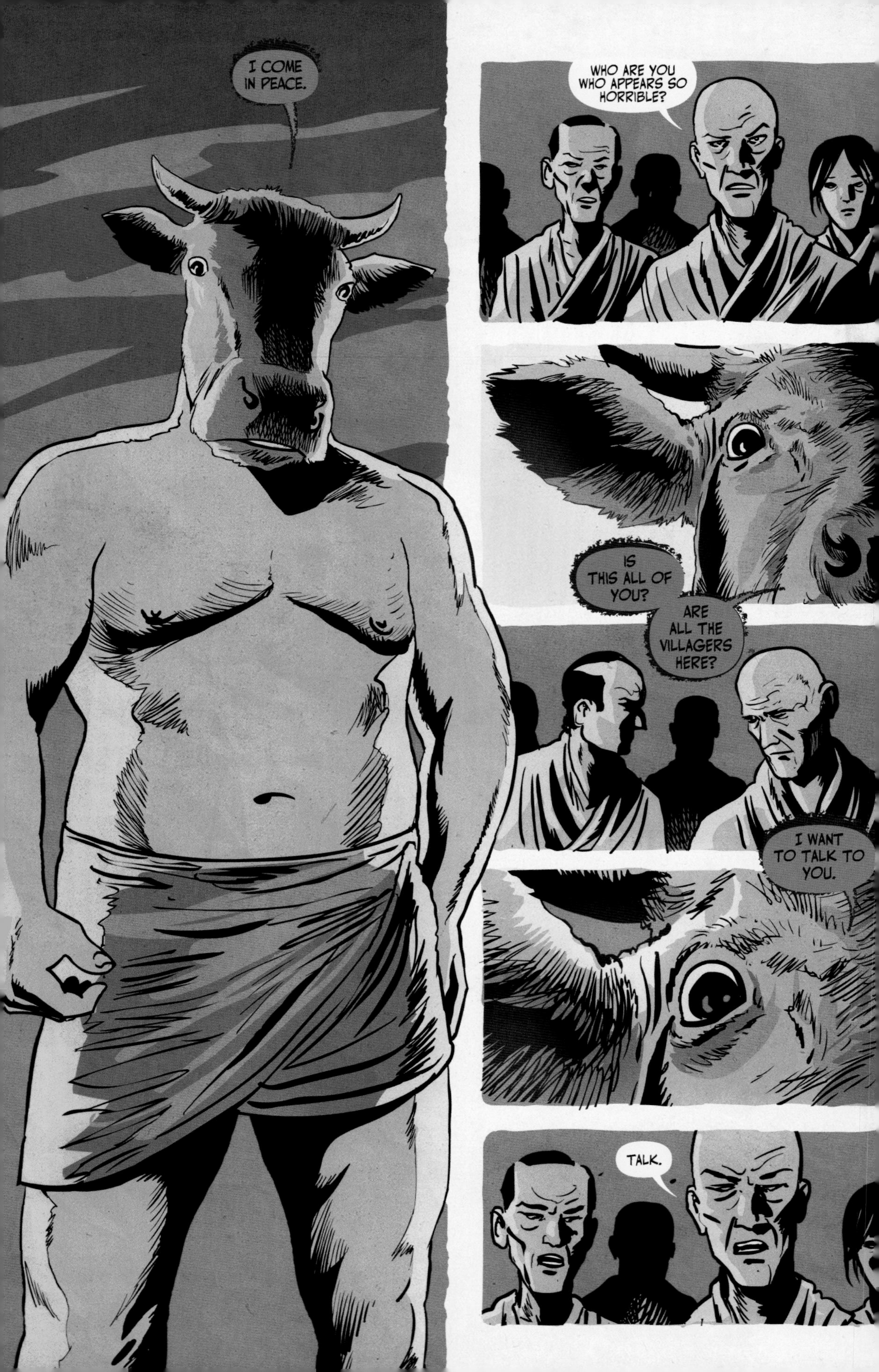
I COME IN PEACE.
WHO ARE YOU WHO APPEARS SO HORRIBLE?
IS THIS ALL OF YOU?
ARE ALL THE VILLAGERS HERE?
I WANT TO TALK TO YOU.
TALK.

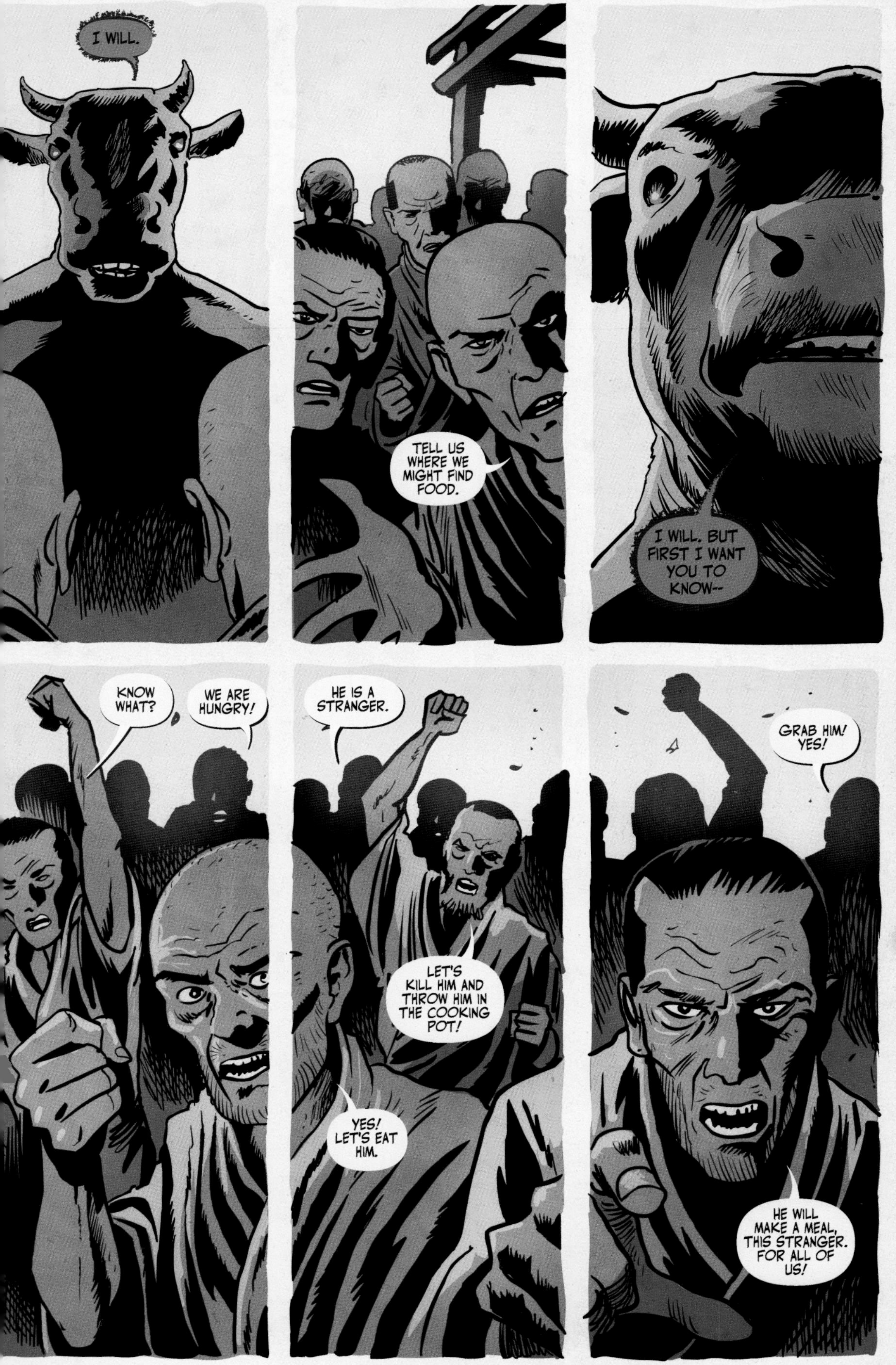
I WILL.
TELL US WHERE WE MIGHT FIND FOOD.
I WILL. BUT FIRST I WANT YOU TO KNOW--
KNOW WHAT?
WE ARE HUNGRY!
HE IS A STRANGER.
LET'S KILL HIM AND THROW HIM IN THE COOKING POT!
YES! LET'S EAT HIM.
GRAB HIM! YES!
HE WILL MAKE A MEAL, THIS STRANGER. FOR ALL OF US!

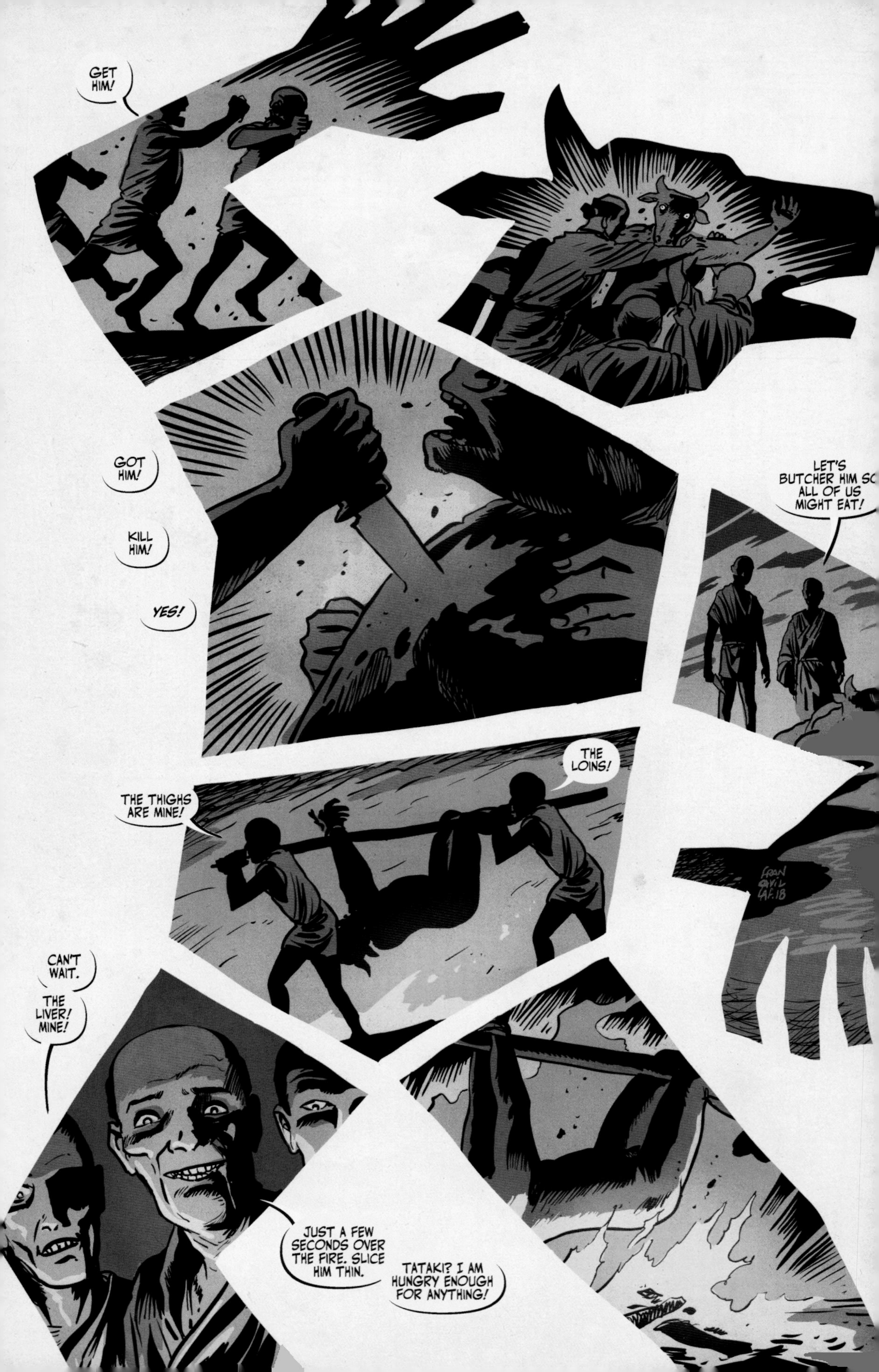
GET HIM!
GOT HIM!
KILL HIM!
YES!
LET'S BUTCHER HIM SO ALL OF US MIGHT EAT!
THE THIGHS ARE MINE!
THE LOINS!
CAN'T WAIT.
THE LIVER! MINE!
JUST A FEW SECONDS OVER THE FIRE. SLICE HIM THIN.
TATAKI? I AM HUNGRY ENOUGH FOR ANYTHING!

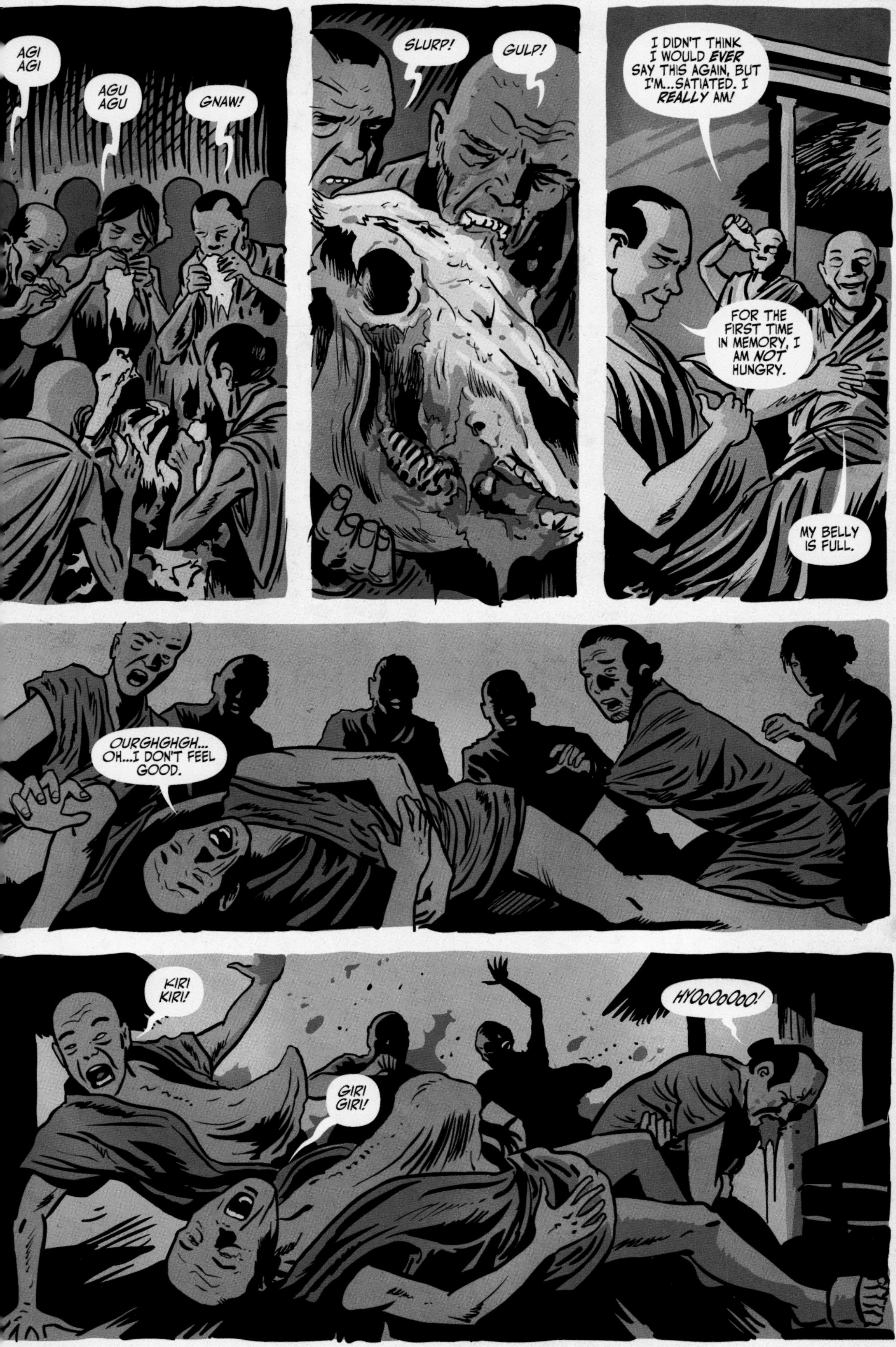
AGI AGI
AGU AGU
GNAW!
SLURP!
GULP!
I DIDN'T THINK I WOULD EVER SAY THIS AGAIN, BUT I'M...SATIATED. I REALLY AM!
FOR THE FIRST TIME IN MEMORY, I AM NOT HUNGRY.
MY BELLY IS FULL.
OURGHGHGH... OH...I DON'T FEEL GOOD.
KIRI KIRI!
GIRI GIRI!
HYOoOoOOO!

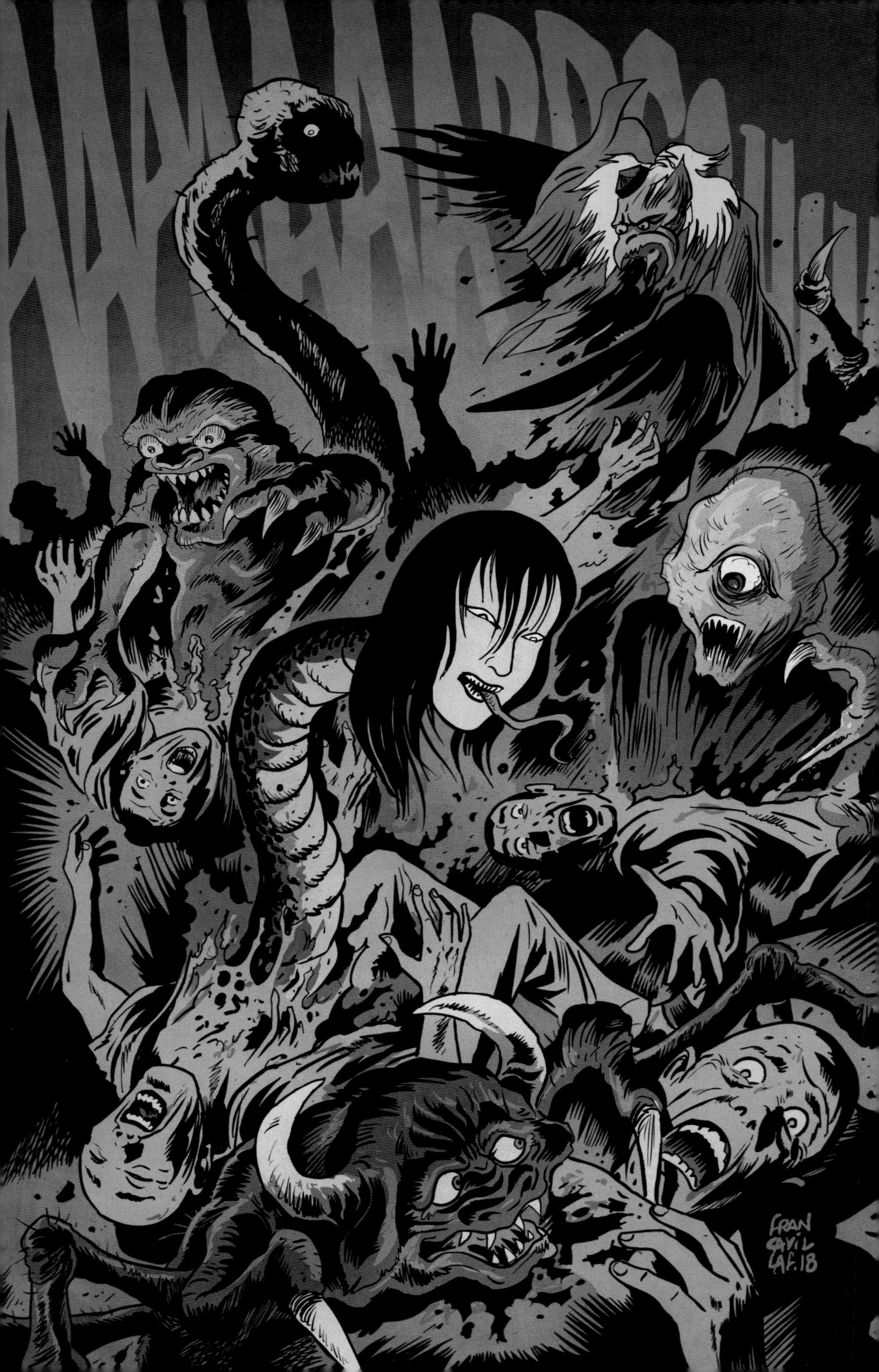

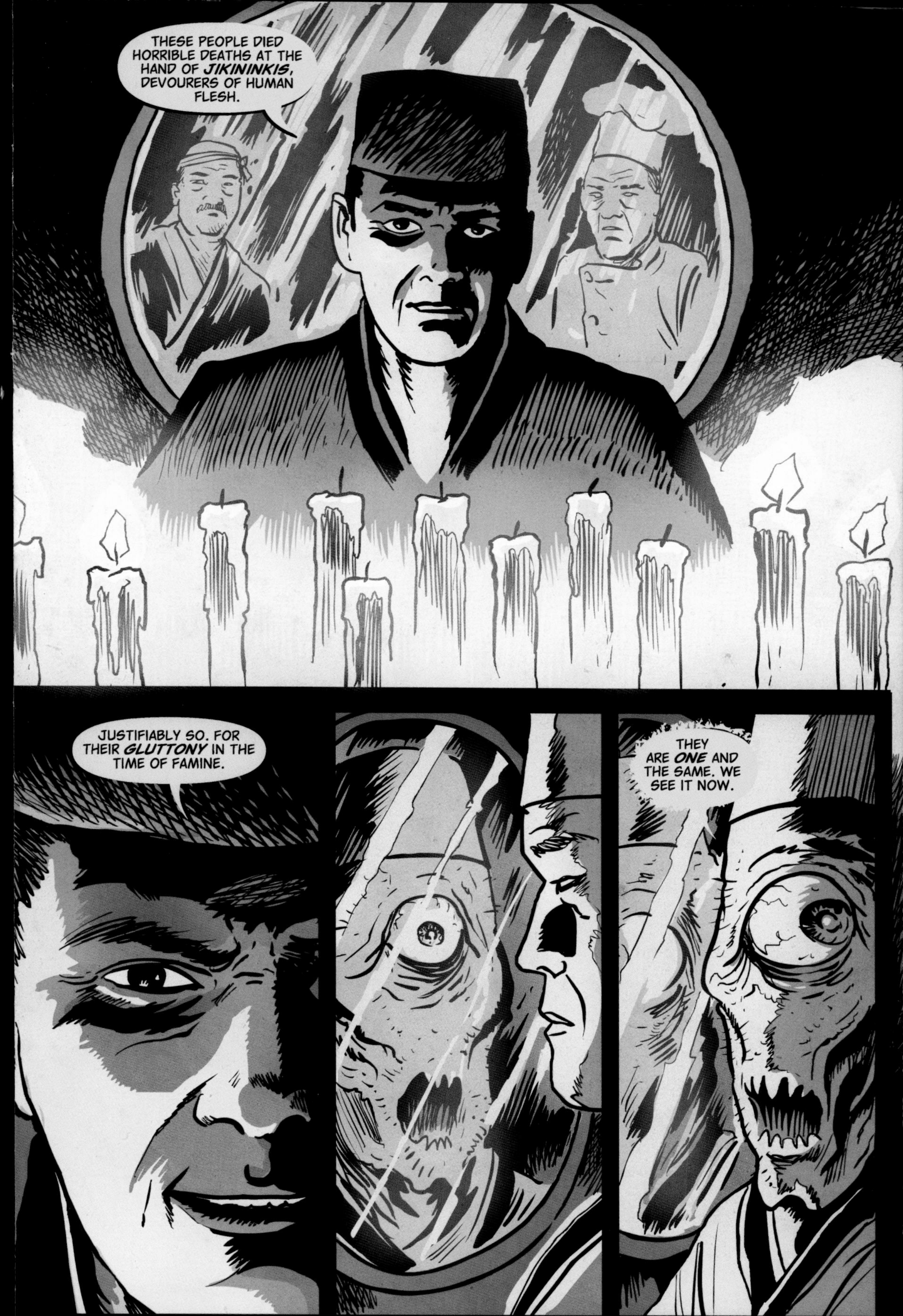
THESE PEOPLE DIED HORRIBLE DEATHS AT THE HAND OF *JIKININKIS*, DEVOURERS OF HUMAN FLESH.
JUSTIFIABLY SO. FOR THEIR *GLUTTONY* IN THE TIME OF FAMINE.
THEY ARE *ONE* AND THE SAME. WE SEE IT NOW.

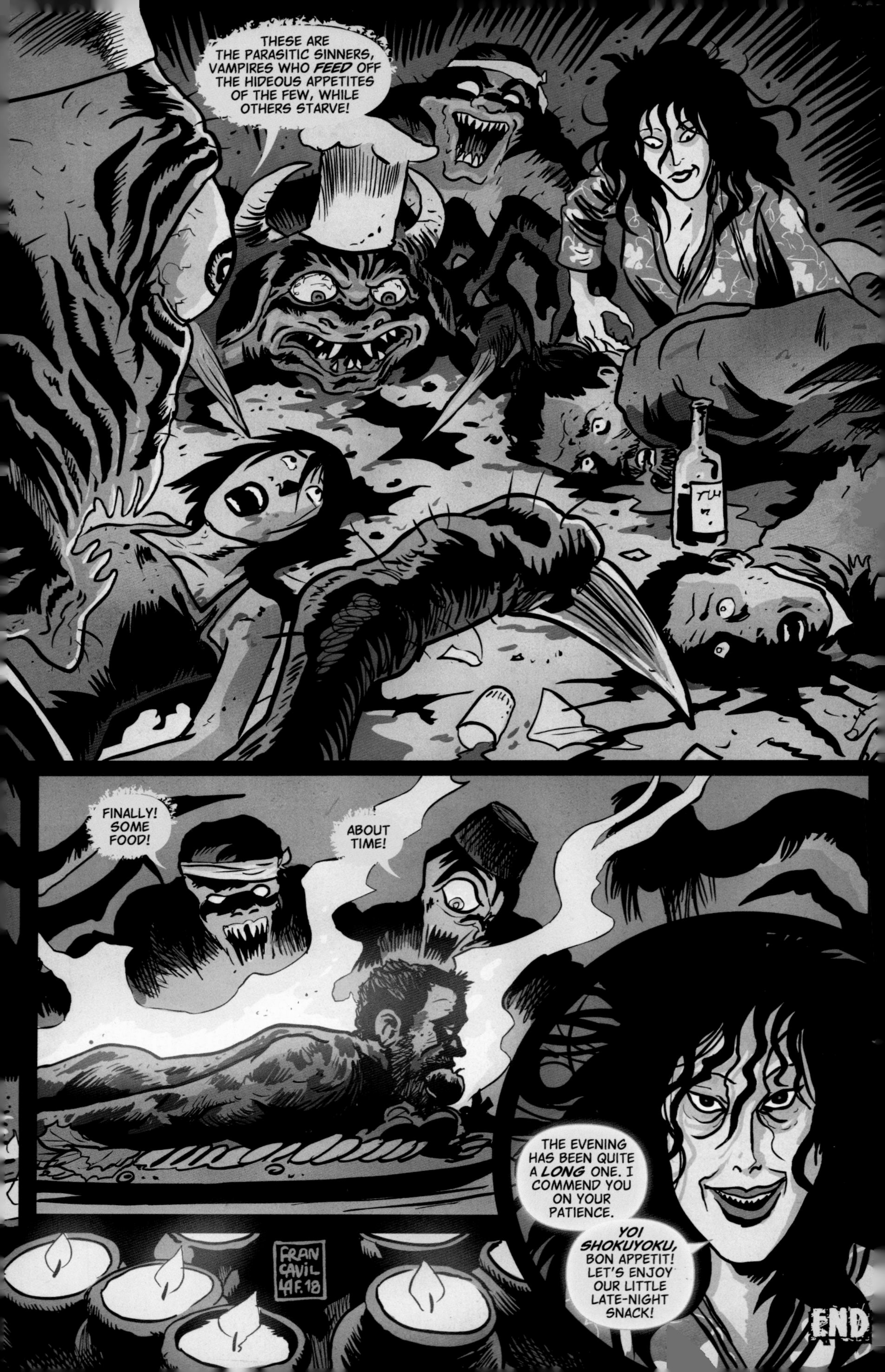
THESE ARE THE PARASITIC SINNERS, VAMPIRES WHO FEED OFF THE HIDEOUS APPETITES OF THE FEW, WHILE OTHERS STARVE!
FINALLY! SOME FOOD!
ABOUT TIME!
THE EVENING HAS BEEN QUITE A LONG ONE. I COMMEND YOU ON YOUR PATIENCE.
YOI SHOKUYOKU, BON APPETIT! LET'S ENJOY OUR LITTLE LATE-NIGHT SNACK!
FRAN CAVIL 14 F. 18
END

Anthony Bourdain

· 1956-2018 ·

This book is dedicated to the memory and enduring allure
of EC Comics and their pre-Comics Code masterworks:
The Haunt of Fear, The Vault of Horror, *and* **Tales from the Crypt**
(née **The Crypt of Terror***), and their master storytellers:*
the Old Witch, the Vault Keeper, and the Crypt Keeper.
May resting in peace not be an option.

—*Anthony Bourdain & Joel Rose*

Tony and I wrote the above dedication a few days before June 8, 2018.
It's the last thing that went back and forth between us.
What I want to add now, however, is this:

For the hungriest ghost of them all: my friend,
my collaborator, my pal, my long-time running mate.
May resting in peace truly not be your option.
Save me a beer, brother, and a seat at the table.

—*Joel Rose*

Stirring the Pot

by Joel Rose

Now you know.

Now you have borne witness. The stories you have just read are true. Or almost so. In the eyes of true horror aficionados, in legend, in culture, in myth, Japan is considered one of the most haunted places on Earth. The ghost and horror stories imbued in the culture are remarkable for their tales of terror, irritable ghosts, and horribly strange beings.

During Japan's seventeenth century Edo Period, a game, *Hyakumonogatari Kaidankai* (100 Candles), was played amongst the samurai class a test of courage. As darkness fell the warriors gathered. The samurai sat in a circle and one hundred andon, or candles, were lit in an adjoining room. One by one the men told ghost and horror stories, tales of eerie, supernatural encounters and unexplained meaning, meant to bring fear into the hearts of their fellow warriors. Upon the end of each kaidan, or tale, the storyteller would stand and make his way to the candles where he would extinguish one, peer in a mirror placed on an adjacent table to make sure the storyteller had not been possessed by a ghost or spirit during the telling, and then return to rejoin his mates. With each passing tale, the room slowly grew darker and darker, the tales scarier and scarier, but as the one hundredth approached fearful participants would invariable abandon the game, too terrified of invoking the wrath of the formidable spirits they had been summoning.

The classic stories told herein are cast around the world and obsessed with love, erotica, and gluttony, more often than not turned into supernatural revenge. Each is a tale of yūrei (ghosts), yōkai (apparitions, spirits and demons) and/or reikon (inner beings residing within each of us and only unleashed at death).

These were Tony's obsessions, not mine. At least, at first. He brought me to their riches, and now I too, am in their throes. When he first mentioned,

"Hey, how about doing this?" I didn't know. First stop, I looked to Lafcadio Hearn, the late nineteenth century esteemed author of *Kwaidan: Japanese Ghost Stories*.

In the 1904 introduction to his book it was written that never has there been such "an interpreter gifted with more perfect insight and sympathy than Lafcadio Hearn. His long residency in that country (Japan), his flexibility of mind, poetic imagination, and wonderfully pellucid style have fitted him for the most delicate of literary tasks. He has seen marvels, and he had told of them in a marvelous way."

"Most of the following Kwaidan, or Weird Tales, have been taken from old Japanese research and books," Hearn wrote. "Some of the stories may have had a Chinese origin. But the storyteller in every case has so recolored and reshaped his borrowing as to naturalize it. One queer tale, *Yuki-Onna, The Snow Woman*, was told me by a farmer of Chofu, Nishitama-gori in Musashi province, as a legend of his native village."

Here is our inspiration, aided by the masterly hands of Sebastion Cabrol, Vanesa Del Rey, Francesco Francavilla, Irene Koh, Leonardo Manco, Alberto Ponticelli, Paul Pope, Mateus Santolouco, and José Villarrubia.

Not only did I go to Hearn for research into *Hungry Ghosts*, but I also read, enjoyed and learned from the online retellings of Zack Davisson. In addition, we drew on *Appartitions, Ghosts of Old Edo* by Miyuki Miyabe, *Japanese Tales of Mystery and Imagination* by Edogawa Rampo, *Tales of Old Japan, Folklore, Fairy Tales, Ghost Stories and Legends of the Samurai* by A. B. Mitford, *The Book of Yokai* by Michael Dylan Foster, and *Japanese Tales from Times Past* by Konjaku Monogatari Shu.

All the stories in *Hungry Ghosts* have been nothing less than a total blast to write. We hope you enjoyed them.

Gachi-gachi-gachi!

Anthony Bourdain's HUNGRY GHOSTS Recipes

TOKYO RAMEN

FOR THE BROTH:
2 pounds chicken bones and/or wings and feet
1 pound pork bones, ideally with some meat attached
2 onions, peeled and coarsely chopped
1 carrot, peeled and coarsely chopped
1 rib celery, coarsely chopped
3 cloves garlic, peeled
Salt to taste
¼ cup soy sauce, or to taste
1 ounce konbu (dried kelp)
1 ounce dried bonito flakes

FOR THE BOWL:
Scant tablespoon canola or other neutral oil
¾ pound ground pork
1 tablespoon white or yellow miso paste
12 ounces fresh ramen noodles
2 soft-boiled eggs, sliced in half lengthwise
Sliced scallions, toasted nori, sesame seeds, and chili oil, for garnish

To make Tokyo-style ramen, you'll actually make two broths: a long-simmered chicken and pork stock, and a quick, light dashi. First, place the chicken and pork bones, onions, carrot, celery, and garlic in a large pot and cover with about 4 quarts of cold water. Bring to a boil, reduce to a simmer, skim off and discard the foam and scum that has risen to the surface, and cook at a simmer for about 3 hours. Strain the broth, discarding the solids. Salt the broth to taste and set aside.

To make the dashi, in a separate pot, cover the konbu with about 1 quart of cold water and bring almost to a boil, without letting the water actually boil. This should take about 8 to 10 minutes. Remove the konbu with tongs, then add the bonito flakes and, watching carefully, bring the water to a boil, removing it from the heat as soon as the water boils to avoid drawing out a strong, bitter flavor from the bonito. Add the resultant dashi to the chicken and pork broth, and bring to a high simmer, then stir in the soy sauce.

In a sauté pan, heat the oil over medium-high heat and add the pork. Cook, stirring, for a few minutes, until any water is released and sizzled away, then add the miso and stir well so that it's evenly incorporated into the meat. Continue to cook until the meat is caramelized. Taste and adjust seasoning with salt as needed, bearing in mind that miso is quite salty.

Bring a medium pot of water to a boil and cook the ramen noodles according to the package directions. Drain, rinse, and strain the noodles, and divide them evenly among four soup bowls. Ladle some of the hot stock over the noodles, reserving any unused broth for another purpose. Add an egg half, some ground pork, scallions, nori, and sesame seeds to each bowl. Serve with the chili oil and additional soy sauce alongside.

Serves 4.

from **THE STARVING SKELETON**

CLASSIC MEATBALLS

3 tablespoons plus ½ cup extra virgin olive oil
1 white onion, peeled and very finely chopped
  to yield about 2 cups
5 cloves garlic, peeled and minced
3 sprigs oregano leaves, finely chopped
3 sprigs thyme leaves, finely chopped
10 sprigs Italian parsley leaves, finely chopped
Salt and pepper to taste

1 pound ground beef
1 pound ground veal
1 pound ground pork
1 cup breadcrumbs
2 large eggs, lightly beaten
1 ½ cups white wine
1 cup prepared tomato sauce
4 ounces grated Parmigiano-Reggiano cheese

In a large sauté pan or Dutch oven over medium heat, warm 3 tablespoons olive oil for a minute or two, then add the onions, garlic, oregano, thyme, and parsley. Season with salt and pepper and cook, stirring, for just a few minutes, until the onions are limp and translucent but before anything begins to brown. You just want to take the bite off the raw vegetables and herbs before adding them to the meatball mixture. Remove the pan from the heat, transfer the mixture to a large bowl, and wash the pan, which you'll reuse to cook the meatballs themselves.

To the mixing bowl with the onions, add the ground meats, breadcrumbs, eggs, and a moderate amount of salt and pepper to season. (If you like, you can safely test the seasoning by cooking a small patty of the mixture in a pan with a bit of oil before tasting and adjusting as desired.) Gently mix it all together by hand—you don't want to crush it together too much, which will result in very dense and heavy meatballs—and form the mixture into approximately 25 two-inch meatballs. Arrange them on a sheet tray or platter, cover with plastic wrap, and let chill in the refrigerator for at least 15 and up to 60 minutes.

Preheat the oven to 400F and remove the meatballs from the refrigerator. If they are refrigerated, let the white wine and tomato sauce come to room temperature while the oven heats up and you seat the meatballs, as per below.

Heat the remaining ¼ cup oil in the sauté pan or Dutch oven and, working in batches, add the meatballs to the pan, take care not to overcrowd it. Sear the meatballs on all sides, gently turning them with tongs and/or a metal spatula, and adding more oil if necessary to keep meatballs from scorching or sticking. As they are cooked, remove the meatballs to a roasting pan large enough to hold them all in a single layer.

Pour the wine and the tomato sauce over the meatballs; the liquid should reach about halfway up the sides of the meatballs. The liquid will become more concentrated, and the volatile alcohol will cook off in the oven. Carefully transfer the pan to the center rack of the oven and cook, uncovered, for about 30 minutes, until the interior of a meatball is 150F, according to an instant-read thermometer. Remove the meatballs to a serving bowl, pour the sauce over, and serve.

Serves 6 to 8, with ostensible leftovers.

*from **SALTY HORSE***
(with a variation on the meat)

OSSO BUCO

6 veal shanks, each approximately 3 inches thick
Salt and pepper to taste
½ cup Wondra flour
½ cup extra virgin olive oil
1 white onion, peeled and diced
3 large carrots, peeled and diced
2 ribs celery, diced
3 cloves garlic, peeled, center sprout and end
   cap removed, finely sliced

1 bottle dry white Italian wine
28-ounce can crushed tomatoes and their
   juices
1 ½ quarts veal stock
Finely grated zest and peeled and coarsely
   chopped flesh of ½ a navel orange
1 bay leaf
3 sprigs fresh rosemary
1 cup whole parsley leaves, for garnish

Use the salt and pepper to season the meat all over. Dredge each shank in the flour, patting off the excess.

Heat half the oil in a large, heavy-bottomed sauté or braising pan over medium-high heat until the surface of the oil shimmers. Place the shanks carefully in the pan, working in batches if necessary to avoid overcrowding the pan—each shank should have its own pan surface area, and there should be room between each one for air to circulate. Overcrowding the pan will lead to a steamy, anemic sear on the meat's surface. Turn the shanks to brown on as many surfaces as possible.

As the shanks are finished searing, use tongs to remove them to a holding pan or plate.

In a Dutch oven or similar vessel large enough to comfortably hold all the shanks, heat the remaining ¼ cup oil over medium heat. Test the temperature of the oil with a piece of onion or carrot – it should sizzle solidly, but not aggressively. Add the onions, carrots, and celery to the pan and season with salt and pepper. Cook, stirring regularly, over medium heat, then add the garlic. Continue to cook for another few minutes, until the vegetables are soft and just beginning to brown.

Add the wine and bring it to a boil. Continue to cook it at a boil, stirring occasionally to keep the vegetables from sticking to the pan, until the liquid has been reduced by half. This will take about 15 minutes, maybe a few more. Once the wine is sufficiently reduced, stir in the crushed tomatoes and veal stock, and let this come to a high boil before adding the oranges, bay leaf, and rosemary. Next, transfer the shanks carefully to the Dutch oven. Once the mixture resumes a boil, reduce the heat to a simmer.

Leave it mostly alone for a about 3 hours, moving things around a little bit every 30 minutes or so to prevent any sticking or uneven cooking. You'll know that the meat is done when it easily yields to the touch of a fork.

To serve, distribute the shanks evenly among 6 shallow bowls. Ladle some of the hot sauce over each portion, taking care not to distribute the bay leaf or herb stems to your guests. Garnish each plate with orange zest and parsley leaves, and serve hot, with saffron risotto (see recipe on next page).

Serves 6.

from **THE HEADS**

SAFFRON RISOTTO

1 ½ quarts chicken stock
6 to 8 best-quality saffron threads
¼ cup Italian extra virgin olive oil
1 small white onion, peeled and finely diced
1 ½ cups carnaroli rice

½ cup dry Italian white wine
4 tablespoons salted butter, cut into chunks
⅓ cup finely grated Parmigiano-Reggiano
  cheese
Salt to taste

Combine half the chicken stock and the saffron threads in a small pan and bring to a simmer to draw the flavor, color, and aroma from the threads into the stock.

In a medium-sized pot, gently heat the oil and stir in the onion, taking care to get each piece coated with oil. Cook gently, stirring frequently, until the onion is soft and translucent; do not let it brown. Add the rice, stirring carefully so that it's well distributed with the onions. Increase the heat to medium-high and cook, stirring occasionally, for 3 to 4 minutes, to gently toast the rice. Stir in the wine and take the heat back down to medium-low. Continue to cook, stirring regularly, as the rice eventually absorbs all the wine and the alcohol smell can no longer be detected.

To this mixture, add a ladleful of the warm saffron-infused stock. Continue to stir and add more stock as it becomes absorbed, eventually also adding the reserved, non-infused chicken stock, a ladleful at a time. Once or twice before all of the stock is absorbed, check the rice for its state of doneness: at the end, it should yield to the bite and be cooked all the way through, but still maintain its structural integrity.

Now, assess the texture of the risotto. Is it runny enough to cover the bottom of a bowl without coaxing? If not, stir in a little more stock until it's the correct consistency.

Now, add the butter chunks and the cheese and beat it with a light hand into the hot rice, incorporating some air and lightening the consistency somewhat as you go. Taste the risotto and season with salt if necessary. Serve immediately with the osso buco (see recipe).

Serves 6 as a side dish.

*from **THE HEADS***

PAN-SEARED DUCK BREAST WITH RED CABBAGE

DUCK:
4 duck breasts, about 6 ounces each

Kosher salt and freshly ground black pepper
to taste

CABBAGE:
2 pieces flat cinnamon bark, rinsed
1 bay leaf
1 sprig fresh rosemary
2 sprigs fresh thyme
½ pound bacon, cut into lardons (1 inch
long by ¼ inch thick pieces)
1 medium white onion, peeled and sliced thinly

½ head red cabbage, cored and thinly sliced
Salt and freshly ground black pepper to taste
1 ¼ cups dry red wine
¼ cup best-quality red wine vinegar
1 teaspoon caraway seeds, toasted
1/4 teaspoon ground allspice
1 tablespoon sugar

SAUCE:
1 tablespoon unsalted butter
2 shallots, peeled and finely chopped
10 to 12 cremini mushrooms, finely chopped
to yield about 2 cups

1 tablespoon all-purpose flour
½ cup dry red wine
2 cups veal stock
Salt and freshly ground black pepper to taste

TO MAKE THE CABBAGE

First, make the bouquet garni – that is, a little packet of herbs and spices that flavors what you're cooking without getting its messy, potentially hazardous bits and leaves everywhere: cut a 5-inch square of cheesecloth and use it to wrap up the cinnamon bark, bay leaf, rosemary, and thyme into a neat package. Secure it with butcher's twine and, for now, set it aside.

In a sauté pan over medium heat, cook the bacon until it has rendered most of its fat and is golden brown, stirring occasionally to make sure that the bacon is cooked evenly. Stir in the onions; cook them in the bacon fat until they're soft and pliable, then stir in the cabbage, making sure it's well coated with the bacon fat. Season it well with salt and pepper and cook over medium-high heat for about 5 minutes, until it begins to soften. Over high heat, add the wine, bring to a boil, then add the vinegar. Scrape the surface of the pan with your spoon to dislodge browned bits, and continue to cook until the liquid is reduced by half. Add the bouquet garni that you've prepared, then stir the whole mixture well and reduce the heat to medium-low, so that the liquid is simmering. Cook, stirring occasionally, until the cabbage is quite tender, about 30 minutes. If at any point the cabbage is sticking to the pan, add a splash of water.

TO MAKE THE DUCK:

While the cabbage simmers, cross-hatch the skin on the duck breasts—meaning, use a very sharp knife to lightly cut a ¼-inch checkerboard pattern into the skin, penetrating the fat layer but not the flesh layer. Season both sides of each breast with salt and pepper.

Place the breasts, skin side down, in a cold sauté pan, working in batches if necessary to avoid overcrowding the pan. There should be space between each breast for air to circulate. Place the pan over medium-low heat and cook for about 15 to 20 minutes, pouring off the excess fat as it is rendered from the breast. When the skin is nicely golden brown and most of the fat has been rendered, increase the heat to high and let the skin sear for one minute, then flip the breasts and let cook on the flesh side for 1 minute to 90 seconds. If you are working in batches, set the cooked duck aside and repeat the process with the remaining duck.

TO MAKE THE SAUCE

Wipe out any excess fat from the sauté pan that you've used to cook the duck, and add the butter. Cook over medium heat until it foams and subsides, then add the shallots and mushrooms. Season well with salt and pepper and cook over medium heat until the liquid from the mushrooms has been released and evaporated, and the vegetables have become browned and fragrant, about 10 minutes. Sprinkle the flour over the mixture and stir well to coat the vegetables; keep scraping the pan with a wooden spoon to keep flour from scorching. Stir in the wine and cook over medium-high heat until it has largely evaporated, then stir in the stock. Bring it to a boil and cook until the liquid has been reduced by half. Strain the sauce into a clean bowl or pot, and taste and adjust the seasoning with salt and pepper as needed.

TO SERVE

Slice the duck breasts thinly and divide the slices, arranged like roof shingles, among four plates. Artfully drizzle or ladle some of the hot sauce over, and arrange some of the cabbage alongside.

Serves 4.

*from **BOIL IN THE BELLY***

A Handy Guide to the Legendary Ghostly Spirits behind our Terrifying Tales

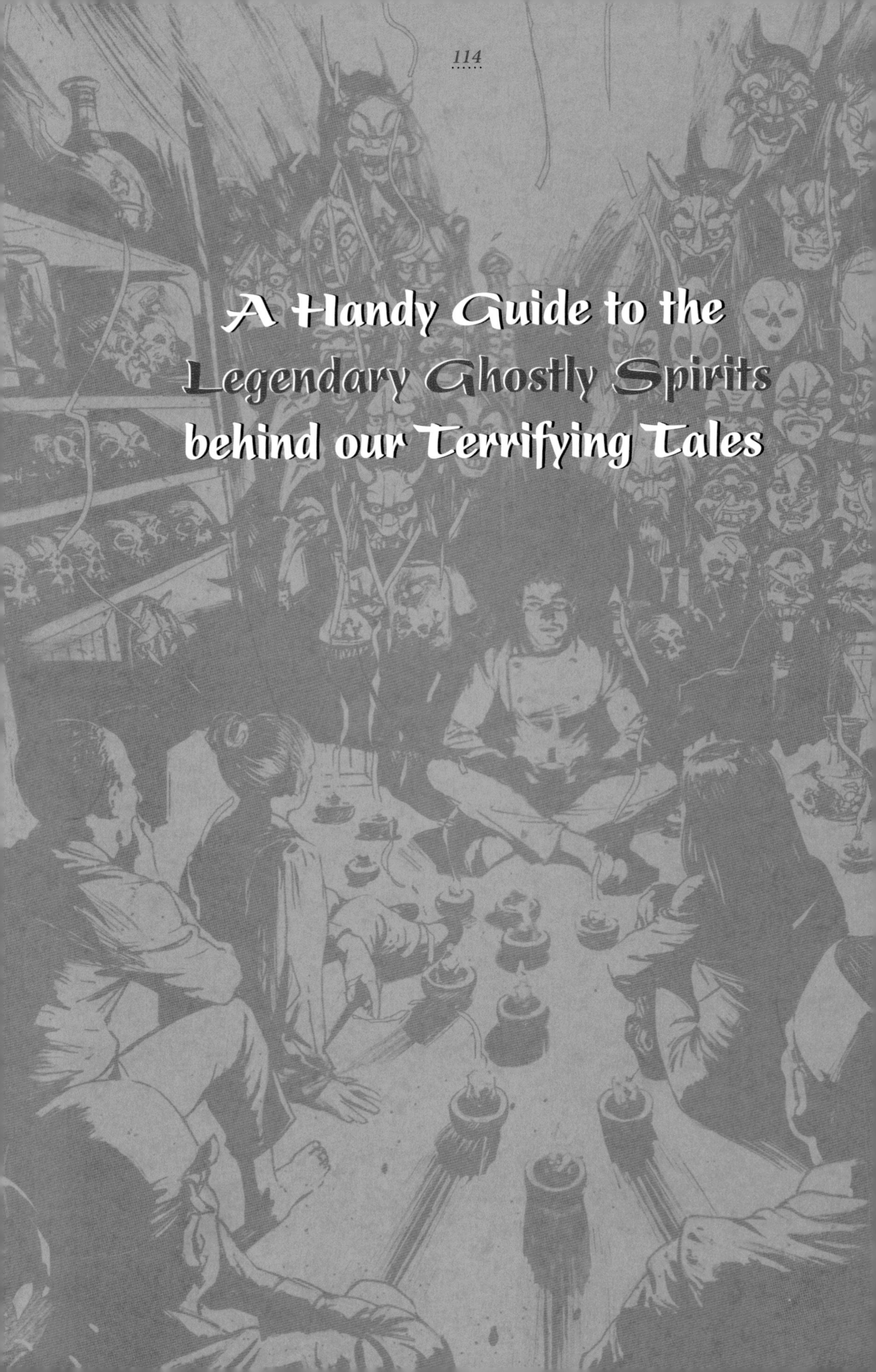

Yōkai

If there is a catch-all name for Japanese ghosts and goblins, it's yōkai. Yōkai are monsters, spirits, and demons, and they are the fixtures of Japanese folklore. Yōkai can be traced back to the 8th century, the beginning of Japanese written language, but came to flourish particularly during the Edo Period of art and culture, which extended from the early 17th century through the mid 19th.

Some yōkai can be characterized as good or funny, but the lion's share are bad to the bone.

Yōkai can be human-like in appearance, or have an animal-like presence.

Some yōkai, like the akuryo, are evil spirits.

Onryo are yōkai with vengeful spirits.

Yūrei

Yūrei always want something. They are yōkai. All yūrei are yōkai, but not all yōkai are yorei.

Yūrei can be ethereal, appearing with white clothing, black hair, and dangling hands and feet. Yūrei often lack legs. Some might have a hitodama surrounding them, a floating, ghostly flame—blue, green, and purple.

Obake

Obake are shapeshifters. They, too, are yōkai. Obake are not considered to be spirits of the dead, but spirits of the living, although sometimes they team with the spirits of the dead. They can take the shape of an animal, a plant, or even an inanimate object.

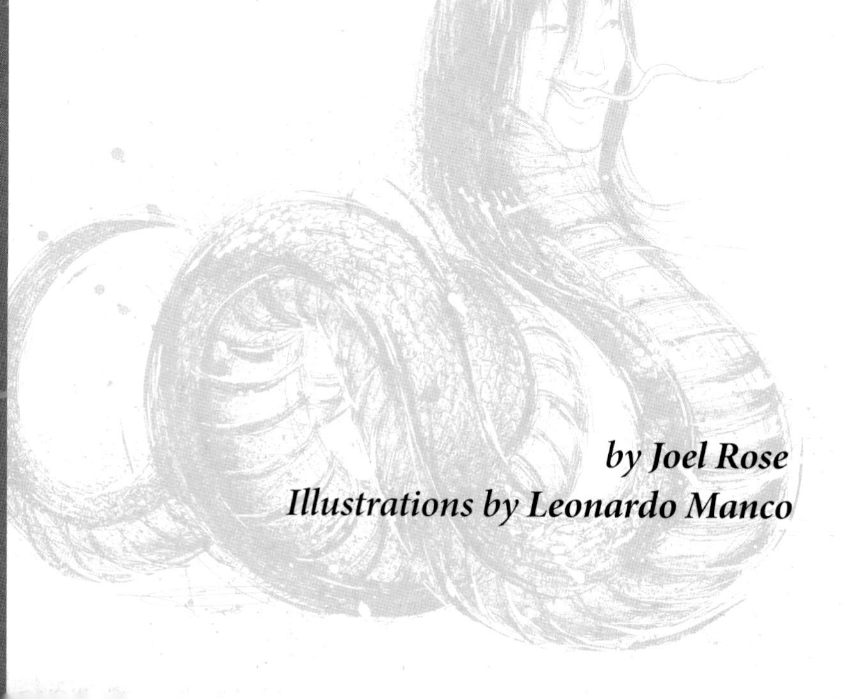

by Joel Rose

Illustrations by Leonardo Manco

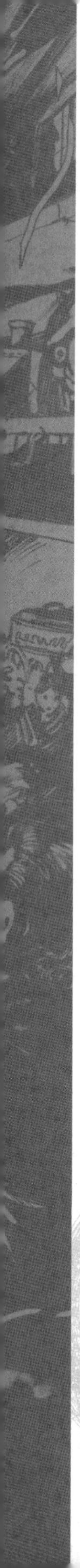

The Starving Skeleton
HIDARUGAMI

Hidarugami are hunger gods, the spirits of those who have starved to death. Hiderugami are vengeful spirits, spiteful and cruel, out to exact their eternal anguish from all.

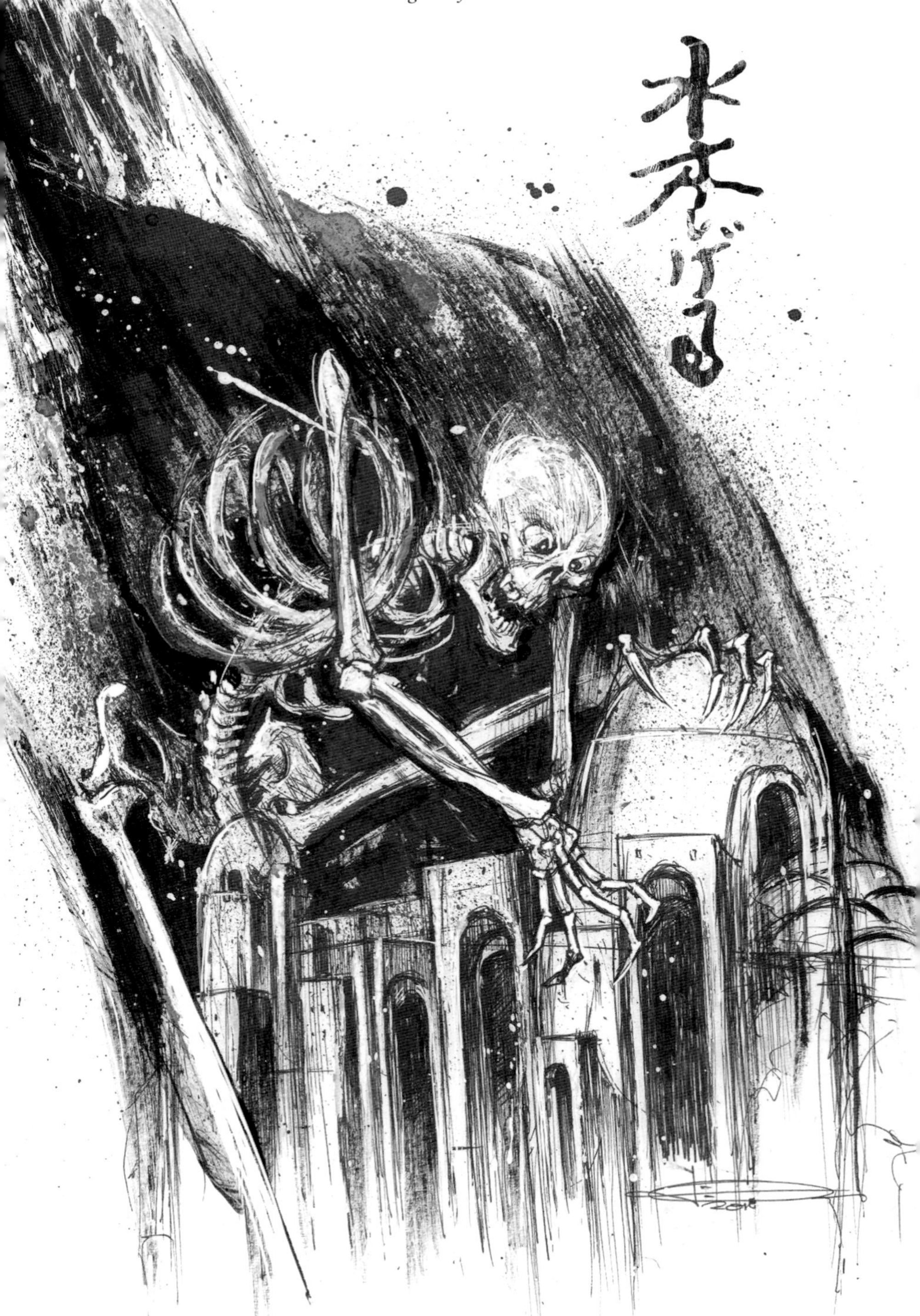
水木しげる

The Pirates

SAZAE ONI

Sazae oni are obake, who take the form of giant shellfish with eyes on their shell and odd arms. They are said to be the ghosts of lustful women who have been thrown into the ocean as punishment for their wanton ways. Sazae oni appear on moonlit nights, dancing on the waves, often with sea dragons. They pretend to be drowning victims, crying out to be saved.

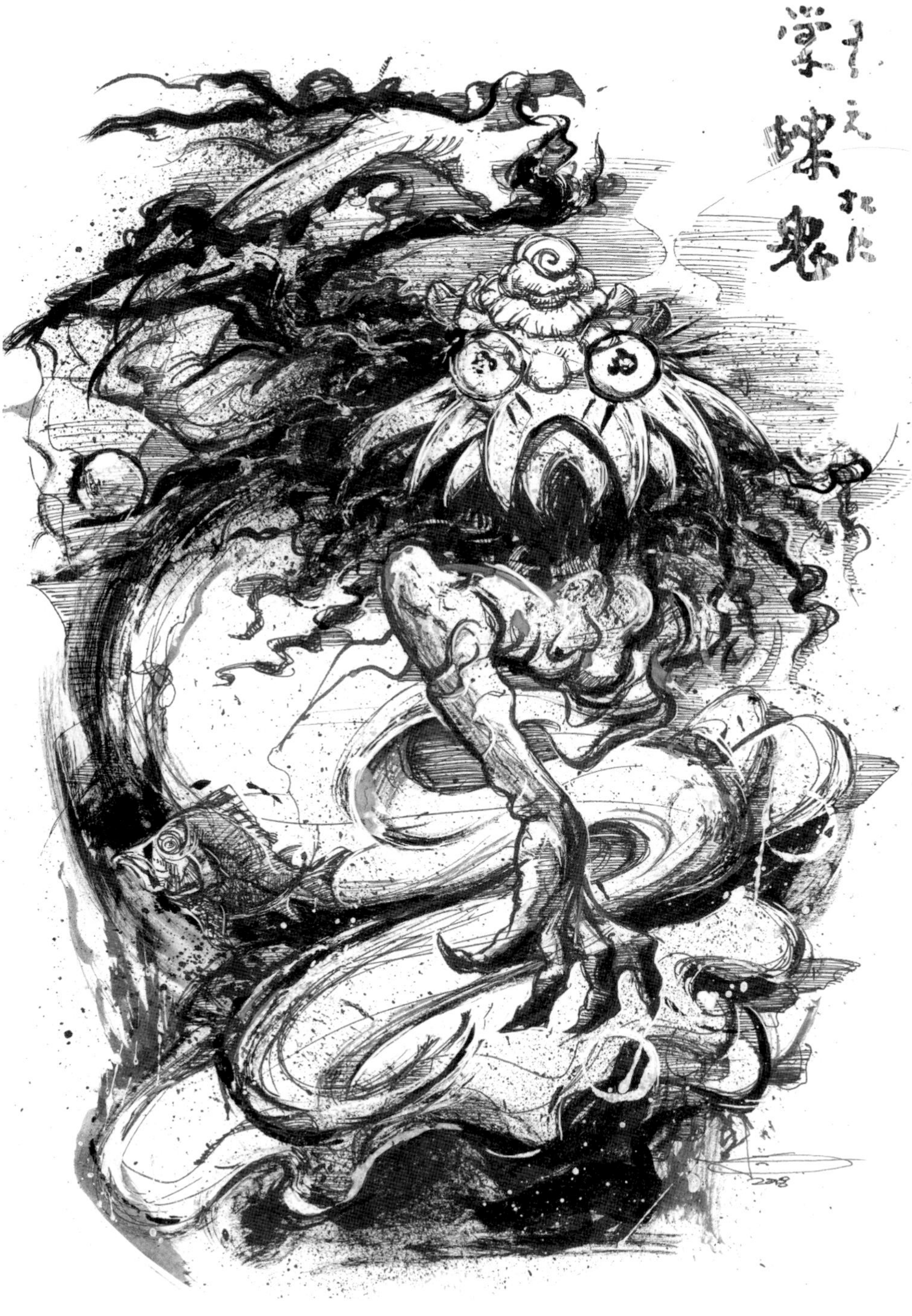
栄螺鬼

Salty Horse

TSUKIMONO

Tsukimono are magical animals that enter the body, sometimes violently, to extract their malevolence by possession of the victim.

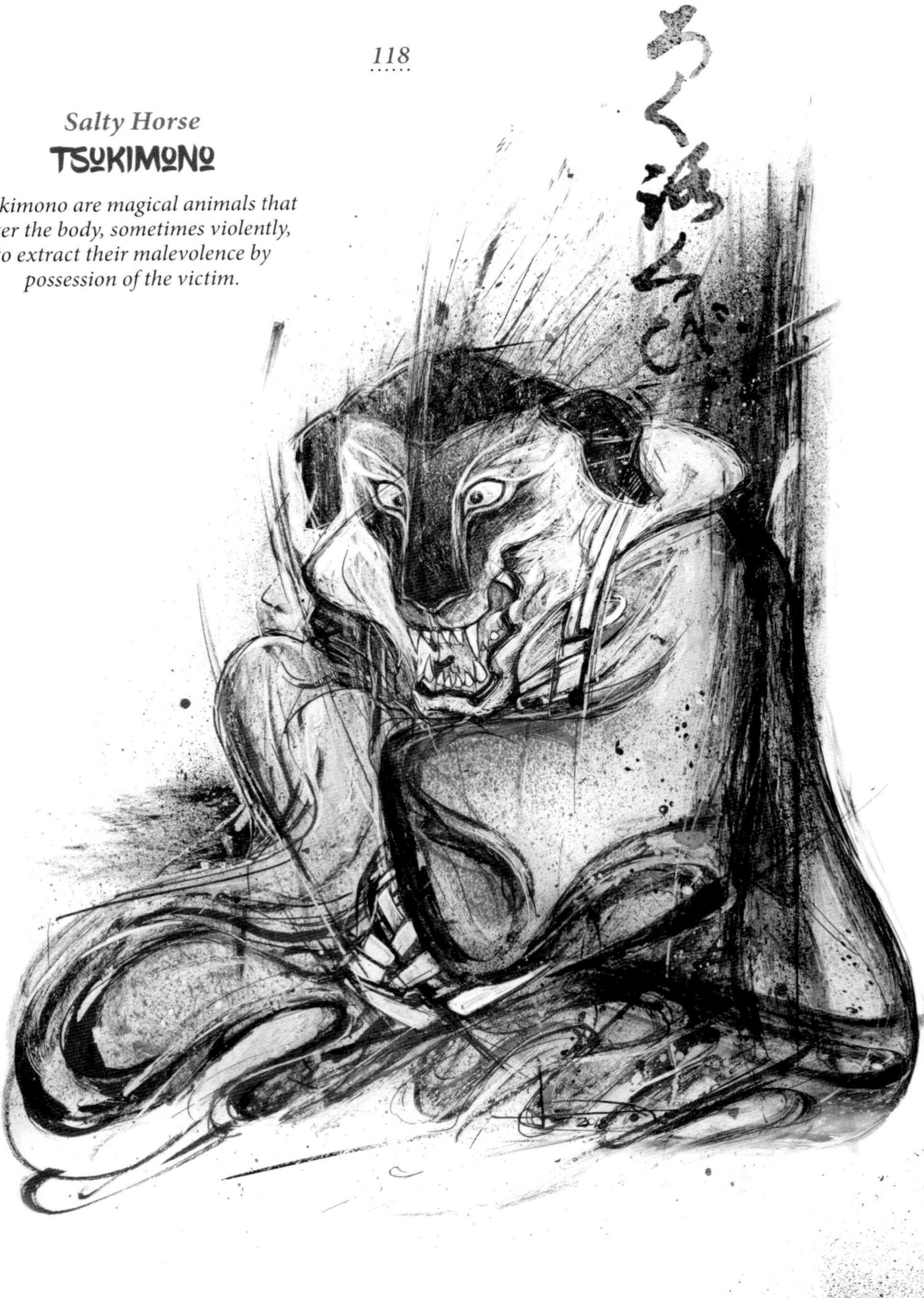

The Heads

ROKUROKOBI

Rokurokobi are yōkai with a human appearance. There are two types of rokurokobi: one whose neck stretches and one (nukekobi) whose head becomes completely disjointed.

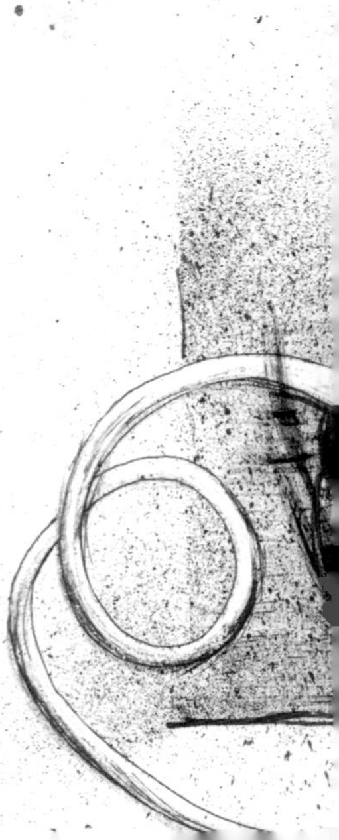

中お見舞い申し上げます。

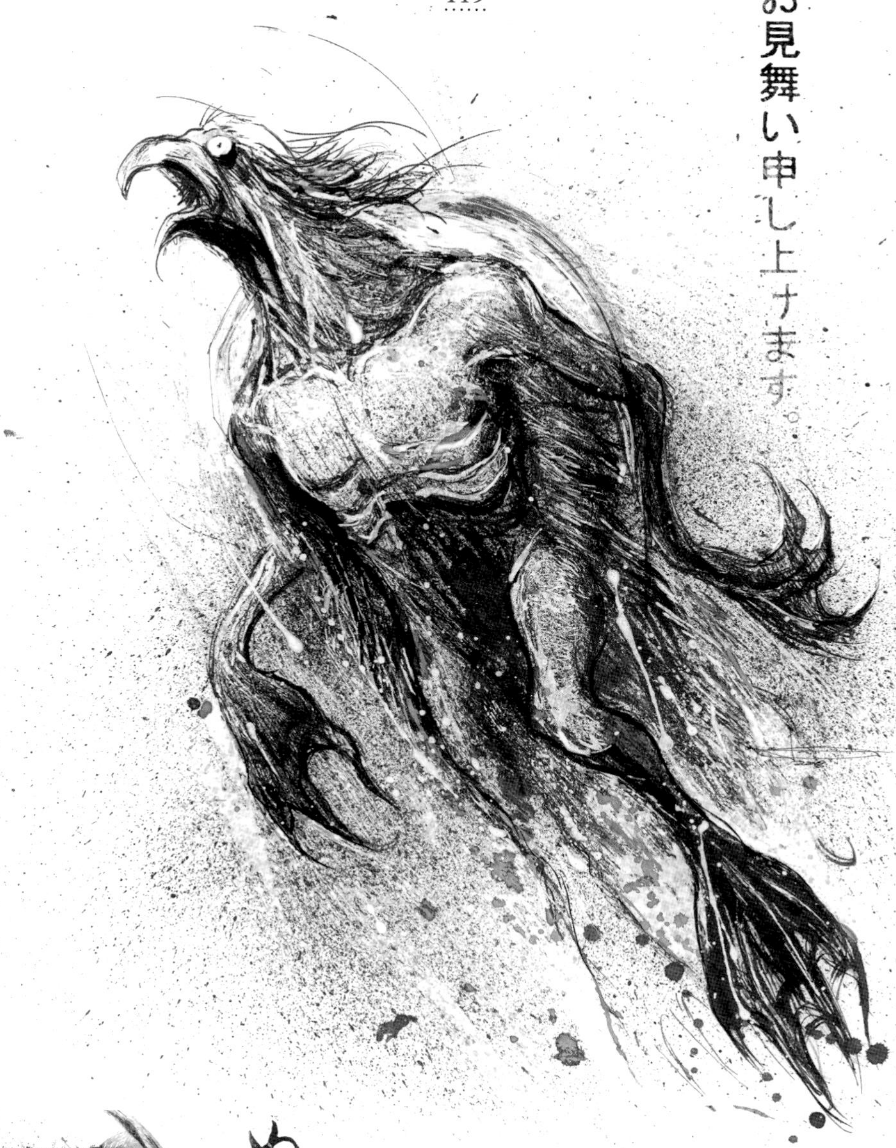

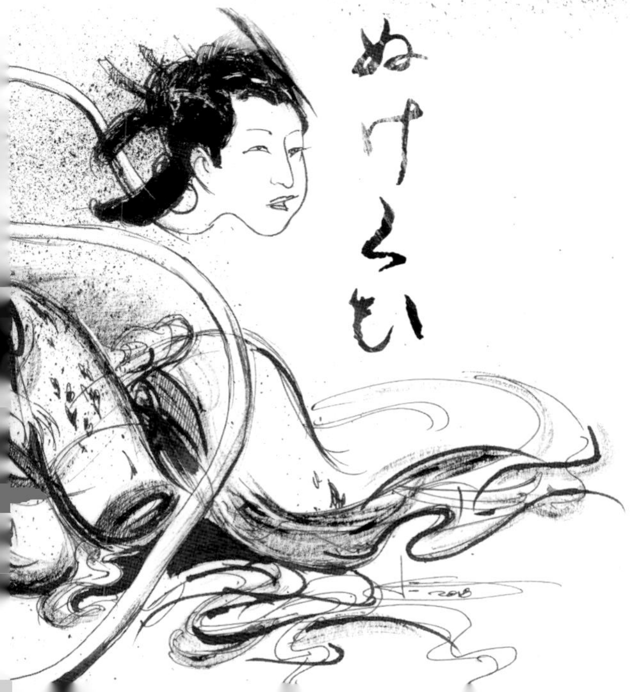

Deep

KAPPA

Kappa are known as turtle ghosts, although they can have elements of monkey and lizard. For the most part, kappas are inhabiters of lakes and rivers, where during the Edo period they were known as a particularly predatory presence. Kappa are usually depicted with a bowl on top of their heads, said to contain a magical liquid giving them supernatural strength.

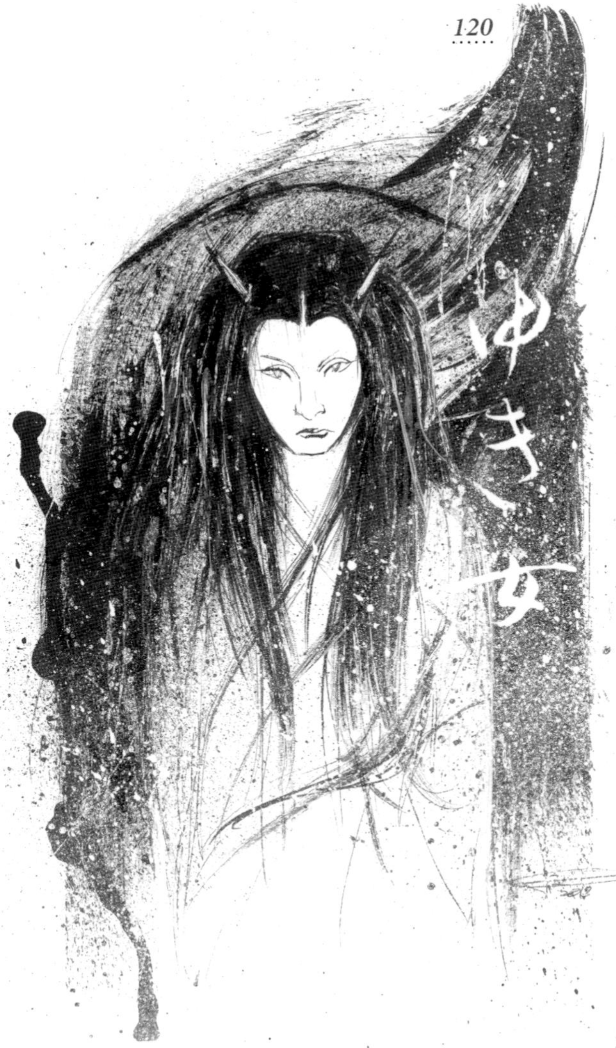
ゆき女

The Snow Woman

YUKI-ONNA

The yuki-onna, the impossibly beautiful snow woman, floats across newly fallen drifts but leaves no footprints. Her kiss, like that of a vampire, draws the life out of her victims. There have been times the snow woman has seen fit to spare her victim, but always for her own purpose.

Boil in the Belly

BAKEMONO

Bakemono are monsters, obake that might appear as animals: a cat, a raccoon, a fox—or a more malicious manifestation, like a snake.

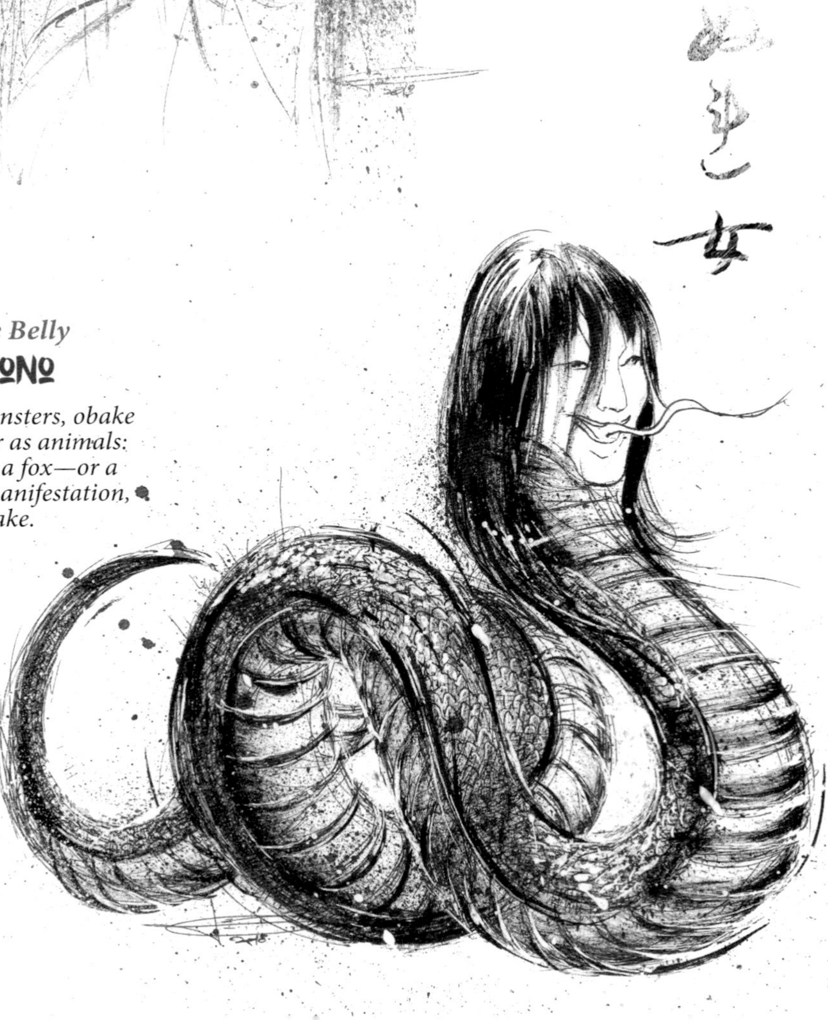

The Cow Head

JIKINIKI

Jikiniki are devourers of human flesh. Damnable in life, in death they are ghouls, cursed to feast on human corpses.

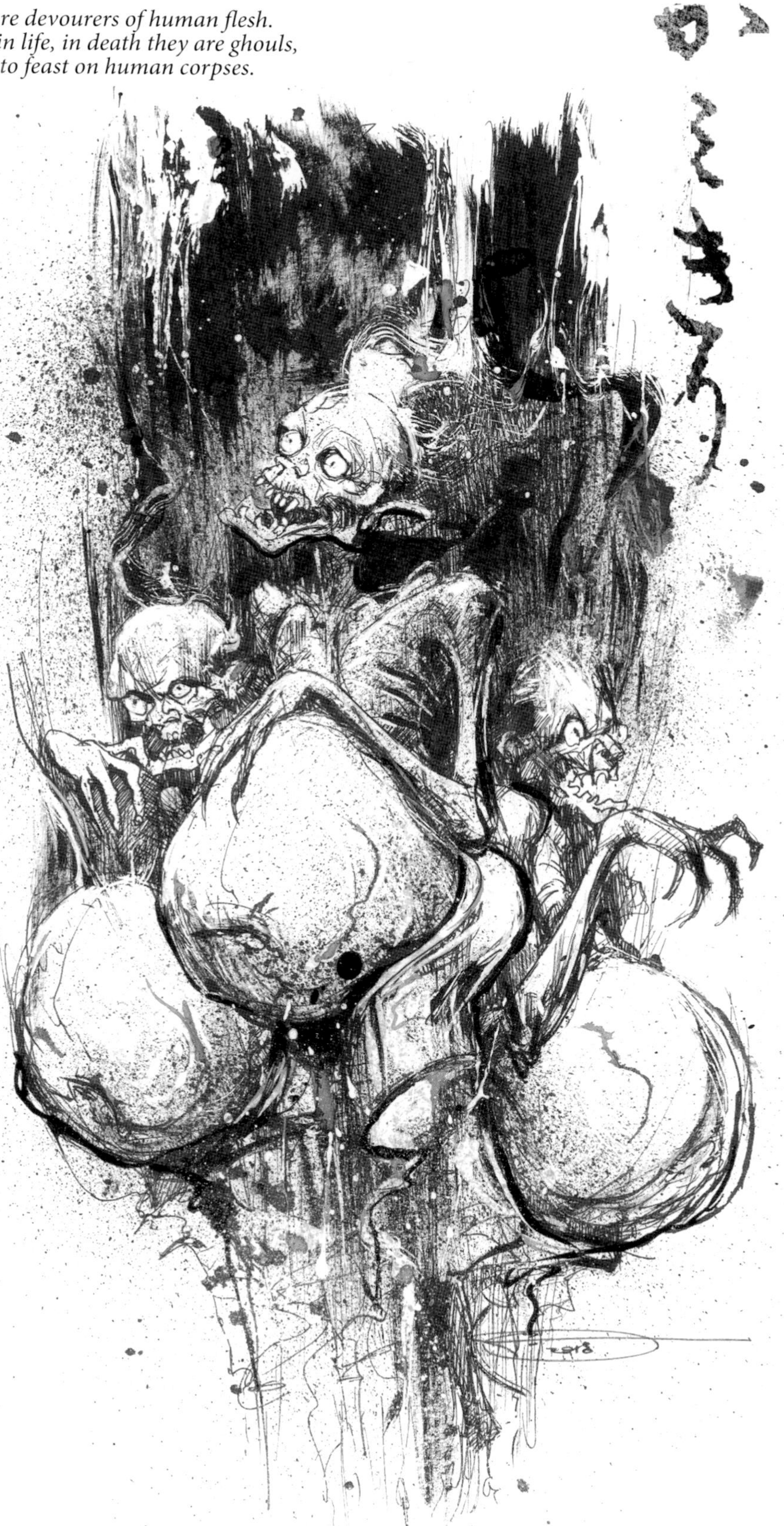

José Villarrubia

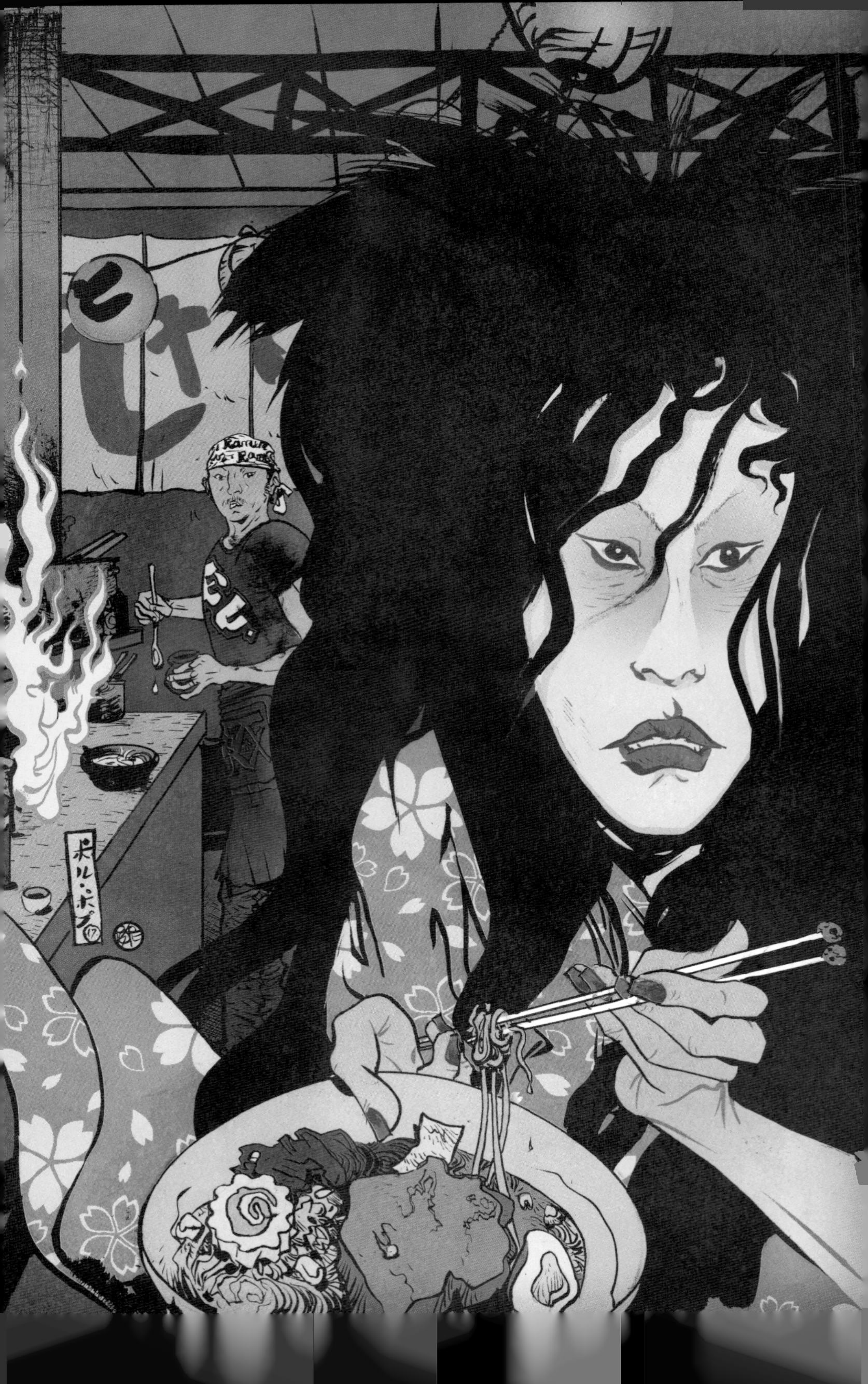

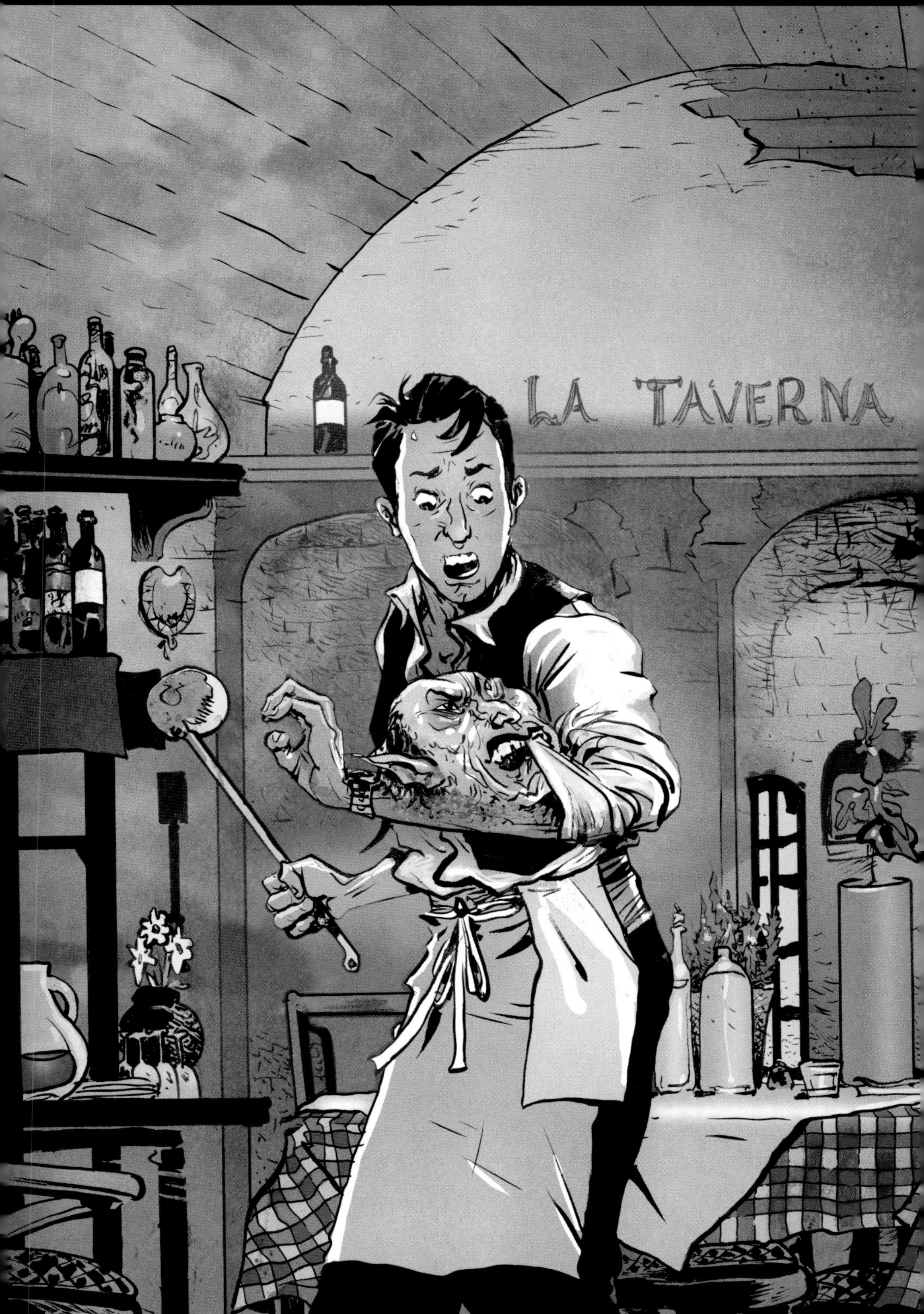
LA TAVERNA

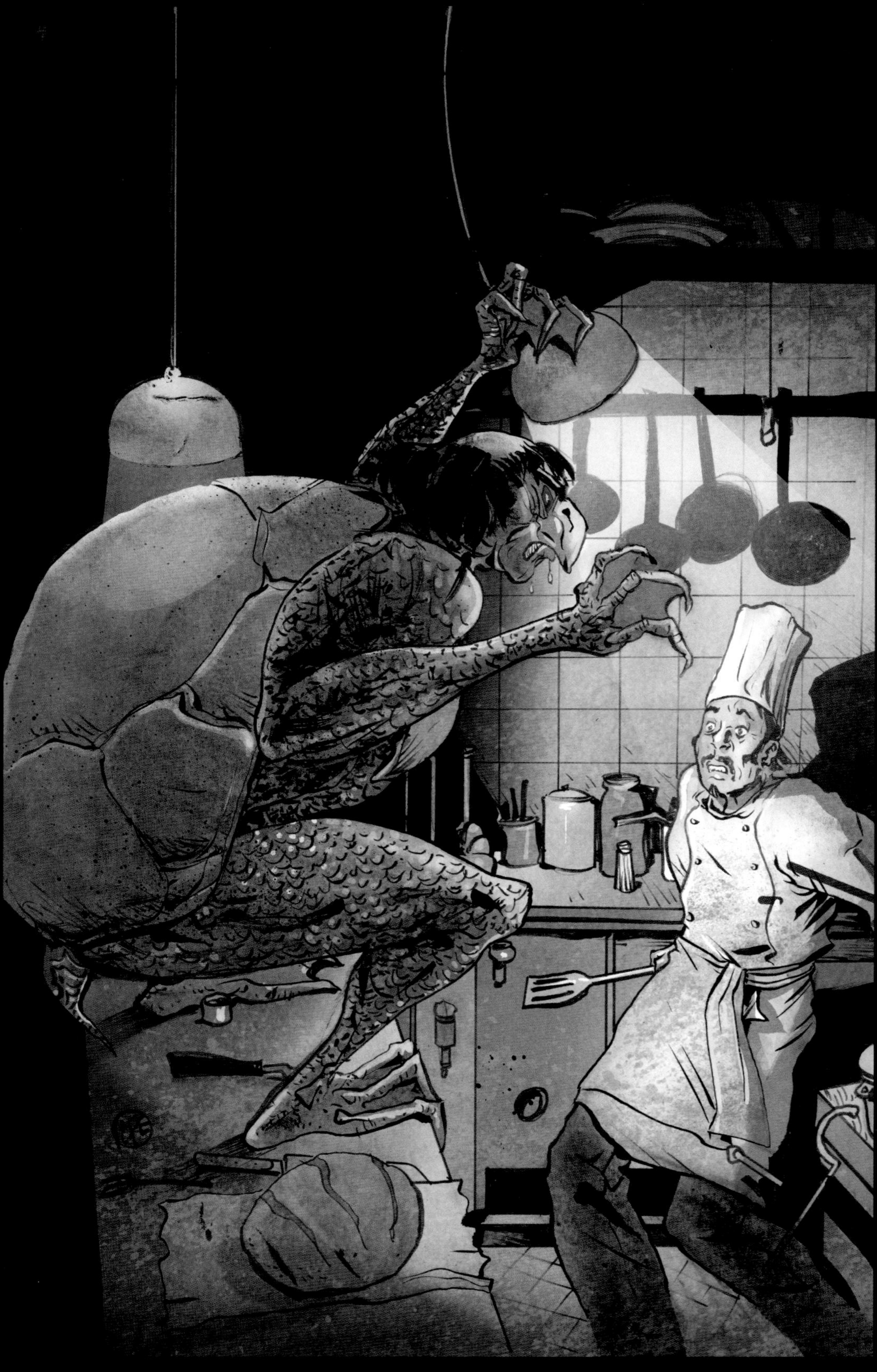

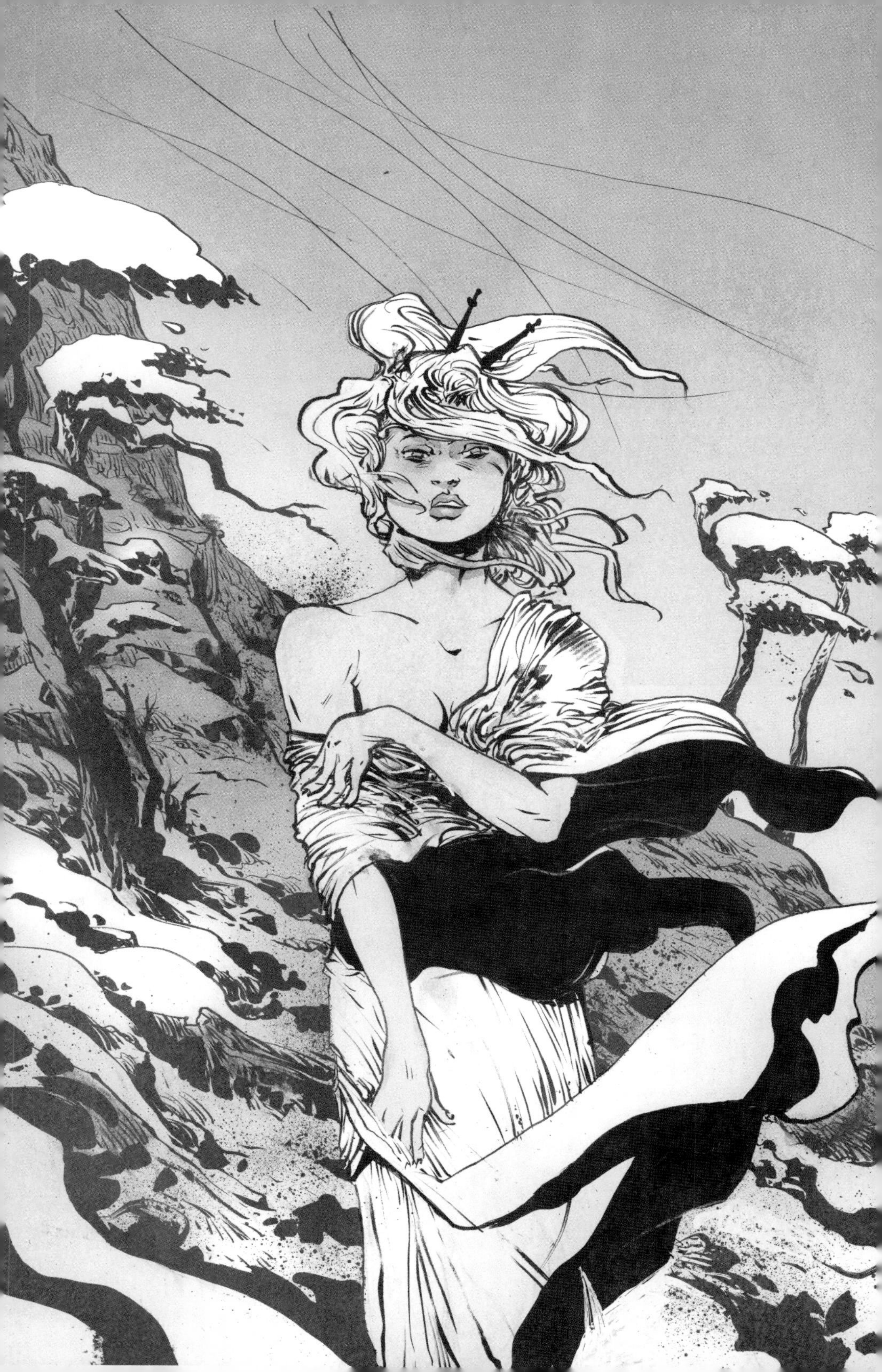

ANTHONY BOURDAIN

Anthony Bourdain was a veteran chef and author of both non-fiction and fiction: the bestselling *Kitchen Confidential, A Cook's Tour, The Nasty Bits, Medium Raw, Appetites: A Cookbook*; the crime novels: *Bone in the Throat, Gone Bamboo, Bobby Gold* and the *Get Jiro!* graphic novel collaboration with writer Joel Rose. His first food and travel show was *A Cook's Tour* on the Food Network, followed by *No Reservations* and *The Layover* on the Travel Channel. In 2013, he joined CNN as a producer, writer and host of the show *Parts Unknown* which received the Peabody Award and five Emmy Awards.

JOEL ROSE

Joel Rose is the author of the novels *Kill the Poor* and *Kill Kill Faster Faster,* both of which have been made into feature films. His other books include *The Blackest Bird, New York Sawed in Half,* and the bestselling graphic novel *Get Jiro!,* co-written with Anthony Bourdain. For DC's Paradox Press he has written *La Pacifica, The Big Book of Thugs,* and *The Big Book of Little Criminals.* Joel was also co-founder and editor of the legendary and influential Lower East Side literary magazine *Between C and D,* published in the 1980s.

JOSÉ VILLARRUBIA

Born in Madrid, Spain, but a long-time Baltimore resident, José Villarrubia is an award-winning artist and colorist best known for his work with Alan Moore (*The Mirror of Love*), Richard Corben (*Cage*), and Paul Pope (*Batman Year 100*). One of his first works in comics was *Veils,* published by Vertigo. Also for Vertigo he colored *Sweet Tooth, Aaron and Ahmed: A Love Story, Gone to Amerikay,* and *Cuba: My Revolution.* He has worked previously with Anthony Bourdain and Joel Rose on *Get Jiro!* and *Get Jiro: Blood and Sushi.*

SAL CIPRIANO

Brooklyn-born Sal Cipriano is a freelance letterer working with a wide range of publishers and creators. His former comic book experiences include writing, drawing, coloring, editing, and publishing. When not lettering, Sal reviews action figures on YouTube, runs a group sketch blog, and drinks gallons of coffee. Better fire up another pot!

PAUL POPE

Born in 1970, Paul Pope is an American artist and designer living in New York City. While he's primarily worked in comics and screen-printing, he's also worked with fashion giants Diesel and DKNY. Other clients include LucasArts, Disney, Cartoon Network, Marvel Comics, DC Comics, Sapporo, Dargaud Editions, the British Film Institute, and many others. The five-time Eisner Award winner has been recognized as a Master Artist by the American Council of the Arts, and has also won the coveted Reuben Award for Best Comic Book for his work on *Strange Adventures.* His latest book, *Battling Boy*—which debuted at #1 on the *New York Times* bestseller list—is currently in feature development at Paramount Pictures.

ALBERTO PONTICELLI

Alberto Ponticelli is the artist behind *Blatta* and *Unknown Soldier*, as well as *Dial H*, *The Dark Knight*, *Second Sight*, *FBP*, and many others. His work has also appeared in *Heavy Metal* and *Frank Frazetta Fantasy Illustrated*.

VANESA DEL REY

Cuban-born creator Vanesa R. Del Rey began her career by doing concept art for animation. Her first sequential works were the *Hit* comic book series and the *Empty Man* series, published by Boom! Studios. She has also illustrated stories for Dark Horse Comics, Marvel Comics, and Image Comics. *Redlands*, which she works on with Jordie Bellaire and Clayton Cowles, has been nominated for an Eisner Award for Best New Series. She works and lives on the beach by the tropics.

LEONARDO MANCO

Born on December 16, 1971 in Argentina, Leonardo Manco started working as a studio assistant at the age of seventeen. At nineteen, he published his first works locally and at twenty-one he debuted in Marvel's *Hellstorm*. Other titles like *Doom*, *Blaze of Glory*, *War Machine*, *Werewolf by Night*, *Hellblazer*, and many more followed. Nowadays he's working on *John Carpenter's Asylum*.

MATEUS SANTOLOUCO

Mateus Santolouco is a Brazilian comic book artist who has worked on titles such as *Zero* for Image Comics, *Dial H* for DC Comics, and *2 Guns* for Boom! Studios, which he co-created with Steven Grant. Since 2011, Mateus has been contributing to IDW's *Teenage Mutant Ninja Turtles*, first as an artist, and eventually a writer.

SEBASTIAN CABROL

Born in Argentina in 1978, Sebastian Cabrol started his work as an inker for titles such as *Caliban*, *God is Dead*, and *Gravel* for Avatar Press, as well as *Thief* from Dark Horse. In 2016, he illustrated a version of W.H. Hodgson's *The House on the Borderland* for Hermida Editores, and in 2018 he created the line art for Marvel's *Falcon: Take Flight*.

IRENE KOH

Born in Seoul in 1990, Irene Koh is a professional comics artist and illustrator who has worked with DC Comics, Marvel Comics, IDW, Riot Games, and Bungie, among others. Her acclaimed creator-owned work *Afrina and the Glass Coffin* was published by Stela in 2016. Most recently, she's been working on *The Legend of Korra: Turf Wars* for Dark Horse Comics, which topped multiple bestseller lists. She currently resides in the San Francisco Bay area.

FRANCESCO FRANCAVILLA

Francesco Francavilla is the Eisner Award-winning writer and artist of *Black Beetle*, and artist of *Afterlife with Archie* and *Batman: The Black Mirror*, among many other titles for every major comics publisher. His editorial illustrations have appeared in the *New York Times Magazine*, and he is also a popular Mondo poster artist.

Cover Artist
Paul Pope

Logo & Book Design
Richard Bruning

Editor
Karen Berger

Associate Editor
Rachel Roberts

Digital Art Technician
Adam Pruett

Publisher
Mike Richardson

ANTHONY BOURDAIN'S HUNGRY GHOSTS

Hungry Ghosts™ © 2018 Anthony Bourdain and Joel Rose.
The Berger Books logo, Dark Horse Books®, and the Dark
Horse logo are trademarks of Dark Horse Comics, Inc.
Berger Books™ is a trademark of Karen Berger. All rights
reserved. No portion of this publication may be reproduced
or transmitted, in any form or by any means, without
the express written permission of Dark Horse Comics,
Inc. Names, characters, places, and incidents featured
in this publication either are the product of the author's
imagination or are used fictitiously. Any resemblance to
actual persons (living or dead), events, institutions, or
locales, without satiric intent, is coincidental.

This volume collects issues #1–4 of
Anthony Bourdain's Hungry Ghosts.

Published by
Dark Horse Books
A division of
Dark Horse Comics, Inc.
10956 SE Main Street
Milwaukie, OR 97222

DarkHorse.com
ComicShopLocator.com

First Edition: September 2018
ISBN: 978-1-50670-669-6
Digital ISBN: 978-1-50670-690-0

10 9 8 7 6 5 4 3 2
Printed in Canada

Library of Congress Cataloging-in-Publication Data

Names: Bourdain, Anthony, author. | Rose, Joel, author. | Ponticelli,
Alberto, artist. | Manco, Leonardo, artist. | Santolouco, Mateus, 1979-
artist. | Cipriano, Sal, letterer.
Title: Anthony Bourdain's hungry ghosts / script, Anthony Bourdain,
Joel Rose; art, Alberto Ponticelli, Leonardo Manco, Mateus
Santolouco [and others];
lettering, Sal Cipriano.
Other titles: Hungry ghosts
Description: First edition. | Milwaukie, OR : Berger Books, September
2018. |
"This volume collects issues #1-4 of Anthony Bourdain's Hungry
Ghosts."
Identifiers: LCCN 2018024030 | ISBN 9781506706696 (hardback)
Subjects: LCSH: Comic books, strips, etc. | BISAC: COMICS &
GRAPHIC NOVELS /
Literary. | COMICS & GRAPHIC NOVELS / Anthologies. |
COMICS & GRAPHIC NOVELS / Horror.
Classification: LCC PN6727.B679 A55 2018 | DDC 741.5/973--dc23
LC record available at https://lccn.loc.gov/2018024030

Published by
Dark Horse Books
A division of
Dark Horse Comics, Inc.
10956 SE Main Street
Milwaukie, OR 97222

Neil Hankerson
Executive Vice President

Tom Weddle
Chief Financial Officer

Randy Stradley
Vice President of Publishing

Nick McWhorter
Chief Business Development Officer

Matt Parkinson
Vice President of Marketing

Dale LaFountain
Vice President of Information Technology

Cara Niece
Vice President of Production
and Scheduling

Mark Bernardi
Vice President of Book Trade
and Digital Sales

Ken Lizzi
General Counsel

Dave Marshall
Editor in Chief

Davey Estrada
Editorial Director

Chris Warner
Senior Books Editor

Cary Grazzini
Director of Specialty Projects

Lia Ribacchi
Art Director

Vanessa Todd-Holmes
Director of Print Purchasing

Matt Dryer
Director of Digital Art and Prepress

Michael Gombos
Director of International Publishing
and Licensing

Kari Yadro
Director of Custom Programs